Pike County Alabama

Index

to

Will Books 1830-1995
Estate Boxes 1830-1955
and
General Estate Book 1-25

Edited By:
Susie K. Senn

Southern Historical Press, Inc.
Greenville, SC   29602

SOUTHERN HISTORICAL PRESS, INC.
PO BOX 1267
Greenville, SC   29601

ISBN #978-1-63914-063-3

Printed in the United States of America

The following is an index to the Will Books from A to Z, the Estate Boxes 1 thru 168, and the General Estate Books from 1 to 25 in the Pike County Courthouse. Book Z of the Will Books had just begun to be used when Probate Judge John W. Gibson went out of office on Jan. 16, 1995. His predecessor, Judge William C. Stone continued in this book until it was completely filled. The Courthouse has now started over with a new set of Will Books which are being indexed in a new book of indexes. It would have been easier to have used the following Will Books if there had been a master index kept of them. Judge Stone is the first Probate Judge in Pike County to start a master index of all Will Books since Jan. 17, 1995 and this will be of great help now and in the future. It is hoped that the index that I have compiled of the Will Books up to Jan. 16, 1995, the index of the General Estate Books, and Boxes will be of help to many people and perhaps it will take some of the wear and tear off of the older Books by people not having to go thru the index in each book every time they look for an old Will or Estate.

To people in other places checking for Wills and Estates in this book, if you should happen to find one that you feel you need, I would suggest you write the Probate Office and find out what the cost would be to get a copy. Of course it is always appropriate to send a S.A.S.E. when writing. The Will Book Indexes from Q to U listed only the first page so you would need to know how many pages need copying. It is hoped that the Probate Office can send you this information and if not they can send you a list of persons who will check for you.

Of course this is not all of the Wills in this Courthouse, some of the earlier ones are in Orphan Court Minute Books and Appraisement Books and other Books of this type. Each section of this book is listed alphabetically. You need to check each section for your ancestor since you do not know how his Estate was handled. At this point I would like to say I hope this helps you find the ancestors you are looking for.

Susie K. Senn

CONTENTS

Will Book	Year
A	1830 - 1862
B	1862 - 1880
C	1880 - 1922
D	1922 - 1952
E	1953 - 1961
F	1961 - 1964
G	1964 - 1968
H	1968 - 1971
I	1971 - 1974
J	1974 - 1978
K	1977 - 1979
L	1977 - 1982
M	1980 - 1982
N	1982 - 1984
O	1984 - 1986
P	1985 - 1987
Q	1987 - 1988
R	1987 - 1989
S	1989 - 1989
T	1989 - 1990
U	1990 - 1991
V	1991 - 1992
W	1991 - 1993
X	1993 - 1994
Y	1994 - 1995
Z	1995 TO JAN. 16, 1995

ABERNATHY, THOMAS S.	P	584 - 595
ACKER, LUCY	H	160
ADAMS, CLEM W.	G	17
ADAMS, CLYDE MINCHENER	F	219
ADAMS, COLSON	A	154 - 155
ADAMS, E.C.	G	141, 324 - 325
ADAMS, G.D.	F	220
ADAMS, GILLIS	W	227 - 239
ADAMS, HARMON	B	184 - 187
ADAMS, JAMES LESTER	V	851 - 864
ADAMS, MAE JEAN RICHBURG	W	165 - 173
ADAMS, MARY DAVIS	T	739 - 747
ADAMS, MARY WILL	W	813 - 821
ADAMS, N.D.	E	465
ADAMS, PHIL A.	J	542
ADAMS, TANNER	Z	18 - 28
ADAMS, WM. H.	B	1
ADAMS, WM. H.	C	107 - 109
ADILL, LUCILLE	I	406
ALBRITTON, SHELTON	W	61 - 90
ALEXANDER, ADA	O	642 - 661
ALEXANDER, JAMES LUTHER	G	143
ALLEN, ANELLA CHAPMAN	M	758
ALLEN, CONNIE PEARL	R	349
ALLEN, DAVID B.	C	37 - 40
ALLEN, ESTELLE S.	R	594
ALLEN, GERTRUDE	V	134 - 146
ALLEN, JAMES	B	18 - 19
ALLEN, JOHN	C	96 - 99
ALLEN, MALLORY JACKSON	Q	349
ALLEN, MARY LIZZIE	Z	1 - 17
ALLEN, RHODA S. GRANT	E	356 - 358
ALLEN, SARAH E.	C	23
ALLEN, WM. ELMER	I	503, 527 - 529
ALLHANDS, JAMES LLEWELLYN	K	621
ALLOWAY, WILLIE FRANK	V	78 - 97
ALLRED, AVIS	D	334
ALLRED, VIOLA	E	178 - 180
AMMONS, JOSH EDWARD	L	551, 640 - 644
AMMONS, JOSH H.	F	223
AMOS, WILLIAM REVILL	V	450 - 462
ANDERSON, A.M.	E	35
ANDERSON, BAMA	D	317

ANDERSON, C.A.	K	10, 153 - 156	254 Trans. to Circuit Ct
ANDERSON, C.P.	C	307 - 308	
ANDERSON, CLEONE A.	W	716 - 790	
ANDERSON, ERNESTINE FOY	Y	233 - 256	
ANDERSON, FRANK S.	I	619	
ANDERSON, FRANK S.	K	362 - 365	
ANDERSON, GRACE MCPHERSON	U	95	
ANDERSON, JAMES W.	D	188	
ANDERSON, RUBY LEE	W	174 - 182	
ANDERSON, SHELBY W.	K	316	
ANDERSON, SHELBY W.	M	78 - 82	
ANDERSON, W.M.	G	147	
ANDRESS, CALLIE E.	C	219 & 226	
ANDRESS, FRANCIS P.	C	11 - 12	
ANDRESS, J.M.	F	1	
ANDRESS, JOHN FRANK	L	125, 229-232	329, 335-337 Circuit Ct.
ANDRESS, JOSEPH M.	C	1	
ANDRESS, MAGGIE B.	C	191 - 193	
ANDREWS, DEWEY	H	568	
ANDREWS, DEWEY	I	175, 176	
ANDREWS, EVA S.	J	318, 386 - 388	
ARMSTRONG, BURNELLE SELLERS	V	698 - 712	
ARMSTRONG, E.C.	C	57 - 58	
ARMSTRONG, LOUISE CLAIBORNE	J	653 - 676	
ARMSTRONG, SALLY	A	108 - 110	
ARWINE, LEWIS H.	D	254	
ASHCRAFT, ANNIE H.	H	171	
ASHCRAFT, ANN ANDERSON	R	709	
ASHCRAFT, GEORGE U.	O	1, 3 - 10	
ASHE, ANNA	D	119	
ASHWORTH, IRENE CLANCY	L	433, 566 - 571	
ASHWORTH, JOHNNY EDWARD	D	291	
ASHWORTH, JOSEPH RUCKER	G	86, 331 - 332	
ASWELL, ROSEVELT R.	E	417 - 419	
ATWELL, MARTHA TOWNSEND	U	570	
AUERBECK, ANNIE T.	D	27 - 31	
AUSBROOKS, BESSIE H.	R	725	
AUSTIN, IRVING O.	H	449	
AUSTIN, Q.P.	O	11, 13, 14	16 - 22
BABCOCK, H.T.	D	281	
BABCOCK, JIMMIE GLEN	G	594	
BAGGETT, EMMETT	H	33, 398 - 400	
BAILEY, MARY A.	C	203 & 221	

2

Name		
BAKER, JIM	U	437
BAKER, JOHN M.B.	A	152
BAKER, SAVANNA	G	155
BAKER, SAVANNAH	E	360 - 362
BALDWIN, ELLA MAE	L	555, 645 - 648
BALLARD, J.E.	D	408
BALLARD, JAMES A.	E	239 - 242
BALLARD, T.V.	D	75
BARBAREE, ALICE E.	W	115 - 131
BARBAREE, P. M.	J	243, 287 - 289
BARBAREE, W.T.	C	372 - 374
BAREFOOT, CAPTAIN MITCHELL	R	569
BARNES, ANNIE GLOVER	M	500, 579 - 582
BARNES, ED S.	D	214
BARNETT, ASA	B	132 - 137
BARNETT, MICHAEL H.	C	90
BARNETTE, ARTHUR	R	366
BARR, ANNIE HENDRICK	K	782
BARR, ANNIE HENDRICK	L	233 - 236
BARR, H.S. SR.	I	514 - 517
BARR, MAGGIE SIMS	E	103 - 105
BARR, MARY E.	C	437 - 439
BARR, RALPH J.	C	420 & 422
BARR, ROBERT E.	S	208
BARR, ROBERT E.	S	619	Estate
BARR, ROBERT E.	T	265
BARR, ROBERT H.	X	803 - 817
BARR, W.L.	C	184 - 185
BARRON, A. ST. C.	J	789, 797 - 801	Trans. to Circuit Ct.
BARRON, ARCHIE	F	242
BARRON, GUSSIE E.	L	207, 696 - 702
BARRON, HERMAN	O	794, 798 - 801
BARRON, HERMAN ED	O	802 - 805
BARRON, LAWRENCE C.	F	245
BARRON, LEON E.	S	437
BARRON, MARTIN	O	329, 332 - 339
BARRON, MARY E.	K	129
BARRON, MARY E.	L	1 - 5
BARRON, MRS. CARRIE	F	237
BARRON, W.H.	R	734
BARRON, W.H.	S	603	Estate
BARTELL, LOUISE	H	63
BASHINSKY, E.B.	G	566, 570

BASHINSKY, E.B.	I	46	final settlement
BASHINSKY, E.B. (final settlement)	H	465, 467 - 470	
BASHINSKY, LEOPOLD M.	D	224	
BASS, ANNIE C.	I	44, 45	
BASS, ANNIE CLOUD	H	540	
BASS, GRADY SHELBY	I	627	
BASS, SALLIE C.	D	259	
BASS, SYLVIA F.	Q	485	
BASS, WALTER A.	K	667 - 687	
BASS, WALTER A.	L	117 - 123	Trans. to Circuit Ct.
BASSETT, EWELL C.	E	298 - 300	
BASSETT, FANNIE H,	I	530 - 532	
BASSETT, FANNY H.	I	363, 364	
BASSETT, J.C.	G	559, 649 - 650	
BASSETT, J.W.	F	250	
BASSETT, JOHN H.	D	142 - 143	
BATTLE, JOHN M.	B	22 - 24	
BATTLE, MINNIE	D	325	
BAXLEY, GUSSIE G.	T	529	
BEALL, LILLIAN CARLISLE	E	380 - 383	
BEAMAN, ABRAHAM SR.	A	25 - 26	
BEAN, ALEXANDER	A	133 - 135	
BEAN, DORCAS	A	133	
BEAN, IDA	E	353 - 355	
BEAN, JAMES F.	B	17 - 18	
BEAN, MOLLIE H.	D	389	
BEAN, WILL	E	307 - 309	
BEARD, IDA W.	D	193 - 194	
BEARD, J.B.	Q	303	
BEARD, J.S.	D	207	
BEARD, LOIS A.	D	348 - 349	
BEARD, ROBERT B.	F	257	
BEASLEY, ED	N	248 - 254	
BEASLEY, MARTHA A.	D	350	
BEASLEY, W.L.	D	404	
BECK, CHESTER K. SR.	L	426, 595 - 598	
BECK, FOSTER C.	J	13	
BECK, JORDAN	B	212 - 213	
BECK, MABEL R.	M	216, 218	364 - 369
BECK, MABEL R.	N	255	
BELCHER, A.S.	I	267, 268	
BELCHER, A.S.	I	534 - 537	final settlement
BELCHER, CORA CLARK	K	94	

4

BELCHER, CORA CLARK	L	135 - 139	
BELL, JOHN E.	O	24, 27 - 37	
BELL, JOSEPH	D	80 - 81	
BELL, LAURA W.	D	77 - 78	
BELL, N.J.	F	203	
BELL, SAMUEL	A	84	
BELSER, C.C.	E	207 - 209	
BENBOW, ANN E.	A	175 - 177	
BERRY, LENA	H	30, 125 - 126	
BERRY, A.F.	F	230	
BERRY, ARMOUR L.	T	324	
BERRY, DAVID A.	E	363 - 365	
BERRY, ELBIRDIE	L	797	
BERRY, ELBIRDIE	M	370 - 374	final settlement
BERRY, EMORY	E	369 - 371	
BERRY, ESSIE G.	T	713 - 723	
BERRY, EWELL EDGAR	K	774	
BERRY, EWELL EDGAR	M	516 - 519	
BERRY, LOUIS	E	403 - 405	
BERRY, LOUIS	M	73 - 75	Trans. to Circuit Ct.
BERRY, WOODROW	N	817 - 824	
BETHUNE, BESSIE	H	121 - 122	
BETHUNE, BESSIE	G	615	
BEVERLY, J.J.	E	275 - 277	
BIGHAM, JOHN	C	67 - 68	
BILLUP, MARTHA A.	C	219	
BISSITT, GEORGE W.	G	309, 312, 316	
BLACK, PETE C.	H	96, 257 - 259	
BLACK, J.K.	P	238, 240 - 247	
BLACK, MARY H.	E	260 - 274	
BLACK, MARY H.	K	260 - 263	final settlement
BLACK, MIRIAM RUSSELL	Y	449 - 475	
BLACK, WALTER C.	D	93 - 94	
BLACKMAN, AGNES SPEER	U	1	
BLACKMAN, JAMES	C	85	
BLACKMAN, LOUIE R.	O	662, 667 - 694	
BLACKMON, ARTHUR J.	I	109	
BLACKMON, ARTHUR JOSEPH	M	277	
BLACKWELL, MARVIN T.	I	91, 179, 180	
BLACKWELL, MARY	C	129 - 130	
BLAIR, JANE P.	D	36 - 37	
BLAIR, L.C.	O	204, 207	209 - 228
BLAIR, TOMMIE	F	261	

BOWERS, BENJAMIN	B	175 - 179
BOWERS, TINIE J.	D	366
BOYD, ALABAMA H.	M	295, 375 - 378
BOYD, ANDREW L.	S	22
BOYD, ANNIE MELL	D	316
BOYD, BETTY M.	G	159
BOYD, CASPER W.	A	249 - 250
BOYD, CHARLES L.R.	C	163
BRADFORD, KRUGER	N	744 - 650
BRADLEY, ANNIE F.	D	70 - 71
BRADLEY, CLARENCE	P	541 - 545
BRADLEY, LILLIE H.	G	533, 599, 600
BRADLEY, MARY	P	535 - 538
BRADLEY, MARY C.	A	188 - 189
BRADLEY, W.A.	D	6
BRADLEY, W.A.	D	6
BRADSHAW, JOHN	A	77 - 79
BRADSHAW, JOHN H.	B	148 - 149
BRADY, DR. JAMES T.	B	203 - 206
BRAGG, JOE DORRILL	J	98, 130,- 133
BRAGG, MARY C.	J	257, 290 - 293
BRANDIS, E.A.	D	392
BRANNEN, EZRA R.	C	353 - 355
BRANNEN, SAMANTHA E.	C	448 - 453
BRANNON, C.C.	D	371 - 372
BRANTLEY, EILEEN GIBSON	H	554, 571 - 572
BRANTLEY, ALEX E.	F	543
BRANTLEY, BETTY GASTON	X	150 - 168
BRANTLEY, CARRIE	G	171
BRANTLEY, EDNA P.	O	40, 42 - 50
BRANTLEY, EMMA MARY	D	69
BRANTLEY, FLAVIA O'NEAL	D	276
BRANTLEY, HERBERT W.	G	517, 521, 522
BRANTLEY, J.A.	D	35
BRANTLEY, J.G.	D	374 - 376
BRANTLEY, JAMES T.	D	382
BRANTLEY, JOE K.	L	582 - 586
BRANTLEY, JOE K.	M	520 - 521 final settlement
BRANTLEY, JUILA WILEY	J	154
BRANTLEY, KYLE M.	O	51, 66 - 74
BRANTLEY, MARY HENDERSON	E	21
BRANTLEY, MARY JOHNSON	R	80
BRANTLEY, T.K.	C	289 - 293

BRANTLEY, W.H.	D	47 - 48
BRASWELL, J.T.	F	247
BRASWELL, JAMES W.	A	90 - 92
BRASWELL, W.R.	I	663 - 664
BRAZIL, JENNIE	G	115, 459, 460
BRAZIL, MYRTLE FAY	F	4
BREWTON, MARK PALMER JR.	W	432 - 451
BRIGGS, MCARTHUR	Q	806
BROOKS, J.M.	R	632
BROOKS, ROBERT	A	20 - 21
BROOKS, WINNIE D.	D	308
BROWDER, H.E.	W	197 - 199
BROWN, W. A.	H	184, 255 - 256
BROWN, ANNIE LAURA	E	321
BROWN, BENJAMIN G.	B	67 - 68
BROWN, CHARLES G.	D	165 - 166
BROWN, CHARLES KANE	E	25
BROWN, FANNIE C.	D	102 - 104
BROWN, HUBERT C.	E	406 - 413
BROWN, HUBERT K.	L	771
BROWN, HUBERT K.	M	83 - 88
BROWN, J. RANDOLPH	C	314 - 315
BROWN, JAMES MARION	T	271
BROWN, JAMES MARION	U	55
BROWN, JIM	F	240
BROWN, JOHN G.	C	120 - 121
BROWN, M. ANDERSON	D	264
BROWN, MAUDE REYNOLDS	D	252 - 253
BROWN, NAN SUE	J	588, 817 - 821
BROWN, PUGH U.	D	108 - 109
BROWN, ROSA LEE	N	384 - 389
BROWN, SAM	G	87
BROWN, W. PETE	G	158
BROWN, WANDA SMITH	G	162
BROWN, WILBUR	D	217
BROXTON, ISAAC I.	B	127 - 129
BRUNDIDGE, IDA MAE C.	E	393 - 396
BRUWINGTON, LEONA	F	244
BRYAN, CLIFFORD C.	H	166, 253 - 254
BRYAN, ROY EVANS	J	4, 163 - 166
BRYAN, BERTHA MAE FOLMAR	I	481
BRYAN, JAMES G.	N	637 - 653
BRYAN, JEANETTE	N	390 - 394

BRYAN, JOHN FREEMAN	V	768
BRYAN, MARCUS W.	F	225
BRYAN, MARGARET J.	Y	589 - 604
BRYAN, YANCEY L.	D	150 - 151
BRYANT, C.L.	D	355
BRYANT, DELL BENSON	E	384 - 392
BRYANT, HARVEY LEE	W	575 - 585
BRYANT, JOHN COLLINS	C	454 - 462
BRYANT, LILLAR C.	K	97
BRYANT, MARY EMMA	Y	289 - 299
BRYANT, SAMUEL	U	129
BRYANT, W.J.	F	235
BULGER, JESSE OLIVER	T	399
BULLARD, HARVEY R.	F	228
BUNDRICK, ELLA	H	330
BUNDRICK, WM. J.	D	65 - 66
BUNTIN, J.C.	M	776
BUNTIN, J.C.	N	13 - 16
BURDEN, JOE LOUIS	U	496
BURDEN, WILL	D	321
BURDICK, BIBB Q	G	383, 461, 462
BURKS, LOUIS C.	P	500 - 534
BURKS, NELLYE T.	H	351, 403 - 404
BURKS, ROBERT TURNER	L	801
BURKS, ROBERT TURNER	M	89 - 92
BURKS, VERA IRENE PRYER	M	383 - 387
BURKS, VERA IRENE PRYOR	L	623
BURKS, VERA IRENE PRYOR	N	17
BURNETT, B.W.	F	556
BURNETTE, WESLEY PAUL	K	346
BURNEY, ARON	K	547
BURNEY, ARON	L	130 - 134
BUSCH, WILLIAM J.	Q	862
BUSH, HENRY	C	207
BUSH, M.C.	C	279 - 281
BUTLER, MYRA G.	D	312
BUTTS, SUSIE	D	223
BYNUM, MARY ENZOR	H	335, 405 - 406
BYNUM, LEVERT DANIEL	J	31, 126 - 129
BYRD, MARION	H	123 - 124
BYRD, BESSIE	P	360, 362 - 367
BYRD, MARVIN	G	579
CADE, IGNATIUS	B	28 - 29

CALDWELL, CLARENCE O.	W	465 - 478	
CALDWELL, CLARENCE O.	X	18 - 30	
CALDWELL, HENRY GRADY	L	625, 653 - 656	
CALDWELL, JAMES E.	J	269, 294 - 296	
CALDWELL, MAMIE	J	262	
CALDWELL, MAMIE	K	380 - 383	
CALDWELL, WILLIAM J.	O	75, 79 - 89	
CALHOUN, J.C.	T	115	
CAMERON, FRED	F	264	
CAMERON, GEORGIA S.	D	314	
CAMERON, W.C.	D	177	
CAMPBELL, CHARLES A.	H	525	
CAMPBELL, ABNER	C	465 - 468	
CAMPBELL, ABNER B.	C	209 - 210	
CAMPBELL, BENJAMIN W.	A	242 - 244	
CAMPBELL, CHARLES A.	I	2 - 4	
CAMPBELL, JAMES R.	W	518 - 530	
CAMPBELL, LUCY E.	T	814	
CAMPBELL, MABEL R.	Y	126 - 135	
CAMPBELL, MAMIE H.	J	460, 771 - 774	
CANTEWELL, JOHNNIE PARNELL	E	93 - 95	
CANTY, G.N.	D	401	
CANTY, LAMON P.	K	134, 387 - 390	
CARDWELL, CLARENCE EUGENE	M	61, 348 - 351	
CARDWELL, E. A.	J	57 - 60	
CARDWELL, E.A.	I	650	
CARDWELL, JOHN N.	I	479, 593, 594	
CARDWELL, RUTH SOMERSET	G	117	
CARGILE, F.P.	D	204	
CARGILE, JASON	A	181 - 182	
CARLISLE, GREEN W.	C	19 - 23	
CARLISLE, IDELLA	O	90, 92 - 115	695 - 712
CARLISLE, JESSIE PRICE	I	573	
CARLISLE, JOHN JR.	U	419	
CARLISLE, MOLLIE	J	161, 222 - 224	Carlisle, Richard Ex'r.
CARNLINE, LEWIS	A	11	
CARROLL, ALLIE M.	D	186	
CARROLL, C.G.	D	280	
CARROLL, EMMETT O.	M	571 - 572	583 - 586
CARROLL, J.S.	C	254 - 259	
CARROLL, JOHN E.	Q	501	
CARROLL, JOSEPH	N	826 - 831	
CARROLL, MAGGIE ANN	E	108 - 110	

CARROLL, NORA	D	252	
CARROLL, W.C.	D	159	
CARSWELL, ADAM	W	861 - 873	
CARTER, MILTON	H	619	
CARTER, ARTHUR P.	I	290	
CARTER, CULLEN BRYANT	M	297, 387 - 392	
CARTER, EDGAR	J	467, 473 - 476	
CARTER, FLOSSIE R.	J	550	
CARTER, FLOSSIE R.	K	352 - 358	Trans. to Circuit Ct.
CARTER, G.B.	F	275	
CARTER, H.J.	J	83	
CARTER, HARVEY J.	J	167 - 170	
CARTER, J.A.	D	287 - 288	
CARTER, JAMES S. SR.	P	876	
CARTER, JOHN LUCIAN	M	327	
CARTER, MAMIE E.	K	350, 706 - 709	
CARTER, MAMIE H.	L	681	
CARTER, MAMIE H.	M	93 - 99	Trans. to Circuit Ct.
CARTER, MARVIN H.	D	386 - 389	
CARTER, MARVIN R.	T	14	
CARTER, MARVIN V.	S	217	
CARTER, MARY F.	N	140 - 141	256 - 260
CARTER, MILDRED ACKER	O	713 - 717	
CARTER, MILTON C.	K	384 - 386	
CARTER, NETTIE	F	272	
CARTER, RAYMOND	G	319, 322 - 323	
CARTER, W.A.	E	375 - 379	
CARTER, W.A.	I	76 - 79	
CARTER, W.A.	K	580, 581	Trans. to Circuit Ct.
CASEY, KATE T.	W	305 - 326	
CASTLEBERRY, SARA F.	N	18 - 23	
CERVERA, PATRICIA S.	L	214, 241 - 244	
CHAMBERS, CODY LEON	R	376	
CHAMBERS, CODY LEON	L	353, 447 - 450	
CHAMBERS, JOE MARK	K	1, 264 - 267	
CHANCELLOR, G. C.	H	341 - 345	final settlement
CHANCELLOR, G.C.	G	584	
CHANCELLOR, RUBY S.	V	628 - 639	
CHANCELLOR, RUBY S.	W	411 - 418	
CHANCEY, ERIE K.	N	705 - 710	
CHANCEY, LAURA J.	E	181 - 185	
CHANCEY, MILDRED	P	4, 6 - 15	
CHANCEY, NAN LOU	E	243 - 246	

CHANCEY, WILLIE G.	D	185
CHANCY, DAVID	C	92 - 93
CHANCY, LUTHER	V	56 - 65
CHANDLER, DORIS E.	R	170
CHANDLER, GEORGE M.	J	96
CHAPMAN, CORLEY SR.	P	108, 117 - 129
CHAPMAN, E.H.	D	260
CHAPMAN, ETHEL C.	I	248 - 251
CHAPMAN, HENRY	P	718 - 733
CHAPMAN, KATHRYN RUSHTON	U	
CHAPMAN, LUCIE C.	R	504
CHATMAN, LAURA W.	M	188, 393 - 397
CHATMAN, SANFORD	Q	261
CHATMON, SANFORD	O	718, 720 - 724 726, 728 - 730
CHESSER, REBECCA R.	C	144 - 145
CHILDS, CLIFFORD L.	H	552
CHILDS, GRACE M.	H	83, 129 - 130
CHILDS, CLIFFORD L.	I	51, 52
CHURCH, MARGARET	J	465, 647 - 651 Trans. to Circuit Ct.
CLARK, DEWEY H.	L	811
CLARK, DEWEY H.	M	64
CLARK, ELIZABETH C.	C	260 - 262
CLARK, JESSIE E.	L	544, 649 - 652
CLARK, JOHN	A	237 - 238
CLARK, W.J.	G	175
CLARY, WILEY S.	B	89 - 90
CLEMENTS, ENTYS THOMAS	Y	563 - 573
COCHRAN, J.R.	D	322
COCHRAN, MRS. CARRIE B.	E	366 - 368
COHN, DORA	D	262
COKER, JOHN M.	R	761
COLE, DORA CRESWELL	O	806, 808 - 823
COLE, KILE P.	V	224 - 235
COLEMAN, GERALDINE BARKER	X	539 - 551
COLLEY, B. JUDSON	I	512
COLLEY, B. JUDSON	J	225 - 227
COLLEY, BERTA H.	G	190
COLLEY, JESSE HALL	J	381
COLLEY, JESSE HALL	J	775 - 778
COLLEY, MYRTIS C.	L	123, 245 - 248
COLLIER, ALLIE	C	356 - 358
COLLIER, JAMES MARSHALL	C	244 - 245
COLLIER, SAMUEL D.	I	637

COLLINS, IDA BELLE	I	132, 181, 182	
COLLINS, KANNIE S.	H	207 -213	final settlement
COLLINS, KANNIE SMYTH	G	587	
COLQUETT, HARRIET A.	S	158	
COMPTON, LOUISE H.	V	767 - 764	
COMPTON, LOUISE H.	X	436 - 459	
CONNELL, EMMA B.	D	377	
CONNOR, EFFIE RODGERS	V	245 - 256	
CONNOR, FRED	G	263, 489 - 490	
CONNOR, J.W.	G	178	
CONNOR, MARTIN	C	251 - 253	
CONRAD, DAVID HOMER	H	452, 478 - 481	
COOK, NETTIE MAE	R	180, 651	
COPE, FLOY R.	U	539	
COPELAND, ANNIE GLENN	D	293	
COPELAND, E.D.	E	197 - 198	
COPELAND, EDITH IRENE	G	102	
COPELAND, EDITH IRENE	G	455 - 456	
COPELAND, EZELL	L	205, 443 - 446	
COPELAND, H. MOSS	D	87 - 89	
COPELAND, J.S.	C	272 - 274	
COPELAND, JOSHUA L.	D	237 - 238	
COPELAND, KATE M.	G	6	
COPELAND, LEE H.	D	278	
COPELAND, LUCY KNOX	M	573 - 574	
COPELAND, LUCY KNOX	N	24 - 28	
COPELAND, MRS. ANNIE L.	D	123 - 124	
COPELAND, SETH	N	636	Trans. to Circuit Ct.
COPELAND, SETH	G	183	CIRCUIT CT. 5/30/1984
COPELAND, VONCILE J.	R	771	
CORKINS, SID	K	391 - 396	
CORLEY, MYRTLE BEARD	L	322, 375 - 378	
COSBY, A.Y.	C	31 - 32	
COSKREY, BERTA	H	61	
COSKREY, BERTA	I	668 - 671	final settlement
COSKREY, D.S.	C	59 - 63	
COSKREY, DAVID	C	52 - 53	
COSTON, JOHN W.	N	261 - 265	
COWART, BESSIE C.	E	39 - 40	
COWART, JAMES	A	9	
COWART, MATTIE LEE	G	131	
COWART, MATTIE LEE	G	329 - 330	
COWLES, T.D.	F	583	

COX, JIM CURTIS SR.	N	395 - 401	
COX, JIM CURTIS SR.	P	134, 137 - 143	446, 448
COX, WILLIAM	F	278	
COX, ZERA	M	486, 587 - 590	
CRAFT, T. W.	H	326, 482 - 484	
CRAFT, JAMES W.	Y	495 - 510	
CRAWFORD, GUSSIE H.	J	259, 482 - 485	
CRAWLEY, ANNIE LAURIE	P	680 - 708	
CRITTENDEN, ELLA M.	J	807, 822 - 826	Crittenden, Roy E. Ex'
CRITTENDEN, ZACK G. SR.	J	389 - 392	
CRITTENDON, SARAH E.	D	118	
CROSS, ODELLE POLLARD	T	804 - 813	
CROSWELL, EDITH	H	127 -128	
CROSWELL, EDITH	G	558	
CROSWELL, WM.	B	142 - 145	
CROW, BEULAH W.	V	121 - 133	
CROW, F.B.	D	211	
CROW, J.R.	X	856 - 867	
CROWDER, R.P.	D	366	
CROZIER, ANNE STARKE	G	457 - 358	
CULPEPPER, CARLOS C.	I	610	
CULPEPPER, CARLOS C.	J	477 - 481	Will located in file.
CULVERHOUSE, CLARENCE W.	M	57, 299 - 314	
CULVERHOUSE, JERRY C.	K	535	
CULVERHOUSE, JERRY C.	L	249 - 252	
CULVERHOUSE, LILLIE L.	M	280	
CUMMINGS, FOY INGRAM	I	134, 230 - 232	
CUNNING, JOHN	A	215 - 222	
CURRY, EULA G.	E	372 - 374	
CURRY, H.M.	D	154	
CURRY, IDA M.	E	414 - 416	
CURRY, MATTIE LEE	I	19, 596 - 598	
CURRY, SHELLIE S.	Q	874	
CURTIS, CATHERINE K.	U	116	
CURTIS, H.C.	K	665	
CURTIS, H.C.	L	379 - 382	
CURTIS, J.A.	G	129, 491 - 492	
CURTIS, J.R.	C	377 - 382	
CURTIS, JOHN M.	T	662 - 680	
DAILEY, DANIEL H.	N	235	
DANIELS, A. J.	G	83, 493 - 494	
DANIELS, MARY P.	H	287	
DANIELS, MARY	C	426 - 428	

DANIELS, MARY R.	K	405 - 408	
DANIELS, THOMAS J.	C	368 - 371	
DANSBY, SMITH	L	114, 253 - 259	
DARBY, CELESTE	D	362 - 364	
DARBY, JAMES	A	56 - 57	
DARBY, M.E.	D	49 - 50	
DARBY, MADGE D.	R	189	
DARBY, MCLEOD	D	49	
DAVENPORT, JIM	D	374	
DAVENPORT, O.L.	I	615	
DAVENPORT, O.L.	K	589 - 594	final settlement
DAVENPORT, O.L. SR.	M	578	Trans. to Circuit Ct.
DAVIS, M. G.	G	196	
DAVIS, W. R.	H	1 -7	
DAVIS, ANNIE PEARL	N	832 - 837	
DAVIS, DACRE GREEN JR.	X	393 - 404	
DAVIS, DUTCH	N	751 - 760	
DAVIS, E.L.	I	438	
DAVIS, E.L.	K	401 - 404	
DAVIS, ELGIEMAE GARLEEN KELLY	M	324, 530 - 534	
DAVIS, H.A.	I	623	
DAVIS, H.A.	K	413 - 416	
DAVIS, HAZEL B.	L	220, 383 - 386	
DAVIS, J.L. JR.	I	566 - 578	
DAVIS, J.T.	E	234 - 238	
DAVIS, JACQUELYN M.	G	193	
DAVIS, JAMES E.	U	733	
DAVIS, JOSIAH	B	146 - 148	
DAVIS, MAGGIE RUTH	W	490 - 496	
DAVIS, MARY ANN	I	340	
DAVIS, MARY ANN	K	397 - 400	
DAVIS, MYRTICE D.	P	202, 204 - 213	
DAVIS, ODESSA JOHNSTON	K	141, 268 - 272	
DAVIS, ODESSA JOHNSTON	L	451 - 464	final settlement
DAVIS, PEARL C.	R	199	
DAVIS, PEARL C.	S	244	
DAVIS, PRESLEY	B	25 - 27	
DAVIS, PRESLEY	Q	245	
DAVIS, ROSEMOND A.	I	93 - 101	
DAVIS, S.C.	D	92 - 93	
DAVIS, SALLIE C.	W	200 - 216	
DAVIS, SARA M.	Q	284	
DAVIS, T. H.	H	569	

DAVIS, T.J.	D	205
DAVIS, TREVELYAN	I	377
DAVISON, MATTIE A.	H	349, 487 - 489
DAVISON, ANN A.	C	32 - 34
DAVISON, J.A.	D	275 - 276
DAVISON, JOHN M.	E	420 - 422
DAVISON, JOHN M.	H	485 - 486
DAWKINS, JOHN C.	N	403 - 408
DAY, MARTIN H.	A	208 - 212
DEAN, JOSEPH EDWARD	P	248, 251 - 259
DEBICE, GILLIS	J	89
DEBICE, GILLIS	K	409 - 412
DEES, CLARA HIX	D	389
DEFEE, J.J.	D	132 - 133
DEJARNETTE, IDA W.	E	455 - 457
DENNIS, CHARLES	B	20 - 21
DENNIS, DANIEL	A	245 - 246
DEVENPORT, ELIZABETH	A	206 - 208
DICKENS, MYRTLE PARKS	W	388 - 401
DICKERT, EVELYN BEASLEY	I	394, 599 - 602
DICKERT, ISIE MARSH	L	371, 465 - 469
DICKERT, J. RALPH	M	561, 591 - 594
DICKEY, CURTIS	R	105
DICKINS, CHARLES WAYNE	S	547
DICKINSON, LENA COLLIER	E	186 - 187
DICKINSON, MRS. ANNIE	D	302
DIETZ, MARY M.	J	568
DIETZ, MARY M.	K	157 - 160
DILLARD, JOHN P.	D	309
DINKIND, J.T.J.	C	118 - 119
DINKINS, ED	B	152 - 155
DINKINS, JANIE	D	307 - 308
DISMUKE, VINEY	C	211 - 212
DISMUKES, MARTHA	D	130 - 131
DIX, LULA	M	575, 682 - 685
DIX, LULA	N	266 final settlement
DIX, RALPH	R	211
DOCKETT, WALTER	U	371
DODSON, IDA F.	Y	476
DODSON, MARVIN N.	J	118, 490 - 493
DONALDSON, CARY DEAM	H	85, 216 - 217
DONALDSON, CAROLYN R.	M	782
DONALDSON, CAROLYN R.	N	29 - 34

DONALDSON, LEORA	M	576 - 577	686 - 689
DORNE, ABNER	A	112 - 113	
DORRILL, DENZIL GARY	H	291, 317 - 318	
DORRILL, GARY G.	Q	513	
DORRILL, J.H.	E	111 - 113	
DORRILL, WESLEY W.	E	400 - 402	
DORRILL, WILLIAM W.	D	215	
DOSTER, BESSIE R.	R	297	
DOTY, LOUISE K.	P	809 - 817	
DOUGLAS, ANNIE LAURIE	G	199	
DOUGLAS, BRYANT J.	D	184	
DOUGLAS, C.B.	C	349 - 353	
DOUGLAS, L.S	G	614, 643 - 644	
DOWLING, ADDIE RUTH	E	231 - 233	
DOZIER, L.L.	N	402	
DOZIER, LINWOOD LAWSON	J	316, 486 - 489	
DOZIER, MRS. NETTIE	D	218 - 219	
DRAGOIN, ANTHONY	K	8, 33 - 36	
DRIGGERS, WILLIAM B.	H	392, 407 - 408	
DRINKARD, L.L.	M	768	
DRINKARD, L.L.	N	35 - 38	
DUBOSE, ETHEL A.	O	436, 439 - 451	
DUBOSE, JEREMIAH	A	75 - 77	
DUBOSE, L.H.	D	106 - 107	
DUBOSE, MAMIE	K	661	
DUBOSE, MAMIE	L	615 - 618	
DUKE, WALTER M.	K	253	
DUNBAR, ROXY M.	G	139, 607 - 608	
DUNBAR, ALICE WOODALL	S	689	
DUNBAR, E.F.	J	337	
DUNBAR, E.F.	L	470 - 473	
DUNBAR, E.F.	N	39	
DUNBAR, MABEL W.	N	530 - 532	536 - 537, 565 - 569
DUNBAR, ROXIE	I	5, 7	
DUNBAR, THOMAS W.	R	227	
DUNBAR, THOMAS W.	S	32	
DUNFORD, BERNICE R.	G	613, 641 - 642	
DUNN, VICTOR	H	301 - 302	
DUNN, C.A.	I	476	
DUNN, C.A.	N	40 - 43	
DUNN, DAVID A.	A	62 - 63	
DUNN, KATIE BELLE	X	703 - 717	
DUNN, VICTOR	G	572	

DUNN, WILLIAM CODY	W	183 - 196	
DUNN, WILLIAM RICHARD	J	61 - 66	final settlement
DYER, SANDRA E.	Q	704	
DYHES, LIZZIE	D	129 - 130	
DYKES, FLORENCE METTA	K	89, 161 - 164	
EAGERTON, CALLIE	R	1, 780	
EAVES, JANE B	B	228 - 230	
ECHEVARRIAS, DIEGO	W	548 - 554	744 - 749
ECHOLS, MARY R.	C	463 - 464	
EDDINGS, ORILEEN	S	783	
EDDINS, HORACE HAYGOOD	I	261	
EDDINS, J.S.	B	113 - 114	
EDGE, EVA	N	126, 142 - 145	
EDGE, OSCAR N.	M	259-268	270-274 Trans. Cir. Ct.
EDMONSON, ALEX C.	C	341 - 348	
EDMONSON, ANNIE BELLE	P	608 - 623	
EDMONSON, ELLA A.	D	188	
EDWARDS, G. B.	G	509	
EDWARDS, G. B.	H	117 - 118	
EDWARDS, H.J.	J	596, 604 - 606	
EDWARDS, JOHN	B	102 - 103	
EDWARDS, LOTTIE LEE	I	562	
EDWARDS, RUTH HILL	L	747	
EDWARDS, RUTH HILL	M	1 - 6	
EIDSON, LORENZO	J	86, 171 - 174	
EIDSON, MITTIE	J	92	
ELLINGTON, CARRIE	U	581	
ELLINGTON, CARRIE	T	694	
ELLIOT, MARGARET ELISE	M	100 - 103	
ELLIOTT, MARGARET ELISE	L	423	
ELLIS, CHARLES FREDRICK	H	328	
ELLIS, CHARLES FREDERICK	K	421 - 424	
ELLIS, EMORY CURRY	F	281	
ELLIT, DAVIS	A	104 - 104	
ELMORE, A.B.	R	380	
ELMORE, OLIVE RAINER	J	560	
ELMORE, V.J.	J	565	
EMFINGER, HENRY W.	C	128 - 129	
ENGLAND, ALTON GRIFFIS	I	571, 672 - 674	
ENGRAM, LILLA	D	277	
ENZOR, MINNIE IDA	H	549, 573 - 574	
ENZOR, ELENOR A.	D	122	
ENZOR, FRANKIE CATHERINE	J	277, 297 - 301	

ENZOR, JOSIAH LANE	I	117	
ENZOR, JOSIAH N.	C	83 - 84	
ENZOR, MINNIE IDA	I	23, 24	
ENZOR, MISS ANNIE	E	397 - 399	
ENZOR, NORMAN C.	M	629, 690 - 693	
ENZOR, TOY FRAZIER	E	11	
ENZOR, VERA ELIZABETH	I	510	
ENZOR, VERA ELIZABETH	K	417 - 420	
ERVIN, ROBERT HUGH	N	555 - 557	570 - 574
ERVIN, VIOLET GROSS	V	580 - 607	
ETHERIDGE, OLINE S.	S	1	
ETHRIDGE, LOVIE	N	409 - 414	
EVANS, JOHNNIE P.	I	28, 56, 57	
EVANS, WM. P.	B	111 - 112	
FAIRCLOTH, A.J.	I	520	
FAIRCLOTH, A.J.	K	425 - 428	
FAIRCLOTH, J.F.	K	3, 165 - 168	
FAIRCLOTH, MARY E.	Q	193	
FAIRCLOTH, MERRILL B.	Y	642 - 651	
FAIRCLOTH, VARA M.	T	247	
FANNIN, EDGAR RIVERS	N	267 - 273	
FANNIN, J.B.	C	402 - 406	
FANNIN, LOUIS R.	I	326, 385, 386	
FARMER, CURREN MONROE	F	288	
FARMER, ROXIE LEE	F	537	
FARNELL, JEFF D.	D	59	
FARNELL, MRS. PEARL	E	430 435	
FARRIS, HILDRETH C.	V	257 - 263	
FAULK, MAGGIE P.	G	486, 544 - 545	
FAULK, BERNARD G.	L	373, 474 - 477	
FAULK, ELLA TAYLOR	W	650 - 655	
FAULK, JAMES THOMAS	M	487, 526 - 529	
FAULK, JESSIE	V	236 - 244	
FAULK, JESSIE	W	149 - 152	
FAULK, LEVI O.	J	791	
FENN, FLORENCE ELIZABETH	X	731 - 740	
FIELDER, LUGENIUS B.	B	9 - 10	
FIELDER, T.L.	B	11 - 13	
FINLAY, FRED G.	E	289 - 291	
FINLAY, MILLIE F.	I	408, 422 - 425	
FINLAY, T.W.	E	114 - 115	
FINLAY, W.R.	C	407 - 412	
FITTS, DORA W.	G	203	

FLEMING, JESSIE M.	H	238, 409 - 410	
FLEMING, A.G.	D	300	
FLEMING, J.S.	K	359	
FLEMING, J.S.	L	607 - 614	
FLEMING, JULIA T.	K	659	
FLEMING, JULIA T.	L	6 - 10	
FLEMING, JULIA T.	R	567	
FLOURNOY, GUS	F	283	
FLOURNOY, J.C.	B	149 - 151	
FLOWERS, ELIZABETH	H	137, 142 - 143	
FLOWERS, JESSIE	G	583, 639--640	
FLOWERS, ARTHUR T.	R	707	
FLOWERS, ELIZABETH	I	187 - 189	190, 191 settlement
FLOWERS, EVELYN E.	O	195, 203	
FLOWERS, EVELYN MOZELLE	I	518, 538 - 540	
FLOWERS, GLORIA G.	X	718 - 730	
FLOWERS, GRADY LEE	Y	700 - 706	
FLOWERS, HILL GRAVES	X	405 - 420	655 - 656
FLOWERS, JACK	N	278 - 285	
FLOWERS, JAS. C.	D	59 - 60	
FLOWERS, JOE TOM	L	367, 478 - 483	
FLOWERS, JOHN	A	101 - 103	
FLOWERS, LORETTA CARTER	I	21, 58, 59	
FLOWERS, R. GRADY	D	401	
FLOWERS, R.C.	D	76, 77, & 92	
FLOWERS, R.C.	D	92 - 76	
FLOWERS, ROSIE CARLISLE	M	618	
FLOWERS, W.C. SR.	F	7	
FLOWERS, WILL	J	120, 175 - 178	
FLOWERS, Z.E.	D	256	
FLOYD JOHNNIE BERTHA HICKMAN	K	105, 429 - 432	
FLOYD, CLIVE WINTON	N	209, 274 - 277	
FLOYD, F.F. (FLETCHER)	K	6, 169 - 172	
FLOYD, LAMAR J.	Q	525	
FLOYD, O.D.	D	365	
FLOYD, RAY	X	225 - 237	
FLYNN, MALLIE	C	202	
FOLEY, JULIA P.	R	386	
FOLEY, WILLIAM D. JR	N	131 - 135	146 - 147
FOLMAR, EMORY	G	318, 542 - 543	
FOLMAR, JESSE T.	H	88, 264 - 265	
FOLMAR, CATHERINE HILLIARD	E	440 - 443	
FOLMAR, CHESTER EARL	M	335, 522 - 525	

FOLMAR, FLOYCE C.	L	809	
FOLMAR, FLOYCE C.	M	110 - 115	
FOLMAR, HELEN	D	160 - 161	
FOLMAR, HENRY W.	X	670 - 681	
FOLMAR, JULIA KNOX	D	99	
FOLMAR, LEOLA INGRAM	K	652	
FOLMAR, LEOLA INGRAM	L	260 - 265	
FOLMAR, LILLY M.	I	228, 345, 346	
FOLMAR, MURRAY	N	138 - 139	199 - 200
FOLMAR, R.E.L.	D	82 - 83	
FOLMAR, RILEY M.	L	807	
FOLMAR, RILEY M.	M	104 - 109	
FOLMAR, ROBERT E.	M	810 - 811	
FOLMAR, ROBERT E.	N	148 - 151	
FOLMAR, SEALY	D	141 - 142	
FOLMAR, SPIN JEWEL WYNN	M	668	
FOLMAR, SPIN JEWEL WYNN	N	44 - 47	
FOLMAR, TOMMIE	F	285	
FOLMAR, W. RALPH	J	639	
FOLMAR, W. RALPH	K	433 - 436	
FOLSOM, BESSIE	H	295, 490 - 492	
FORD, ANNIE WEAVER	J	590	
FORD, ANNIE WEAVER	K	37 - 40	
FORDHAM, MARY B.	G	525	
FORDHAM, H.B. SR.	F	183	
FORDHAM, MARY B.	H	53 -54	
FOREMAN, EMMA J. R.	H	51 - 52	
FOREMAN, EMMA JAN RIVERS	G	512	
FOREMAN, LILLA (alias Lillia)	D	326	
FORTUNE, ASBERRY	E	444 - 446	
FORTUNE, LEAMON	S	334	
FOSTER, KIRK	H	262 - 263	
FOSTER, JOHN L.	C	25 - 26	
FOSTER, JOSSIE E.	X	460 - 473	
FOSTER, ORA TURNER	N	711 - 716	
FOWLER, JOHN L.	N	152 -155	
FOWLER, JOHN LEWIS	M	780	
FOWLER, VELMA	X	741 - 755	
FRANCE, RAY ERNEST	V	608 - 617	
FRANK, FLORENCE ROSENBERG	F	290	
FRANKLIN, CHARLES M. JR.	G	111	
FRAZER, WM. A.	A	2	
FRAZIER, ALBERT	J	578	

FRAZIER, EVIE	I	287	
FRAZIER, MARTHA	D	23 - 24	
FREDRICK, E.M.	G	1	
FREEMAN, FANNIE D.	D	260	
FREEMAN, GEORGE M.	M	220, 398 - 401	
FREEMAN, IRENE PILLEY	D	412	
FREEMAN, JAMES C.	C	91	
FREEMAN, JAMES ELLIS	N	415 - 420	
FREEMAN, JOHN HENRY	L	627, 703 - 706	
FREEMAN, TOMMIE LEE	J	244 - 246	
FRENCH, CYRIL G.	G	85	
FRYER, DICK	D	344 - 345	
FRYER, GENIE	O	824, 826 - 842	
FRYER, GENIE	Q	1	
FRYER, JOHN	D	290	
FRYER, MAE W.	I	80, 183, 184	
FRYER, S.A.	D	12	
FRYER, WILLIAM E.	F	301	
FULFER, MINNIE BROWN	E	423 - 426	
FULLER, GRADY J.	H	551, 575 - 576	
FULLER, CLETIA C.	U	619	
FULLER, HARRIET	C	277 - 278	
GAFFORD, VETENIA	D	135	
GALLOWAY, H.H.	D	125 - 126	
GALLOWAY, JAMES	C	17	
GALLOWAY, LEO M.	N	761 - 766	
GALLOWAY, W.L.	D	267	
GANO, GORDON H.	U	760	
GARDNER, CATHERINE C.	J	101, 779 - 785	final settlement
GARNER, FLORENCE	G	221	
GARRETT, CLAYTON W.	U	777	
GARRETT, J.F.	P	327, 329	331 - 339
GARRETT, J.F.	Q	367	
GARRETT, M.J.	I	164, 295 - 297	
GASTON, LULLINE EMBRY	G	80, 495	
GAY, LURLINE	I	387 - 390	
GAYLARD, JAMES W. JR.	J	9, 67 - 70	
GELLERSTEDT, PEARL	F	306	
GELLERSTEDT, ROBERT S.	H	278	
GELLERSTEDT, ROBERT S.	I	486 - 490	
GELLERSTEDT, RUTH D.	H	440	
GELLERSTEDT, RUTH D.	I	484, 485	
GERRALD, POLINA	B	166 - 167	

GIBBS, BILLIE SPELLS	O	116, 118	120 - 128
GIBSON, ALLYNE M.	R	19	
GIBSON, BEULAH R.	K	137, 148 - 152	Trans. to Circuit Ct.
GIBSON, C.S.	M	223, 226, 227	402 - 405
GIBSON, CARL B. SR.	O	254, 257 - 263	
GIBSON, I.D.	X	788 - 802	
GIBSON, J. RUSSELL JR.	T	353	
GIBSON, J. RUSSELL SR.	E	438 - 439	
GIBSON, LIDA C.	X	109 - 130	
GIBSON, LUTHER A.	M	510, 595 - 598	
GIBSON, RAY	P	624 - 648	
GIBSON, RAY	R	787	
GIBSON, SAMUEL ROYAL	A	239 - 241	
GIBSON, SYLVANUS	B	140 - 142	
GIBSON, W.B.	D	413	
GIDDENS, JACK L. SR.	H	397, 579 - 580	
GIDDENS, JAMES F.	D	174	
GIDDENS, JAMES F.	M	511, 599 - 600	
GIDDENS, JULIUS C.	C	275 - 276	
GIDDENS, MARY F.	F	558	
GIDDENS, MARY MARGARET	H	527, 577 - 578	
GILCHRIST, MALCOLM W.	I	285, 347, 348	
GILCHRIST, MARJORIE E.	R	393	
GILFORD, REBECCA	E	205 - 206	
GILLIS, JOHN	J	503 - 507	
GILLIS, MARY E.	D	157	
GILMORE, GEORGE W.	G	207	
GILMORE, FRANCES	E	451 - 453	
GILMORE, JULIA W.	D	293 - 294	
GILMORE, VELMA BRAZIL	E	255 - 259	
GILMORE, WILLIS GLEN	F	303	
GINRIGHT, ANNIE G.	U	487	
GINYARD, IDA	Q	781	
GLAWSON, JAMES	A	196 - 198	
GLENN, EVA BAKER	N	286 - 291	
GLOVER, ADDIE G.	D	207	
GODWIN, ALBERT M.	E	220 - 224	
GODWIN, BENJAMIN F.	N	767 - 772	
GODWIN, JORDAN	C	35 - 37	
GODWIN, WYLEY	A	33 - 34	
GOFF, SARAH J.	D	116	
GOLDEN, CLARENCE D.	J	679	
GOLDEN, CLARENCE D.	K	41 - 44	

GOLDEN, ELIZABETH	A	223 - 234
GOLDEN, SALLY V.	R	402
GOLDTHWAITE, C.B.	E	427 - 429
GOLDTHWAITE, JOHN R.	C	64 - 66
GOLDTHWAITE, JULIA	R	410
GOMILLION, HENRY	A	113 - 115
GRAHAM, JIMMY E.	N	128 -129
GRANBERRY, JENNIE	E	447 - 450
GRANGER, JOHN C.	A	86 - 87
GRANT, C. C.	G	78
GRANT, C.A.	D	314
GRANT, COMMIE P.	W	141 - 148
GRANT, J.O. SR.	D	120
GRANT, JERRY CLARK	Y	333 - 341
GRANT, LAURA I.	D	329
GRANT, M.L.	I	398
GRANT, MATTIE K.	D	346
GRANT, SARAH	B	65 - 66
GRANT, WILSON	C	99 - 103
GRAVES, A.L.	C	6 - 10
GRAVES, ARCHIBALD	A	127 - 128
GRAVES, DAVID	A	183 - 185
GRAVES, FRANCIS	U	379
GRAVES, HARVIE R.	T	439
GRAVES, HARVIE REX	U	529
GRAVES, HELEN KOENIG	M	647
GRAVES, JAMES	A	185 - 187
GRAVES, JOHN	A	121 - 122
GRAVES, JOHN B.	U	199
GRAVES, PALMIRA T.	U	534
GRAVES, PALMIRA T.	T.	452
GRAVES, SUSANNAH	D	65
GRAY, MARY	B	192 - 195
GREEN, W. P.	G	135, 609 - 610
GREEN, FLORENA SHIRLEY	J	329, 499 - 502
GREEN, G.T.	J	443, 494 - 498
GREEN, HARMON T.	F	309
GREEN, INDIA MAERIAN	M	283, 406 - 409
GREEN, MARY EMMA	U	1
GREEN, N.F.	D	318
GREEN, R.H. JR.	L	749
GREEN, R.H. JR.	M	7 - 10
GREEN, R.T. (Final Settlement)	G	209, 397

GREEN, RILEY P.	D	391
GREEN, S.E.	Y	
GREEN, STEPHEN H.	H	25, 57 - 58
GREENE, ANNIE B.	P	368, 370 - 377
GREENE, ANNIE B.	Q	13
GREENE, FRANCES B.	R	308
GREENE, GROVER GILLIS	F	314
GREENE, JOE C.	T	367
GREENE, JOHN GAVIN	Q	538
GREENE, MILDRED F.	U	548
GREENE, RUPERT D. SR.	F	312
GRIDER, ALVA H.	K	86, 173 - 176
GRIDER, BENJAMIN	A	60 - 61
GRIDER, KATE	D	367
GRIFFIN, ALEX	F	179
GRIFFIN, ERIN G.	E	436 - 437
GRIFFIN, FRED LOUIS	R	420
GRIFFIN, FRED LOUIS	S	420
GRIFFIN, L.H.	E	217 - 219
GRIFFIN, MRS. M.L.	D	307
GRIFFIN, STANLEY W.	S	657, 721
GRIFFIN, W.E.	D	10
GRIMES, ALBERT W.	H	149, 231 - 232
GRIMES, EDLO	H	204, 411 - 412
GRIMES, MAE OLA	H	557
GRIMES, WALTER	G	564
GRIMES, WALTER	H	276 - 277
GRIMES, CORA MAE	L	342, 387 - 392
GRIMES, ELLIE MAE PRICE	S	679
GRIMES, ELLIE MAE PRICE	T	737 - 738
GRIMES, FRONIE B.	L	428, 591 - 594
GRIMES, HENRY THOMAS	I	270
GRIMES, MAE OLA	I	53, 55
GRIMES, ROXIE ANN	K	741
GRIMMER, IRENE	F	10
GRIMMER, JULIA IVANELL	S	388
GRIMMER, MRS. M.J.	D	294 - 295
GRISSETT, MATTIE MAE G.	P	41, 43 - 50
GRISSETT, WILLIE W.	V	718 - 735
GRISWALD, ROY	G	82
GRISWOLD, JEWEL SORRELL	K	127
GRISWOLD, JEWEL SORRELL	M	51
GRUBBS, DAN	H	113, 115 - 116

GRUBBS, EMMIE C.	D	18	
GRUBBS, MARY	D	292	
GRUBBS, MINNIE L.	I	102, 233 - 236	
GUNNELS, J.H.	D	337	
GUNTER, ERA	L	537, 657 - 658	
GUTHERY, DONALD RAY	M	44	
HAAK, AARON FRANK	G	227	
HAISTEN, ALBERT F.	H	496, 498 - 500	
HAISTEN, FRANCES W.	I	192 - 200	
HAISTEN, H.H. SR.	F	172	
HAISTEN, HELEN S.	O	129, 142, 143	145 - 149
HAISTEN, MARTHA B.	L	338, 484 - 487	
HAISTEN, THOMAS W.	C	142 - 143	
HALL, OLA	F	14	
HALLFORD, DOROTHIENE A.	V	170 - 186	685 - 688
HALLFORD, HUBERT J.	X	509 - 525	
HAM, B.A.	C	208	
HAMIL, GEORGE W.	D	46	
HAMMERLY, EDWIN TERRY	D	411	
HAMMERLY, PEARLE ROSS	D	383	
HANCHEY, W.E.	C	239 - 242	
HANCHEY, WILLIE BLAN	E	247 - 248	
HARDEN, F.M.	D	68	
HARDEN, GEORGE W.	D	295	
HARDEN, J.A.	J	815, 831 - 834	
HARDY, EUNICE K.	E	249 - 251	
HARGROVE, ANNIE J.	E	210 - 216	
HARMON, ANNA	C	294 - 296	
HARMON, J.F.	C	122 - 123	
HARMON, LEO C.	R	521	
HARMON, LEO C.	T	333	
HARMON, T.B.	D	45	
HARPER, P.O.	C	447	
HARRELL, C.A. (GUS)	O	498, 501, 502	504, 506, 508 - 513
HARRELL, EUGENE A.	J	114, 179 - 182	
HARRELL, H.M.	D	372	
HARRELL, J.E.	I	404, 405	447, 448
HARRELL, L. CLARENCE	M	285, 410 - 413	
HARRELL, T.J.W.	D	271 - 272	
HARRELL, VONZELL P.	W	217 - 226	
HARRELSON, AUSTIN	O	757 -759	
HARRELSON, AUSTIN	O	731, 738 - 749	751 - 756
HARRELSON, CONNIE MAE	P	450, 452 - 466	

HARRIN, SARAH	A	35 - 37	
HARRIS, AMANDA M.	F	328	
HARRIS, CHARLES PORTER	P	146, 147	
HARRIS, CODY W.	R	324	
HARRIS, DANIEL MONROE SR.	R	795	
HARRIS, DORIS M.	Q	375	
HARRIS, ELLA CLEONE	Q	388	
HARRIS, FELIX	N	562, 575 - 578	
HARRIS, FELIX	P	260 - 263	Order final settlement
HARRIS, HILDRETH C.	U	161	
HARRIS, JAMES E.	D	161	
HARRIS, JOHN C.	Q	760	
HARRIS, JOHN W.	D	380 - 381	
HARRIS, LILLIE E.	P	749 - 768	
HARRIS, LUDIE WILLIAMS	U	276	
HARRIS, MRS. GEORGIA	D	194	
HARRIS, NANNIE V.	R	240	
HARRIS, NOLIE NANNIE V.	T	558	
HARRIS, TIM	F	319	
HARRISON, BENJAMIN F.	J	727	
HARRISON, BENJAMIN F.	K	49 - 52	
HART, W.D.	F	343	
HARTSFIELD, WILEY W.	A	59 - 62	
HARVELL, J.W.	B	37	
HARVEY, CEPHUS	D	271	
HARVEY, VIOLET WINTON	V	676 - 684	
HARVEY, WM. HENDERSON SR.	D	323	
HARVIL, W.N.	C	473 - 474	
HASSON, ISRAEL	N	292 - 297	
HASSON, SARA C.	P	264, 266 - 270	272, 274, 275
HASTEY, ALICE L.	J	546, 607 - 609	
HATAWAY, CONLEY	J	597, 827 - 830	
HATAWAY, LUTHER L.	F	317	
HATAWAY, MARTHA P.	D	22 - 23	
HATTAWAY, JAMES L.	G	266, 499 - 500	
HATTAWAY, BERNIE	N	298, 303 - 307	
HATTAWAY, CHARLES E.	O	453 - 456, 458	460 - 464
HATTAWAY, FLORENCE R.	K	118, 441 - 445	
HATTAWAY, GLADYS	O	760, 762, 764	765
HATTAWAY, MYRTLE BELLE	O	514, 516 - 525	
HATTAWAY, O. BRANTLEY	L	437	
HATTAWAY, W.B. II	H	39 - 44	Trans. to Circuit Ct.
HATTAWAY, W.B. III	M	67, 352 - 355	

HATTAWAY, W.B. JR.	F	17	
HAY, S.E.	I	565, 579 - 582	
HAYES, WALTER HOBSON	K	344	
HAYES, WALTER HOBSON	L	140 - 144	
HAYNES, BEN	O	352, 354 - 356	465 - 469
HEAD, CLYDE	S	737	
HEAD, CLYDE	T	623	
HEAD, DOROTHY HENDERSON	L	559, 564	
HEAD, DOROTHY HENDERSON	M	123 - 129	
HEAD, LOUIS L. JR.	G	387, 635 - 637	Trans. to Circuit Ct.
HEARD, MYRA ANN	L	638, 707 - 710	
HELMS, ALLENE Y.	V	518 - 529	
HELMS, D.L.	F	331	
HELMS, FLORENCE BRYAN	H	581 - 584	
HELTON, JOHN T.	H	179, 413 - 414	
HELTON, ERIN T.	I	172, 349, 350	
HENDERSON, ALEX	D	304	
HENDERSON, CHAS.	D	167	
HENDERSON, ELI	A	172 - 175	
HENDERSON, ELIZABETH B.	H	292, 315 - 316	
HENDERSON, FOX	C	388 - 393	
HENDERSON, FRED	D	228 - 232	
HENDERSON, FREDRICK	Q	31	
HENDERSON, G.R.	F	340	
HENDERSON, GERALD A.	E	313 - 318	
HENDERSON, J.C.	D	90	
HENDERSON, J.E.	X	868 - 884	
HENDERSON, JAMES	D	34	
HENDERSON, JERE AUGUSTUS	D	11	
HENDERSON, JOSIE F.	W	273 - 281	
HENDERSON, JUILA BROOK	N	137	Trans. to Circuit Ct.
HENDERSON, JULIA BROCK	M	318, 414 - 417	
HENDERSON, M.E.	C	232 & 236	
HENDERSON, MARGARET C.	D	55 - 57	
HENDERSON, MARY VINING	J	383	
HENDERSON, MARY VINING	K	16 - 27	Appeal to Circuit Ct.
HENDERSON, MRS. M.E.	C	232 - 235	
HENDERSON, SALLIE E.	D	51 - 52	
HENDRICH, MARY	N	423 - 429	
HENDRICK, MARY	P	149 - 164	
HENDRICK, W.L.	C	154 - 155	
HENRY, VERNE B.	P	549 - 554	
HERBERT, JAMES D.	I	272	

HERLONG, FRANK T.	N	48 - 51
HERLONG, FRANKLIN T.	M	743
HERNDON, ADDISON L.	N	539 - 546
HERNDON, BURRELL	B	125 - 127
HERNDON, JAMES SR.	A	67 - 69
HERNDON, JOHN P.	B	69 - 71
HERNDON, OKLEY C.	F	338
HERON, NONNIE WOOD	Q	850
HERRINGTON, W.H.	D	296
HESTER, SALLY A.	G	237
HICKMAN, A.E.	F	22
HICKS, GLADYS F.	I	407
HICKS, GLADYS F.	K	437 - 440
HICKS, IDA B.	V	290 - 294
HICKS, LILLIE L.	V	287 - 289
HICKS, STEPHEN WASHINGTON	V	284 - 285
HICKS, STEVE H.	V	295 - 305
HICKS, W.A.	V	279 - 283, 286
HIGHTOWER, C.W.	D	24
HIGHTOWER, HAROLD T.	D	329
HIGHTOWER, J. WILLIAM	E	301 - 303
HIGHTOWER, J.E.	E	167
HIGHTOWER, LIZZIE L.	H	365, 493 - 495
HILBURN, WM. DEWEY	P	378 - 389
HILDRETH, ANNIE LESTER	O	479, 482 - 488
HILDRETH, ANNIE LESTER	P	214 - 216 Pet. for final settlement
HILDRETH, MATTIE L.	K	736 - 738
HILDRETH, MATTIE L.	L	11 - 15
HILDRETH, MATTIE L.	O	237 -242
HILDRETH, PAUL	O	489, 491 - 497
HILDRETH, PAUL	Q	116
HILL, BENJAMIN A.	I	13
HILL, IRENE P.	F	28
HILLIARD, ELIZABETH	Q	397
HILLIARD, J.B.	D	165
HILLIARD, KATE H.	D	152
HILLIARD, SUSIE H.	I	27
HILLIARD, W.L.	D	319
HILLIARD, WM.	B	72 - 76
HIMBERG, A.A.	C	135
HINES, FLAVIA INGRAM	F	31
HINES, FRANK D.	L	349, 488 - 491
HINSON, THOMAS LAFAYETTE	T	423

HINSON, THOMAS LAFAYETTE	U	415	
HIXON, ANNIE BRABHAM	I	130, 276, 277	
HIXON, J.M.	D	328	
HIXON, JOHN D.	F	527	
HIXON, JOHN R.	J	440, 508 - 511	
HIXON, SAMUEL	A	230 - 231	
HIXON, SAMUEL WALTER JR.	K	303	
HIXON, W.L.	B	40 - 41	
HOBBS, DONALD S.	G	125, 497 - 498	
HOBDY, FRANK	H	323, 415 - 416	
HOBDY, JANE A.	C	79 - 80	
HOBDY, WILLIE L.	H	282	
HODGES, JAMES C.	F	326	
HOISTEN, H. H. JR	N	430 - 436	
HOLDER, CHARLIE P.	Q	729	
HOLLADAY, JOHN W.	H	562	
HOLLAN, LOTTIE M.	V	10 - 24	
HOLLAN, W.L.	F	322	
HOLLIS, M. R.	G	137 469 - 470	
HOLLIS, WILL TOM	G	223	
HOLLIS, EDWIN M.	J	11, 134 - 137	
HOLLIS, LUCY D.	K	177 - 180, 614	619 - 620 Trans. Cir. Ct
HOLLIS, LUCY D.	L	266	final settlement
HOLLIS, NELL F.	M	11-14, 631 -641	Trans. to Circuit Ct.
HOLLOWAY, WM. FRANKLIN	C	40 - 42	
HOLMES, FERNEY	L	689, 711 - 714	
HOLMES, FERNIE	M	121 - 122	final settlement
HOLSEY, JORDAN	K	239	
HOLSEY, JORDAN	M	116 - 120	
HOLT, OTIS	N	308 - 313	
HOOD, FRED	M	497	Shirley Hood, Admrx.
HOOKS, C.G.	D	220	
HOOKS, ESTER C.	P	16, 18 - 27	
HOOKS, GEORGE	A	204 - 205	
HOOKS, MELVIN LESLIE	X	526 - 538	
HOOKS, TAMAR	C	56	
HOOTEN, HENRY	A	65 - 66	
HOOTEN, JAMES	N	838 - 843	
HOOVER, FLORENCE GRACE	U	347	
HORN, OLIVER P.	E	228 - 230	
HORTMAN, RACHEL V.	S	415	
HORTON, LONNIE C	N	773 - 779	
HOSMER, MARGARET A.	D	133 - 134	

HOSMER, SAMUEL MONROE	C	315 - 317
HOUSTON, QUINT L.	P	467 - 476
HOWARD, BYRON H.	G	233
HOWARD, JAMES ROSS	G	241
HOWARD, JOHN HENRY	G	359
HOWARD, FRED R.	L	203, 267 - 270
HOWARD, HARRIS	D	73
HOWARD, HARRY H.	U	653
HOWARD, HERBERT R. SR.	J	677, 835 - 838
HOWARD, J.D.	M	245, 418 - 423
HOWARD, J.H.	D	46 - 47
HOWARD, MINNIE P.	M	130 - 133
HOWELL, J.W.	B	37
HOWELL, THOMAS J.	F	35
HUBBARD, ANN G.	C	363 - 365
HUBBARD, G.J.	H	185, 346 - 348
HUBBARD, JOHN P.	C	228 - 231
HUDSON, JULIA	X	777 - 787
HUDSON, WILLIAM R.	K	743
HUDSON, WILLIAM R.	L	145 - 149
HUEY, J. A.	H	155
HUFF, BESSIE L.	N	844 - 851
HUFF, V.B.	T	147
HUGGINS, ANDREW H.	H	563
HUGGINS, ANDREW H.	I	60, 61
HUGGINS, BOBBY G.	I	17, 62, 64
HUGGINS, JIMMIE W.	I	675 - 677
HUGGINS, WM.	C	319 - 321
HUGHES ELIZ. NAOMI SANDERS	K	96, 181 - 184
HUGHES, KEYTON	I	400, 412, 413
HULEN, LOIS IRENE	V	473 - 486
HULEN, ROBERT LEE	K	710 - 715
HUNER, STANLEY HENRY	J	569
HUNT, AMY T.	H	22, 269 - 270
HURTT, JOHN	A	12 - 13
HUSSEY, CALLIE C.	K	551
HUSSEY, LOUIE BARFIELD	H	357
HUSSEY, LOUIE BARFIELD	K	45 - 48
HUSSEY, M.J.	P	390, 394 396 - 410
HUSSEY, PEARL H.	M	747
HUSSEY, PEARL S.	N	52 - 57
HYBART, JOHN HUGH	C	47 - 50
INGRAM, GRADY L. SR.	V	324 - 336

JINKINS, J. H.	G	255
JINRIGHT, JAMES THOMAS	W	327 - 338
JINRIGHT, JOEL D.	I	167, 201, 202
JINRIGHT, L.A. SR.	M	773
JINRIGHT, L.A. SR.	N	62 - 65
JINRIGHT, MILDRED P.	W	822 - 830
JOHNSON, A.C.	Q	548
JOHNSON, ADDIE K.	K	693
JOHNSON, ARTHUR LEE	D	324
JOHNSON, DONALD	H	331, 417, 418
JOHNSON, F.B. SR.	C	329 - 333
JOHNSON, GRADY	M	489, 535 - 538
JOHNSON, JAMES	C	264
JOHNSON, JOHN A.J.	A	135 - 136
JOHNSON, LEONA	J	7, 183 - 186
JOHNSON, LOUIS FRANCIS	L	150 - 154
JOHNSON, M.C.	X	840 - 849
JOHNSON, MANUEL H. SR.	W	372 - 386
JOHNSON, MARY C.	D	17
JOHNSON, MARY TOM	H	72
JOHNSON, MARY TOM	J	610 - 615
JOHNSON, MILTON	R	115
JOHNSON, MOSES	L	496 - 501
JOHNSON, MRS. MATTIE G.	D	378 - 379
JOHNSON, NICIE	E	118 - 119
JOHNSON, OTHA W.	N	654 - 661
JOHNSON, R. GRADY	J	462, 692 - 695 Trans. to Circuit Ct.
JOHNSON, THOMAS HOLLOWAY	W	844 - 860
JOHNSON, TRUMAN R.	V	618 - 627
JOHNSON, WILL	H	55 - 56
JOHNSTON, FANNIE PRESTWOOD	G	554
JOHNSTON, WILL	G	511
JOHNSTON, ALONZA E.	E	194 - 196
JOHNSTON, ALTO L.	D	247
JOHNSTON, BERTHA G.	F	366
JOHNSTON, CAMELLA T.	M	782
JOHNSTON, CAMILLA T.	N	76 - 79
JOHNSTON, CHARLES D.	W	892 - 901
JOHNSTON, F. T.	G	119, 453 - 454
JOHNSTON, FANNIE P.	N	72 - 75
JOHNSTON, FOX H.	F	361
JOHNSTON, FOX H.	O	872 - 883
JOHNSTON, FOX HELMS	Q	30

JOHNSTON, FOY C.	E	310 - 311	
JOHNSTON, G.F.	V	25 - 45	
JOHNSTON, GLADYS ADKINS	K	664	
JOHNSTON, GLADYS ADKINS	L	16 - 20	
JOHNSTON, JOE RAY	L	183, 271 - 274	502-504 settlement
JOHNSTON, JOHN DAVID	E	171	
JOHNSTON, JOHN DAVID JR.	E	116 - 117	
JOHNSTON, L.Q.	R	433	
JOHNSTON, LILLIAN M.	Y	690 - 699	
JOHNSTON, LORETTA W.	P	734 - 748	
JOHNSTON, MITCHELL D.	F	363	
JOHNSTON, RALPH B.	H	530	
JOHNSTON, RALPH B.	I	8 - 10	
JOHNSTON, T.E.	D	109 - 110	
JOHNSTON, WILLIAM O.	V	463 - 472	
JONES, ANDREW JACKSON	G	13	
JONES, GUSSIE HENDERSON	G	103, 501 - 502	
JONES, A.J.	H	363	
JONES, A.J.	K	446 - 449	
JONES, ADA S.	I	474, 541 - 543	
JONES, ADELAIDE	N	579 - 590	
JONES, AMANDA	D	131 - 132	
JONES, AMANDA	D	393	
JONES, BRITTON	A	167 - 168	
JONES, CHARLES GLENN	F	193	
JONES, DOCK	D	4	
JONES, DOCK	D	111	
JONES, DOCK (new Trustee)	D	249	
JONES, DOCK (Trustee Settlement)	D	251	
JONES, FLORA	X	911 - 929	
JONES, GUSSIE H.	H	133	final settlement
JONES, H.R.W.	E	120 - 122	
JONES, J.M.	F	166	
JONES, J.S.	B	77 - 78	
JONES, JAMES HARRISON	U	559	
JONES, JOSEPH	W	555 - 574	
JONES, LIZZIE LOVE	I	383, 545, 546	
JONES, NETTIE KING	F	355	
JONES, PARTHENIA	F	41	
JONES, PAUL S.	V	530 - 542	713 - 717
JONES, ROBERT W.	V	894 - 912	
JONES, S.B.	D	376 - 377	
JONES, S.E.	I	442, 583 - 586	

JONES, SUSIE C.	D	395
JONES, V.D.	D	62 - 63
JONES, VALDA	K	273 - 276
JONES, VALDA M.	J	573
JONES, W.A.	F	358
JONES, W.A.	R	426
JONES, W.W.D.	D	15
JONES, WILLIAM HARRISON	K	565, 595 - 598
JORDAN, CURRY C.	Y	76 - 93
JORDAN, J.J.	D	105 - 106
JORDAN, L.L.	J	470
JORDAN, LAMON LEE	J	616 - 618
JORDAN, MARVIN E.	K	780
JORDAN, MARVIN E.	L	155 - 159
JORDAN, MARY E.	D	64
JORDAN, ROSA LEE	V	
JUSTICE, H.N.	D	399
KEENER, JAMES M.	A	251 - 252
KEITH, PEARLLENA C.	T	569
KEITH, W.J.	T	119
KELLEY, DANIEL	I	393, 493, 494
KELLEY, LEVIE CURTIS	F	349
KELLEY, MIRIAM J.	N	156 - 161
KELLY, B.F.	F	47
KELLY, EDNA M.	M	287, 428 - 431
KELLY, GEORGE W.	I	430
KELLY, GEORGE W.	L	659 - 662
KELLY, J.A.	K	255
KELLY, J.A.	L	21 - 25
KELLY, J.C.	N	780 - 785
KELLY, QUEENIE	O	357, 359 - 374
KELSEY, PAUL SEYMORE	R	61
KENDRICK, JOHN MOSLEY	C	213 - 217
KENDRICK, SARAH E.	D	101
KENNEDY, MARTHA A.	C	180 - 181
KENT, GLENN	V	805 - 817
KENT, KIRBY R.	I	169, 351, 352
KERN, ABRAHAM K.	F	50
KETCHUM, MATTIE D.	R	31, 654
KEY, FOREST C.	F	373
KEY, LERA GERTRUDE	O	768, 770 - 779
KEY, MARY LOU BAXTER	S	561
KILLINGSWORTH, BRUCE	S	344

KILLINGSWORTH, ROSANNA D.	D	114	
KILLINGSWORTH, VONNIE W.	X	756 - 765	
KILLINGWORTH, NOAH W.	G	142, 605 - 606	
KILPATRICK, L.B.	I	337, 495, 496	
KILPATRICK, RALPH L.	V	865 - 893	
KILPATRICK, RALPH L.	X	31 - 68	
KILPATRICK, THOS. J.	D	35 - 36	
KINARD, EULA B.	D	249	
KINDRED, G.A.	D	112	
KINDRED, JOHN B.	D	174	
KING, M. F.	G	267	
KING, C.L.	H	537, 585 - 588	
KING, FRANKLIN E.	D	315	
KING, GILBERT C.	U	78	
KING, J.P.	M	620, 694 - 697	
KING, JOHN F.	B	87 - 88	
KING, L.A.	N	549 - 550	717 - 720
KING, MAGGIE L. BERRY	H	361	
KING, ROBBIE H.	X	629 - 645	
KING, T.B.	D	13	
KING, THELMA W.	V	156 - 169	543 - 569
KING, W.E.	C	282 - 284	
KIRBY, LORETTA GOOCH	J	107, 393 - 396	
KIRKLAND, HUGH J.	L	738	
KIRKLAND, HUGH J.	M	15 - 18	
KLASING, MRS. N.W.A.	D	61 - 62	
KLEINHEIDER, VIVIANE C.	V	657 - 666	
KNIGHT, CHARLIE L.	Q	558	
KNIGHT, W.C.	I	333	
KNIGHT, W.C.	K	450 - 453	
KNOTTS, CLEVELAND I.	L	557, 663 - 666	
KNOWLES, ROBERT	B	106 - 107	
KNOX, HENRY	D	163 - 164	
KNOX, O.F.	B	179 - 182	
KNOX, RICKIE LEE	F	352	
KOENIG, DENA IDA	L	91	
KOENIG, ERNEST JACOB	J	39	
KYZAR, SUSIE	G	477, 660 - 661	
KYZAR, CHARLES G.	K	5, 53 - 56	
KYZAR, MAGGIE L.	V	507 - 517	
KYZAR, MAHALIE	D	2	
KYZAR, MARY	D	1	
LAKE, JAMES W.	P	28 - 40	

LAMBERT, CHARLES R. JR.	U	428	
LAMPLEY, HENRY	I	334, 497, 498	
LANEY, ANNIE JO M.	J	156	
LANGFORD, COHEN HAY	K	553	
LARKIN, LULA MAE BERRY	L	799	
LARKIN, LULA MAE BERRY	M	432 - 436	final settlement
LAW, OLA	G	271	
LAW, ADA	J	158, 516 - 519	
LAW, CORA PETREY	E	1 - 2	
LAW, JOHN A.	C	86 - 89	
LAW, MATTIE E.	D	263	
LAW, VERA	P	649 - 658	
LAW, W.H.	D	212	
LAWRENCE, SARAH	B	30 - 32	
LAWRENCE, WM.	C	15 - 16	
LAWSON, FRANCES LOU	D	33 - 34	
LAWSON, LOLA	K	279 - 283	final settlement
LAWSON, M.J.	D	32	
LAWSON, VERNON D. JR.	R	440	
LEATHERWOOD, RALPH EDWARD	V	404 - 418	
LEDBETTER, L.J.	X	190 - 202	850 - 855
LEE, FITZHUGH	J	376, 512 - 515	
LEE, HOMER D.	F	61	
LEE, J.B.	S	54	
LEE, J.B.	T	261	
LEE, LIZZIE H.	K	145, 458 - 461	
LEE, ROBERT E.	L	546, 572 - 575	
LEE, RUTH PARDUE	J	379	
LEE, RUTH PARDUE	K	57 - 60	
LEE, VERA B.	U	745	
LEE, WILLIE E.	D	242 - 243	
LEE, WM.	B	156	
LEE, WOODSON P.	A	125 - 126	
LEIGHTON, JOHN W.	C	322 - 328	
LEONARD, ANNIE B.	F	378	
LEONARD, ELIZA	L	223, 505 - 508	
LEONARD, EUGENE	L	226, 509 - 512	
LESLIE, FELIX	D	364	
LESLIE, JAMES B.	F	381	
LESLIE, JAMES BOOTH	E	127 - 128	
LEVERETT, CLEMMIE G.	U	209	
LEVERETTE, HIRAM J.	K	767	
LEVERETTE, KYLE RAMAGE	W	282 - 293	

LEVERETTE, LAURA	K	241, 288 - 294
LEVERETTE, WILLIE W.	L	26-31, 112-113 Trans. to Circuit Ct.
LEWIS, CHELLIE	W	402 - 410
LEWIS, ELIZABETH K.	N	66-67, 162-165
LEWIS, JOHN F.	D	296 - 298
LEWIS, JUDGE	E	190 - 193
LEWIS, W.P.	M	76, 356 - 359
LIFFORD, W.E.	E	129 - 130
LIGHTFOOT, B.H.	K	223, 284 - 287
LIGHTFOOT, GEORGIA VIOLA	F	56
LIGHTFOOT, JAMES H.	S	751
LIGHTFOOT, JOSEPH I.	D	326
LIGHTFOOT, OLENE L.	Y	280 - 288
LIGHTFOOT, RICHARD M.	Q	406
LILES, ALVIN D.	J	94, 187 - 190
LINTON, AVIS H.	O	150, 152 - 159
LINTON, WOODROW	N	314 - 319
LITTLE, JAMES C.	U	318
LITTLE, JAMES E.	Y	656 - 664
LITTLE, MARY E.	L	79, 160 - 164
LITTLE, W.H.	J	810, 843 - 846 Little, Mattie Lou ex'r.
LIVINGS, CLENDER S.	M	340, 539 - 544
LIVINGS, M.J. SR.	M	491, 545 - 548
LIVINGSTON, A.T.	F	53
LIVINGSTON, KIRBY	F	187
LIVINGSTON, ROY	Y	319 - 332
LIVINGSTON, WM. R.	I	684
LOCKARD, MRS. M.J.	D	40
LOCKE, E.H.	D	19 - 20
LOCKE, RICHARD	B	44 - 46
LOCKLEY, OMER	U	217
LOFLIN, DOZIER	L	365, 393 - 396
LOFLIN, H.D.	Y	1 - 11
LOFLIN, KLEOB N.	F	578
LOGAN, ELLENE S.	X	646 - 654
LOGAN, JAMES L.	E	124 - 125
LOGAN, JOHN WALTER	Q	126
LOGAN, LEX HAROLD	J	548, 619 - 621
LOGAN, LEX HAROLD	M	134, 135
LONG, C.R.	X	314 - 339
LONG, E.E.	E	285 - 288
LONG, JACK W.	R	447
LONG, JACK W.	T	132

LONG, LILLIE B.	V	835 - 850	
LONG, MELBA S.	T	830	
LOTT, JULIA B.	O	264, 266 - 272	
LOTT, KENNETH RAY	K	690	
LOTT, KENNETH RAY	L	32 - 36	
LOTT, STELLA	K	107, 454 - 457	
LOVE, JAMES WALTER	L	576 - 581	
LOVE, JAMES WALTER	L	435	
LOVE, WALLACE	F	375	
LOVE, WM. M.	C	138 - 139	
LOVEJOY, H.L.	F	580	
LOW, H. MICHAEL	U	605	
LOW, H. MICHAEL	V	570 - 579	
LOWER, WILLIAM J.	V	818 - 834	
LOWERY, J. ROBERT	Q	650	
LOWERY, R.A.	D	313	
LUCAS, JAMES	G	274	
LUCAS, BESSIE L.	O	273, 277 - 279	282 - 288
LUDLAM, JEREMIAH	B	59 - 61 & 91	
LUMPKIN, DORA	J	805	Walker, Lee ex'r.
LUMPKIN, DORA	L	165 - 169	
LUNSFORD, GRADY FOY	M	190, 437 - 440	
LUNSFORD, RUTH B.	P	340 - 345	350 - 359
LYNCH, P.A.	H	37, 49, 50	
MACK, JOHN	E	137 - 138	
MACON, L.W.	D	198	
MADARIS, WILLIE R.	R	454	
MADDEN, JESSIE TAFT	S	254	
MADDEN, JESSIE TAFT	T	464	
MADDOX, EDGAR MOORE	N	454 - 459	
MADDOX, LUCY JERNIGAN	I	84, 205, 206	
MADDOX, MYRTLE T.	W	1	
MAHONE, ELIZABETH P.	T	385	
MAIN, VERNA	F	540	
MALLETT, CHARLES A.	P	51 - 64	
MALLETT, CHARLES N.	D	178	
MANN, JAMES C.	V	272 - 278	
MANNING, E.M.	K	470 - 473	
MANNING, J.H.	I	103, 207, 208	
MARRON, PETER G.	A	199 - 200	
MARSH, FREDERICK C.	H	545, 591 - 600	
MARTIN, LUCIOUS M.	H	111, 220, 221	
MARTIN, WALTER RAY	Z	29 - 42	

MARTIN, WILLIE PHENIX	P	65, 68 - 97	555 - 566, 769 - 772
MARY, S.E.	I	185, 186	
MARY, SEBASTIAN E.	I	353, 354	
MASSEY, DAR LEE WALTERS	J	249, 302 - 305	
MASSEY, J.A.	D	361	
MATHEWS, ANNIE L.	H	242	
MATHEWS, ANNIE L.	K	462 - 465	
MATHEWS, B.W.	H	240	
MATHEWS, JAMES H.	I	432, 449, 450	
MATHIS, CLARA CARGLE	G	76	
MATHIS, MARIE	G	653, 654 - 655	
MATHIS, G. RAY	M	237, 441 - 445	
MAUGHON, MITCHELL D.	C	247 - 250	
MAUGHON, RUFUS DAYNOR	O	376, 379 - 386	
MAUGHON, RUFUS DAYNOR	P	219, 220, 222	
MAULDEN, LORENZA	N	512 - 513	662 - 667
MAULK, MARY VIC	F	65	
MAY, WILLIAM EARL	G	123, 467 - 468	
MAY, BARBARA S.	C	366 - 368	
MAY, CHASTINE	D	236	
MAY, FRANCES WALTERS	I	227, 318, 319	
MAY, JAMES	A	201 - 203	
MAY, MARY MYRTLE	F	76	
MAY, THELMA H.	I	25, 237 - 239	
MAY, W.H.	D	384	
MCARDLE, LAWRENCE E.	H	369, 506 - 508	
MCBETH, WALTER	A	39 - 42	
MCBRIDE, BETTY S.	G	277	
MCBRYDE, A.J.	C	359 - 363	
MCBRYDE, B.R.	H	456	
MCBRYDE, B.R.	I	209 - 210	
MCBRYDE, BETTY S.	M	50 - 51	final settlement
MCBRYDE, MATTIE E.	D	394	
MCBURNEY, HUGH	B	2 - 8	
MCCAA, ALEX J.	M	289, 452 - 455	
MCCALL, CHARLES R.	C	124 - 125	
MCCALL, GEORGE A.	C	54 - 55	
MCCALL, KATHERINE R.	D	301	
MCCALL, LULA MAE	M	627	
MCCALL, LULA MAE	N	80 - 83	
MCCALL, LULA MAE	N	80 - 83	
MCCALL, SARAH	A	74 - 75	
MCCANN, BESS	S	579	

MCCARLEY, JACK D.	J	652
MCCARTHA, CLARENCE L.	C	440 - 443
MCCARTHA, CLARENCE L.	D	357 - 358
MCCARTHA, MABLE M.	M	233, 456 - 459
MCCASKILL, ALEX	K	348, 724 - 727
MCCLAIN, HARMON WESLEY	M	140 - 143
MCCLELLAN, ANGUS R.	K	531, 599 - 601
MCCLENDON, MAURINE	W	656 - 671
MCCOLLUM, BESSIE H.	K	311
MCCOLLUM, W. HARDY	M	787
MCCORMICK, LESSIE	G	535
MCCORMICK, FULTON O.	J	851
MCCORMICK, FULTON O.	K	732 - 735
MCCORMICK, G.W.	E	202 - 204
MCCORMICK, JOHN C.	B	11
MCCORMICK, LESSIE	H	59, 60
MCCRARY, JOHN B.	X	930 - 941
MCCULLOUGH, ESTELLE	Q	151
MCDONALD, J.H., Margaret, Fannie	D	160
MCDOUGH, MARION E.	L	818
MCDOUGLE, MARION E.	M	152 - 155
MCDOWELL, WM. D.	A	82 - 83
MCEACHERN, FLOY JONES	V	423 - 434
MCEACHERN, HADLEY A.	D	279
MCEACHERN, JOHN A.	C	304 - 306
MCFARLIN, ROBERT B.	V	368 - 377
MCGEHEE, WINNIE Y.	F	383
MCGHEE, ROBERT	G	393
MCGHEE, LULA BELL	K	698 - 705
MCGILVRAY, JOHN ARCHIE	V	66 - 77
MCGOWAN, ALGIE SR.	X	214 - 224
MCGRADY, BRUDEIS	G	290
MCGRADY, LAWSON	S	74
MCGUIRE, DAN SR.	C	265 - 268
MCILHENNY, SARAH G.	C	175 - 177
MCKEE, W. G.	G	286
MCKEE, EUNICE	H	321, 501 - 504 final settlement
MCKEE, HETTIE	K	688
MCKEE, HETTIE	L	715 - 719
MCKENNY, J. M.	M	19 - 22
MCKENZIE, ETHEL W.	I	269, 278, 279
MCKENZIE, ROYCE B.	S	517
MCKINNEY, J.M.	K	617

MCKINNEY, WILLIE GREEN	V	306 - 323
MCKINNON, ALEXANDER CHARLES	E	132 - 133
MCKINNON, ANN J.	K	100
MCKINNON, ANN J.	M	601 - 604
MCKOWN, JOHN	B	182 - 184
MCLANE, CHARLES	B	35 - 36
MCLANE, DUNCAN	A	19
MCLANE, HENRY A.	C	237, 238, & 243
MCLANEY, JAMES	B	222 - 224
MCLAUGHLIN, SICY H.	T	507
MCLAUGHLIN, WOODROW	I	682, 683
MCLEAN, MARY VENITA	G	282
MCLENDON, GEORGIA RUTH	Y	268 - 269
MCLENDON, NANCY	C	72 - 73
MCLEOD, AUDREY WIGGINS	M	144 - 147
MCLEOD, C.F.	D	333
MCLEOD, C.F.	D	354
MCLEOD, EULA MAE	L	692
MCLEOD, EULA MAE	M	148 - 151
MCLEOD, EVELYN KNOX	H	337, 601 - 606
MCLEOD, H.C.	D	98
MCLEOD, HUBERT	D	273 - 274
MCLEOD, IRENE P.	F	63
MCLEOD, JACK BRANTLEY SR.	K	248, 602 - 605
MCLEOD, JAMES A.	K	482 - 485
MCLEOD, JAMES ALEXANDER	H	297
MCLEOD, KATE	F	385
MCLEOD, NORMAN	B	164 - 166
MCLEOD, WALTER J.	H	187, 266, 268
MCLURE, GUSTAVUS Y.	C	131 - 132
MCLURE, JOE H.	I	642
MCLURE, JOHN R.	I	414, 499, 500
MCLURE, M.K.	C	133 - 134
MCLURE, MARTHA ANN	C	132 - 133
MCLURE, MILLIE	F	388
MCLURE, SALLIE LE BOYD	L	546, 667 - 670
MCLURE, WM. RANKIN JR.	Q	416
MCLURE, WM. RANKIN JR.	S	86
MCMILLIAN, EDWARD	B	84 - 86
MCNAIR, LUCILLE	N	510 - 511 595 - 600
MCNAIR, T.D.	K	334
MCNEAL, W.M.	F	169
MCNEIL, A.O.	F	390

MCNEIL, MATTIE E.	P	411, 414 - 417
MCNEILL, I.H.	D	37 - 38
MCNEILL, LIZZIE	D	10 - 11
MCNEILL, W.M.	D	175 - 176
MCPHERSON, ELI ALONZA	D	199
MCPHERSON, JAMES L.	L	180, 275 - 278
MCPHERSON, SARA	N	166 - 169
MCPHERSON, SARA GUNNELS	M	812 - 813
MCQUEEN, HATTIE	J	310
MCQUEEN, HATTIE	M	23 - 26
MCROY, JOHN	A	68
MCSWAIN, BETTIE F.	G	3
MCSWAIN, CECIL	G	507
MCSWAIN, CECIL	H	47, 48
MCSWAIN, MRS. ELIZABETH	D	250
MCSWEAN, C.	C	218
MCSWEAN, DR. COLIN	C	222
MCVAY, ERNEST	K	578
MCVAY, ERNEST	L	37 - 41
MCVAY, FRED	M	53 - 56 136 -139
MCVAY, JOHNNIE	E	339
MCVAY, OLGIE S.	N	533 - 535 591 - 594
MCVAY, UNOLA etal.	E	329
MCWHORTER, JOHN	A	16 - 17
MEADOWS, BEUNA MAE	I	283, 341, 342
MEADOWS, FOREMAN	V	498 - 506
MEADOWS, GARY	K	117, 185 - 188
MEADOWS, JIMMIE D.	H	442
MEADOWS, JIMMY D.	I	343, 344
MEEKS, SARA LORRAINE	G	89
MEEKS, LORAINE HUGHES	X	818 - 839
MERRITT, EDITH ANN	H	110
MESSICK, G.W.	E	134 - 136
MESSICK, LILLIE MAE R.	S	65
MESSICK, LOUIE M.	D	386
MILES, DAVID	A	42 - 47
MILEY, JAMES E.	G	475, 656 - 657
MILLER, THOMAS	B	160 - 162
MILLER, U.L.	D	381
MILLS, BARBAREE	D	196 - 197
MILLS, JAMES WALTER	U	469
MILLS, LENA P.	H	94, 218, 219
MILLS, NORMAN	X	579 - 595

MILLS, SARAH STRAHORN	U	641
MILLS, WILLIAM E.	W	153 - 164
MINCHENER, FRANCIS	C	399 - 401
MINCHENER, GRACE LEE	V	772 - 787
MINCHENER, MRS. W.H.	D	284
MINCHENER, W.H.	D	113
MINCHINER, MARY E.	C	200 - 201
MING, NELSON	D	87
MITCHELL, J.F.	D	3
MITCHELL, JOHN M.	Y	257 - 267
MOLL, HERMAN H.	E	304 - 306
MONEY, JUANITA F.	O	243 - 252
MONEY, JUANITA F.	P	130 - 133
MOODY, GERTRUDE JORDAN	Y	707 - 730
MOODY, V. ALTON	L	363, 513 - 516
MOORE, B.F.	B	33 - 34
MOORE, JOHN W.	B	100 - 101
MOORE, L.D.	A	257 - 259
MOORE, MILDRED B. WRIGHT	I	563, 678 - 681
MOORE, MYRTLE	F	392
MOORE, PETE	H	93
MORELAND, E.N.	B	38 - 39
MORGAN, MICHEAL T.	G	592
MORGAN, MICHAEL T.	H	303, 304
MORGAN, S. MONROE	D	208
MORRISON, DANIEL HUEY	X	568 - 578
MORRISON, EVA MARIA	T	340
MOSELEY, ALICE DUNBAR	L	631
MOSLEY, TAMMIE W.	U	451
MOSLEY, TOMMIE W.	V	419 - 420
MOSLEY, WM.	B	103 - 105
MOSSER, BELINDA	A	136 - 137
MOSSER, SAMUEL	B	138 - 140
MOTES, D.H.	D	320
MOTES, J.A.	D	141
MOTES, M.A.	D	338
MOTES, MORRIS	C	77 - 79
MOTES, ONA	M	228, 446 - 449 698
MOTLEY, MAMIE HARLAN	H	531, 589, 590
MOTLEY, NELL M.	E	18
MOULTRY, SANFORD	N	868, 870 - 873
MOULTRY, SANFORD	O	780 -782
MOZLEY, IDA WILL	X	942 - 953

MOZLEY, PAUL E.	N	345 - 349	450 - 453
MULICAN, VERA L.	E	278 - 279	
MULICAN, W.H.	D	245	
MULLINS, WILLIAM H.	Y	305 - 317	
MULLIS, A.B.	F	394	
MULLIS, E.G.	F	414	
MULLIS, F.E.	I	107	
MULLIS, F.E.	K	474 - 477	
MULLIS, LYDIA M.	K	101, 478 - 481	
MULLIS, NETTIE C.	K	250, 466 - 469	
MURPHREE, AMY H.	F	396	
MURPHREE, DORA	F	69	
MURPHREE, ELIZABETH B.	K	61 - 64	
MURPHREE, J.D. (Trustee)	D	140	See Bk. C, Pg. 164
MURPHREE, J.H.	I	246, 355, 356	
MURPHREE, JOEL D.	C	164 - 166	
MURPHREE, JOEL D.	D	285	
MURPHREE, KATHRYN G.	S	797	Estate
MURPHREE, KATHRYN G.	U	185	
MURPHREE, KEY	D	261	
MURPHREE, LILA	D	201	
MURPHREE, LUNA W.	E	31	
MURPHREE, MARY ELIZABETH	F	72	
MURPHREE, MELANIE W.	N	232, 320 - 323	
MURPHREE, MRS. E.A.	C	140 - 141	
MURPHREE, MRS. T.F.	C	429 - 436	
MURPHREE, T.E.	D	265 - 266	
MURPHREE, THOMAS T.	C	285 - 287	
MURPHREE, WILLIAM H.	V	388 - 403	
MURPHREE, WILLIAM H.	W	874 - 879	
MURPHREE, WILLIE BELLE	I	381	
MURPHREE, WILLIE BELLE	J	191 - 198	
MURPHREE, WILLIE PURCELL	F	399	
MURPHY, C.A.	Q	669	
MYERS, WILBUR R.	N	206 - 207	324 - 327
MYHAND, DOROTHY L.	Y	94 - 125	
NANCE, O.B.	H	109	
NANCE, O.B.	K	486 - 489	
NARAMORE, RUBY MERLE	L	315	
NEEL, ANGUS D.	O	538, 541 - 549	
NETTLES, HENRY H.	U	676	
NETTLES, HENRY H.	V	264 - 271	
NEWBERRY, W. D.	G	297	

NEWBERRY, MYRTICE A.	J	697	
NEWBY, SAM	I	426, 451, 452	
NICHOLS, ADDIE S.	F	560	
NICHOLS, MAJOR	M	646, 699 - 706	
NICHOLS, PAYTON	D	175	
NIXON, LOCHRAN C.	I	396, 501 - 502	
NOLEN, EDNA R.	F	587	
NONNENMAN, JOSEPH E.	T	280	
NORMAN, GRACE SHIRLEY	U	141	
NORRELL, MARGARET W.	Q	570	
NORRIS, JOE TOM	M	664, 703 -706	
NORRIS, MARY E.	X	657 - 669	
NORRIS, ROBERT GUY	F	416	
NORRIS, THOMAS M.	Y	12 - 45	
NORWOOD, MANASSA	C	10 - 11	
O'DEA, ANDREW	B	171 - 172	
O'NEAL, GEORGE R.	E	347 - 348	
O'NEAL, MURRAY D.	Q	717	
OAKES, LOUIE	L	430, 603 - 606	
ODOM, MINNIE A.	M	666, 707 - 710	
OKEL, LUCILE B.	J	112, 397 - 400	Benj. Boyd Okel, Ex'r.
OLIVER, NEAD S.	R	675	
ORME, E.C.	S	709	
ORME, MYRTILINE D.	S	195	
OSTEEN, EMMA B.	F	574	
OSTEEN, H.A.	D	347 - 348	
OUSLEY, MERTIE	F	419	
OUTLAW, WM. E.	N	170 - 176	
OWENS, A.B.	F	422	
OWENS, ARTHUR H.	E	37 - 38	
OWENS, B.M.	D	358 - 359	
OWENS, C.A.	D	145 - 146	
OWENS, GEORGE E.	D	412	
OWENS, GEORGE E.	E	139 - 141	
OWENS, MILTON J.	N	786 - 791	
OWENS, OLEAN	Y	300 - 303	605 - 641
OWENS, PERRY S.		132, 490 - 495	
OWENS, ROBERT L.	L	720 - 725	
PACE, M.D.	D	310 - 312	
PACE, MATTIE LOIS T.	N	558 - 561	601 - 605
PACE, SARAH C.	H	390, 518 - 520	
PANHORST, G. M.	G	326, 327 - 328	
PARK, JOE C.	D	216	

PARK, ORA LEE	P	418, 423 - 426	428 - 432, 820 - 843
PARK, ORA LEE	Q	256	
PARKER, LIZZIE	G	528, 603 - 604	
PARKS, ALBERT D.	E	5 - 7	
PARKS, ALEX	F	436	
PARKS, ALTO L.	D	406	
PARKS, EVA MCCREARY	F	90	
PARKS, JERRE BURR	F	441	
PARKS, LELA NALL	D	353	
PARKS, MINNIE HELMS	V	98 - 120	
PARKS, RALPH	F	80	
PARKS, RICHARD H.	C	301 - 302	
PARKS, ROY F.	G	385, 465 - 466	
PARKS, SUE ROSALIND	W	479 - 489	
PARTRIDGE, KENNETH B.	K	562	
PARTRIDGE, KENNETH B.	L	42-46, 397-398	final settlement
PAUL, J.L.	D	100	
PAUL, JAMES T.	J	275, 306 - 309	
PAUL, LULA	F	93	
PAULK, THOMAS H.	A	225 - 230	
PAULK, W.A.	B	97 - 99	
PEACOCK, FLORRIE	F	426	
PEACOCK, JOHN L.	E	29	
PEACOCK, JOHN P.	L	222, 399 - 402	
PEACOCK, MYRTIS POWELL	L	695, 726 - 729	
PEACOCK, PEARL SMITH	N	629 - 635	672 - 675
PEACOCK, PEARL SMITH	O	160 - 164	
PEACOCK, RAYMOND G.	R	534	
PEARSON, CLARENCE POE	F	86	
PEAVY, GRADY	F	429	
PEEK, ALFRED	H	325, 419, 420	
PEEK, ROZELLA	I	403, 547 - 550	
PENERTON, CARRIE	L	218, 517 - 520	
PENNICK, ROY "JACK"	M	751	
PENNICK, ROY (JACK)	N	84 - 87	
PENNINGTON, ANNIE K.	D	31 - 32	
PENNINGTON, C.	C	383 - 387	
PENNINGTON, CLYDE	E	145 - 147	
PENNINGTON, JAMES HENRY	H	189, 395	final settlement
PENNINGTON, M.W.	D	84	
PENNINGTON, ROSCOE	O	229 - 236	
PENNINGTON, VERA VASHTI	H	174	
PENNINGTON, VERA VASHTI	J	622 - 624	

PERKINS, JARDINE C.	D	234
PERKINS, WILLIAM LEONARD	G	463, 658, - 659
PETERS, HARRIETT	A	138 - 147
PETERS, SUSAN S.	C	376
PHELPS, WILLIAM J. JR.	P	569 - 581
PHILLIPS, ANNIE	D	320
PHILLIPS, CEPHUS A.	I	1, 65, 66
PHILLIPS, E.M.	H	151
PHILLIPS, JAMES	Y	412
PHILLIPS, STELLA FOWLER	J	325, 401 - 404
PHILLIPS, STEWART M.	I	211 - 214 final settlement
PHILLIPS, STUART M.	H	271 - 273
PHILLIPS, ZELMA	Y	483
PICKET, LAURENTINA N.	C	68 - 69
PICKETT, H.F.	A	246 - 249
PICKETT, RICHARD M.	A	256 - 257
PICKETT, ROBERT	A	57 - 60
PIERCE, T. C.	G	333, 334 - 335
PIERCE, FOY NELSON	O	550 -558
PIERCE, KATE C.	X	885 - 910
PIERCE, MARIE W.	N	852 - 859
PIERCE, T.E.	D	74
PIERCE, W.E.	D	243
PIERSON, GUS	E	143 - 144
PIERSON, WM. R.	C	220 - 221
PINCKARD, J.W.	F	431
PINCKARD, JAMES H.	C	125 - 127
PINCKARD, RAY	Y	511 - 554
PIPPIN, EVA N.	M	814
PIPPIN, EVA N.	N	177 - 180
PIPPIN, L. DEVON	N	460 - 467
PITTMAN, E.H.	D	195
PITTMAN, NOLA MAE	F	190
PLATT, HARMON	A	98 - 100
POLLARD, VIOLA S.	F	439
POPE, R.T.	D	151
POPE, SARAH	A	253 - 254
POTTS, BABE	H	389, 509 - 511
POTTS, COUTIE	W	715 - 732
POWELL, ANN T.	G	336, 337 - 338
POWELL, CARRIE H.	G	264
POWELL, ALBERT M.	K	537
POWELL, BERYL	S	446

POWELL, BERYL	T	724 - 736	
POWELL, CARRIE H.	M	711 - 714	
POWELL, CECIL C.	U	663	
POWELL, D.M.	N	328 - 333, 564	Trans. to Circuit Ct.
POWELL, GENIE L.	X	596 - 605	
POWELL, HELEN	C	110 - 111	
POWELL, JAMES E.	D	403	
POWELL, JOHN	A	110 - 111	
POWELL, JOHNNIE M.	J	767	
POWELL, JOHNNIE M.	K	189 - 192	
POWELL, L.C.	D	400	
POWELL, L.K.	D	57 - 58	
POWELL, LEX ARNOLD	U	333	
POWELL, MARY EMMA	T	600	
POWELL, PURCER A	G	339, 340 - 341	
POWELL, ROBERT F.	C	421 - 423	
POWELL, WHITTIE GASTON	K	770	
PRESCOTT, ALTO	J	285	
PRESTWOOD, GARRETT F.	J	585	
PRESTWOOD, LOUIS MARSHALL	I	301 - 314	
PRICE, ANNIE SMYTH	E	199 - 201	
PRICE, JAMES P.	K	224, 295 - 298	
PRICE, JOSEPH C.	D	323	
PRITCHETT, HOSEY	M	315	
PRUETT, WYCHE GREENE	J	273, 520 - 523	
PRUETT, WYCHE GREENE	K	65 - 68	
PRUITT, FRANCIS M.	B	56 - 58	
PRUITT, MARY	D	116 - 117	
PUGH, BURRELL B.	A	129 - 132	
PUGH, FREEMAN	F	83	
PUGH, JESSE	A	105 - 108	
PYLANT, ISHAM SR.	B	225 - 227	
QUALLS, CLAUDE A. SR.	W	609 - 625	
QUALLS, GILLIS D.	W	294 - 304	
QUARLES, WILLIAM H. JR.	V	212 - 223	
QUEEN, ERNEST LESTER (SONNY)	S	130	
RABB, ROBERT S.	A	119 - 120	
RAFFERTY, FRANCES L.	K	243	
RAFFERTY, MAXWELL LEWIS JR.	N	88 - 91, 208	Trans. to Circuit Ct.
RAFFERTY, MAXWELL LEWIS JR.	M	678	
RAIFE, LEROY	Q	771	
RAIFORD, ADDIE	D	359 - 360	
RAINER, GEORGE	H	274, 275	

RAINER, MRS. MOLLIE	D	221	
RAINER, OLIVIA K.	J	102	
RAINER, ROSS	H	227, 228, 305	final settlement
RAMAGE, O. K.	G	356, 360 - 361	
RAMAGE, BENJAMIN	C	70 - 72	
RAMAGE, BURR	D	157 - 158	
RAMAGE, HATTIE L.	F	446	
RAMAGE, JAMES T.	D	180	
RAMAGE, WILLIE M.	I	330, 453 - 455	
RAMSAY, JOHN A.	B	62 - 65	
RAMSEY, LENA	J	30, 145 - 147	
RAY, L.E.	N	474 - 479	
REDDOCH, ANNIE B.	I	505	
REDDOCH, CAROL D.	G	362, 368 - 369	
REDDOCH, J.T.	G	351, 354 - 355	
REDDOCH, M.G.	J	635	
REDDOCH, MARY BELLE	T	212	
REDDOCK, JOHN D.	D	145 - 147	
REDDOCK, MARY BELLE	V	736 - 746	
REDMON, JAMES DOUGLAS	P	224, 227 - 235	
REDMON, JOHN	A	1	
REDMON, LUCINDA	K	546, 606 - 609	
REDMON, SIMON	B	220 - 223	
REED, BABE	J	250 - 256	Trans. to Circuit Ct.
REEVES, C. O.	G	343, 344 - 345	
REEVES, FATE O.	M	156 - 159	
REEVES, MARY ANNA	G	346, 349 - 350	
REEVES, BEN	M	715 - 718	
REEVES, CARLISS A.	P	276, 278 - 280	288, 289, 291 - 293
REEVES, CARLISS A.	P	296, 297	
REEVES, COLUMBUS OLIN JR.	W	250 - 261	
REEVES, EDNA Y.	X	203 - 213	
REEVES, FATE O.	L	816	Linda G. Reeves, Ex'r.
REEVES, JOHNNIE R.	O	387, 399 - 403	408 - 410
REEVES, JOHNNIE R.	P	582, 583	
REEVES, MARY ANNA	K	777 - 778	Trans. to Circuit Ct.
REEVES, RUSHIE J.	L	541, 671 - 675	
REEVES, SAMFORD E.	N	341 - 346	
REEVES, SARA M.	K	772	
REEVES, SARA M.	L	279 - 281	
REEVES, W.W.	F	95	
REGENTINE, MARGARET J.	Q	579	
REGETINE, MARGARET J.	R	143	

REGISTER, ALEX	T	201	
REGISTER, BENJAMIN	C	56 - 57	
REISMAN, MAURICE	V	187 - 196	
RENFROE, A.J.	F	102	
RENFROE, A.J. JR.	P	846 - 855	
RENFROE, EMMA L.	J	268, 405 - 408	
RENFROE, GLEN	N	334 - 340	
RENFROE, JOHN A.	X	421 - 435	
RENFROE, QUINTON C.	O	470, 472 - 473	475 -477
RENFROE, ROY GLEN	K	309, 496 - 502	
RENFROE, SARA M.	W	16 - 60	
REVILL, B.F.	N	468 - 473	
REVILL, BEULAH MAE	I	560	
REVILL, BEULAH MAE	J	71 - 78	final settlement
REVILL, RABON AUGUSTUS	F	121	
REYNOLDS, FRED D.	I	113	
REYNOLDS, G.C.	F	114	
REYNOLDS, HENRY	X	340 - 356	
REYNOLDS, J. L.	M	345	
REYNOLDS, JAMES W.	D	33	
REYNOLDS, LONIE	F	452	
REYNOLDS, MAUDE H.	J	3, 79 - 82	
RHODES, BEN M.	M	507, 553 - 556	
RHODES, CLEVELAND	F	535	
RHODES, GILBERT ALFRED	J	581	
RHODES, HAROLD N.	M	488, 540 - 552	
RHODES, LAVANIA T.	O	289, 291 - 297	
RHODES, MARY PAULINE	J	591, 786 - 789	
RHODES, MATTIE B.	H	293, 421, 422	
RHODES, NANCY	A	153 - 154	
RICE, LUCY M.	W	802 - 812	
RICE, ROBERT N. SR.	L	431, 599 - 602	
RICHARDSON, ALICE B.	K	124	
RICHARDSON, ALICE B.	L	282 - 285	
RICHARDSON, E.W.	N	522 - 525	668 - 671, 860 - 867
RICHARDSON, EDWARD HURON	X	766 - 776	
RICHARDSON, MARY	A	50 - 52	
RICHARDSON, SAM	M	644, 719 - 722	
RICHARDSON, VELLA	N	792 - 797	
RICHBURG, J.W.	E	148 - 149	
RICHBURG, JESSIE RUTH	U	173	
RICHBURG, JOE BOB	I	436, 456, 457	
RICHBURG, JOE COSTON	H	451	

RICHBURG, JOE COSTON	K	503 - 506
RICHBURG, MARY C.	F	118
RICHBURG, PERRY H.	F	106
RICHBURG, RALPH C.	I	40, 215, 216
RICHBURG, W.R.	F	99
RICKS, JESSE	A	87 - 90
RIDDICK, JENNIE	D	16
RIDDLE, C. M.	M	241, 460 - 463
ROBBINS, ELLA MAE	X	682 - 702
ROBERTS, JOSEPH BAXLEY JR.	U	593
ROBERTSON, J. W.	G	373, 376 - 377
ROBINSON, LOTTIE	D	86
ROBINSON, PAULINE MCSWAIN	Y	136 - 232
RODGERS, EARNEST	D	360 - 361
RODGERS, MARY JACKSON	U	302
RODGERS, ROBERT	A	22 - 25
RODGERS, THOMAS HUGH	F	108
ROGERS, JOHN HENRY	R	332
ROLING, JOHN	A	4
ROLLIN, JIM	G	370, 371 - 372
ROLLING, C. FREEMAN	H	86, 423, 424
ROLLING, D.E.	H	559
ROLLING, D.E.	I	357, 358
ROLLING, ETHEL CURRY	H	515 - 517
ROLLING, ROBBIE E.	H	437
ROLLINS, DILCY	U	393
ROLLINS, LILLIE MAE	I	315, 359, 360
ROLLINS, LOUISE	W	638 - 649
ROLLINS, WILLIAM C.	L	221, 403 - 406
ROOD, FRANCIS G.	W	359 - 371
ROSE, HELEN W.	H	19, 512 - 514
ROSE, JAMES L.	F	450
ROSE, LACEY D.	P	773 - 781
ROSE, MARSHALL GLEN SR.	I	86, 320, 321
ROSEBERRY, ESTELLA	K	103
ROSEBERRY, ESTELLE	N	92 - 95
ROSEBERRY, JOHN T.	C	288 - 289
ROSENBERG, ABRAHAM	D	233
ROSENBERG, ADOLPH H.	J	374, 625 - 627
ROSENBERG, JESSE	E	280 - 284
ROSENBERG, JOSEPH S.	F	111
ROSENBERG, SIGMOND	I	688, 700
ROSENBERG, SIGMOND	K	69 - 73

ROTEN, PAUL W.	J	1	
ROUSE, WM. H.	A	254 - 255	
ROWE, J.P.	C	44 - 46	
ROWE, MELISSA A.	C	412 - 419	
RUDD, DANIEL W.	G	278, 379 - 380	
RUSHING, MITCHELL P.	R	148	
RUSHING, RENDER	V	788 - 804	
RUSHING, WILLIE R.	F	448	
RUSSELL, ELLEN L.	K	582	
RUSSELL, ELLEN L.	L	286 - 289	
RUSSELL, SAREPTA A.	D	121	
RUTLEDGE, CHARLES E.	I	521, 607 - 609	
RUTLEDGE, CHARLES E.	J	142 - 144	521 - 522
RYALS, ELIZABETH F.	P	670 - 679	
RYALS, J.D.	H	319	
RYALS, J.D.	I	252, 253	
SALISBURY, WM. L.	B	208 - 211	
SANDERS, J. GILLES	G	55, 56	
SANDERS, WILLIE S	G	407 - 409	
SANDERS, ALICE	F	454	
SANDERS, ANNIE C.	H	450	
SANDERS, ANNIE C.	I	219, 220	
SANDERS, ANNIE LOU	E	27	
SANDERS, BERTRAM L.	L	71-78, 290-293	
SANDERS, DORSEY	J	266, 311 - 315	Remove to Circuit Ct.
SANDERS, EMMA LAW	F	159	
SANDERS, FLORA R.	K	532, 716 - 719	
SANDERS, FRANCIS E.	A	71 - 72	
SANDERS, HERMAN	M	333, 557 - 560	
SANDERS, ISAAC	B	130 - 132	
SANDERS, J.G.	J	641	
SANDERS, J.G.	K	28 - 32	Trans. to Circuit Ct.
SANDERS, J.M.	C	334 - 340 & 371	
SANDERS, JOHN M.	D	342	
SANDERS, MANDY BARRON	J	281	
SANDERS, NAN P.	L	344, 411 - 414	
SANDERS, RUBY	T	781	
SANDERS, RUTH F.	M	230, 464 - 467	
SANDERS, W.S.	D	206	
SANDERS, WILEY S.	H	538	
SANDERS, WILEY S.	I	217, 218	
SANDERS, WILLIE S.	F	"464	
SASSER, HENRY	B	187 - 191	

SATIRAS, GEORGE E.	D	333	
SAWTELL, SIDNEY BLAN	R	265	
SCARBROUGH, LOUIE F.	Q	435	
SCARBROUGH, R.W.	D	135 - 136	
SCHOFIELD, MANCIL K.	K	655	
SCHOFIELD, MANCIL K.	L	296 - 299	294 - 295
SCOGGIN, JOHN	A	14	
SCOTT, HOLLAND	C	365	
SEAL, THOMAS J.	L	814	
SEAL, THOMAS J.	M	168 - 171	
SEALE, LITTLETON	A	37 - 38	
SEALS, JOHN M.	C	168 - 169	
SEALS, MRS. L.J.	C	246 - 247	
SEARCY, HARVEY L.	F	487	
SEAY, A.G.	D	242	
SEAY, EMMA B.	C	262 - 263	
SEGARS, CHARLIE G.	E	155 - 156	
SEGARS, MYRA L.	I	105, 298 - 300	
SEGARS, SARAH A.	C	29 - 30	
SEGARS, SUSIE	F	137	
SELLERS, GERTRUDE	C	172 - 173	
SELLERS, HEPSEBETH	C	195 - 196	
SELLERS, HERBERT	H	233	
SELLERS, HUBERT	J	199 - 202	
SELLERS, LEMMA C.	J	384	
SELLERS, LEMMA C.	L	170 - 174	
SELLERS, LOWNDES YANCY	X	300	
SELLERS, NELL COX	S	533, 729	
SELLERS, ROBERT LEON	J	331, 528 - 533	
SELLERS, S.J.	F	470	
SELLERS, SAMUEL	A	155 - 158	
SELLERS, SIDNEY H.	I	324, 458 - 470	
SELLERS, VIRGINIA	D	5 - 6	
SELLERS, VIVIAN	M	252, 468 - 471	
SELLERS, W.R.	D	54	
SELMAN, MARY M.	D	335	
SELMAN, MARY W.	T	491	
SENN, ADDIE B.	M	202 - 214	
SENN, C.T.	D	190 - 192	
SENN, EMORY	L	47 - 51	
SENN, EMORY W.	K	84	
SENN, HUME	J	854	
SENN, HUME	L	52 - 55	

SENN, WILLIAM R.	F	467
SHACKELFORD, E.M.	D	257
SHACKLEFORD, JULIA J.	F	571
SHACKLEFORD, RUTH	F	156
SHARP, J. T.	G	410 - 412
SHAVER, BETTY K. etal	K	115
SHAVER, LOLA D.	P	98, 100 - 107
SHAVER, ROY G.	N	727 - 732
SHAVER, YANCEY E. SR.	K	113, 193 - 196
SHAVER, ZACK	E	91 - 92
SHAVERS, WILLIAM A.	O	559, 561 - 568
SHAW, MARY ELIZABETH	V	689 - 697
SHEALY, THOMAS LAMAR	I	567, 568
SHEALY, THOMAS LAMAR	K	515 - 518
SHEHANE, EULA LEE	F	473
SHEHANE, JAMES ANDREWS	L	300 - 303, 212
SHELL, JOHN W.	B	115 - 116
SHEPARD, J.B.	F	485
SHEPARD, M. C.	O	298, 300 - 309
SHEPHERD, J.A.	D	107 - 108
SHEPHERD, KATE ABNER	P	168, 170 - 180
SHEPHERD, KATE ABNER	R	50
SHEPHERD, MARY LIZZIE	J	795
SHEPHERD, MARY LIZZIE	K	197 - 200
SHEPPARD, ALLEN	N	721 - 726
SHEPPARD, ARRIE V.	Q	180
SHEPPARD, BENJAMIN MOSES	U	61
SHERWOOD, ROGERS	V	147 - 155
SHIELDS, ISABELL	L	680
SHIPMAN, J. MELTON	E	162 - 164
SHIPMAN, ROBERTA	G	547 - 553
SHIPMAN, ROBERTA P.	H	147, 147
SHIRLEY, EMMA E.	G	73, 503 - 504
SHIRLEY, FLOYD	T	583
SHIRLEY, FLOYD	U	245
SHIRLEY, JAMES ROBERT	H	28, 251, 252
SHIRLEY, LUCILE B.	R	686
SHIRLEY, S.H.	D	355 - 356
SHIRLEY, SHELBY S. SR.	J	571
SHIVER, M.A.	D	351
SHOFNER, SAVANNAH	C	116 - 117
SHULTZ, FREDERICK	A	213 - 214
SIKES, JESSIE	J	409 - 413

SIKES, NELL J.	V	421 - 422
SIKES, NELLE J.	T	611
SILER, MINNIE O.	D	41, 53 - 54
SILER, MYRA GRIFFIN	L	424, 586 - 590
SILER, SOLOMON	A	93 - 97
SIMMONS, CORA	F	478
SIMMONS, FANNIE	C	302 - 303
SIMMONS, MARGARET	D	115
SIMMONS, MILDRED HARPER	W	419 - 431
SIMMONS, WILLIE M.	R	545
SIMPSON, C.C.	F	483
SIMPSON, MAMIE D.	J	123
SIMS, B.F.	D	38 - 39
SIMS, ISAAC J.	E	150, 152 - 154
SIMS, JAMES B.	I	325, 391, 392
SIMS, JAMES T.	P	181, 183 - 190
SIMS, MRS. A.E.	D	26 - 27
SIMS, WILLIAM M.	J	763
SIMS, WILLIAM M.	K	201 - 204
SIMS, WM. A.	C	299 - 300
SINQUEFIELD, MOSES	B	53 - 55
SKINNER, SEABORN J.	C	74 - 76
SKINNER, SEABORN J.	D	255
SLAUGHTER, ALVARADA J.	T	1
SLAYTON, C.L.	F	131
SMART, CHARLES	F	532
SMART, ED F.	E	9 - 10
SMART, LOUIE S.	J	110
SMART, MARY W.	H	288, 425, 426
SMART, WILLIAM C.	T	749
SMITH, BEN S.	F	175
SMITH, BERNICE T.	U	710
SMITH, CASHIA SMYTH	G	399, 402 - 405
SMITH, DIXIE	N	487 - 491
SMITH, DONALD L.	J	802
SMITH, DONALD L.	K	511 - 514
SMITH, EMRY MELVINA	F	134
SMITH, ETHEL E.	J	116, 237 - 239
SMITH, EUNICE	W	531 - 547
SMITH, HUGH H. SR.	Q	199
SMITH, J.D.	H	104, 222, 223
SMITH, J.D.	K	563 - 564 Trans. to Circuit Ct.
SMITH, JORDAN	A	190 - 193

SMITH, KING L.	N	347 - 353	
SMITH, LOLA	D	346	
SMITH, LUCIOUS	O	843 - 846	862 - 871
SMITH, M.O.	I	427	
SMITH, MAHONE	V	1 - 9	
SMITH, MRS. LESLIE D.	N	497 - 503	
SMITH, RAY P.	S	89	
SMITH, RUBY	P	477, 480 - 489	
SMITH, W.W.	D	13	
SMITH, WILL	N	492 - 496	
SMITH, WILLIAM T.	D	203	
SMITH, WILLIE DELIA	X	373 - 392	
SMYTH, ENZOR	F	459	
SMYTH, SAMUEL M.	B	158 - 160	
SMYTH, SARAH C.	C	269 - 271	
SNEED, BESSIE	N	480 - 486	
SNEED, CAREY	O	784, 789 - 792	
SNEED, CAREY	U	517	
SNEED, HARRIET	E	319 - 320	
SNEED, PEARL E.	D	356 - 357	
SNEED, RAPHAEL	J	599	
SNIDER, JULIA ANN	C	50 - 51	
SNYDER, MARY LOUISE	G	616, 623 - 624	
SNYDER, MARY LOUISE	H	224 - 226	
SOMERSET, A. R.	M	746	
SOMERSET, A.L.	N	96 - 99	
SOMERSET, A.S.	D	272 - 273	
SOMERSET, CARL B.	G	413 - 415	
SOMERSET, ELIZABETH HARRIS	J	261	
SOMERSET, ELIZABETH HARRIS	K	519 - 522	
SORREL, ANISE J.	K	228 , 230 - 233	236, 237 demand trans
SORRELL, ANISE J.	J	349, 534 - 541	645, 706 - 724
SORRELL, ANISE J.	J	681, 730 - 759	
SORRELL, SUSIE MAE	M	27 - 31	
SORRELL, W. J.	M	503 - 506	
SORRELL, W.J.	I	365	
SORRELL, W.J.	J	203 - 215	451 - 455 Circuit Ct.
SORRELLS, SUSIE MAE	L	740	
SPAFFORD, EMILY S.	C	137	
SPAFFORD, MOSES	C	136 - 137	
SPARDLEY, RAY R.	G	416 - 418	
SPEIGHTS, CLEO HOYT	N	676 - 683	
SPEIGHTS, GRACE HILL	O	569, 571 - 574	576

SPEIR, JOHN	A	52 - 54	
SPENCER, CALLIE MAE	J	87, 148 - 150	
SPENCER, LEVI A.	F	480	
SPENCER, PETER	B	169 - 174	
SPENCER, RUTH W.	F	530	
SPICER, J.D.	N	185 - 188	
SPIVEY, HENRY D.	E	292 - 294	
SPIVEY, HILLARD	M	160 - 163	
SPIVEY, HILLIARD	L	812	
SPIVEY, HOLLAND	L	549, 676 - 679	
SPIVEY, JOHNNY KYE SR.	F	457	
SPIVEY, M.S.	D	171	
SPRADLEY, MARY W.	K	657	
SPRADLEY, MARY W.	M	605 - 609	final settlement
SPRINGS, LAURA LOUISE	V	46 - 55	
SPURGER, MELBA D.	N	124, 181 - 184	
SPURLOCK, OLLIE B.	J	327, 628 - 631	
ST. JOHN, HENRY SEWELL SR.	W	672 - 714	
ST. JOHN, HENRY SEWELL SR.	X	606 - 628	
STAFFORD, MURRELL NEWTON JR.	P	1, 3	
STALLINGS, DR. H.S.	D	282	
STALLINGS, J.J.	C	156 - 158	
STALLINGS, JOHN L.	S	267	
STALLINGS, MRS. EADIE	F	475	
STALLINGS, S.A.F.	D	8	
STALLSWORTH, JAMES	A	169 - 171	
STANDLEY, J.E.	L	351, 407 - 410	
STARKE, FANNIE C.	C	424 - 425	
STARKE, GEORGE C.	J	437	
STARKE, MAMIE M.	D	248	
STARKE, MARY A.	D	289	
STARKE, SAMUEL J.	D	405	
STARKE, WILLIAM C.	D	94 - 95	
STARKS, LUCINDA	Q	815	
STARKS, MARY ELLA	M	164 - 167	
STARLING, CLARA R.	N	203 - 205	210 - 230
STARLING, DOROTHY C.	I	621	
STARLING, DOROTHY C.	J	231 - 233	
STARLING, HUGH D.	J	234 - 236	
STARLING, HUGH DENT	I	625	
STARLING, J.B.	H	547	
STARLING, J.B.	I	67 - 70	
STARLING, J.J.	F	127	

STARLING, MAGNUS J.	T	682 - 691	
STEED, ARVIS	M	291, 472 - 475	
STEED, ARVIS	T		
STEED, CHARLES EDGAR JR.	W	626 - 637	
STEED, TOMMIE	K	779	
STEED, TOMMIE	L	65 - 70	
STEELE, N.D.	S	699	
STEPHENS, LAMON	F	163	
STEPHENS, THOMAS OTIS	Q	688	
STEVENS, H.V.	D	226 - 227	
STEWART, CEPHALIE	M	215	
STEWART, WILLIAM KNOX	G	663	
STEWART, ANNIE MAE	M	673, 723726	
STEWART, ELIZABETH W.	W	791 - 801	
STEWART, GEORGE W.	C	2 - 3	
STEWART, J.H.	H	300	
STEWART, LILLIAN H.	V	348 - 367	
STEWART, LOUISE G.	N	526 - 529	500 - 503
STEWART, MARGARET S.	W	132 - 140	
STEWART, MATILDA	D	72 - 73	
STEWART, SAMUEL W.	K	258, 507 - 510	
STEWART, W.L.	K	79	
STEWART, W.L.	L	197 - 202	
STEWART, WILLIAM ALVA	V	378 - 387	
STEWART, WM. BRAXTON	Q	829	
STEWART, WM. KNOX	H	144, 145	
STEWART, Z.D.	J	794	
STEWART, Z.D.	K	74 - 78	
STEWART, ZEDA	K	313	
STEWART, ZULA	L	189 - 196	
STINSON, CHARLES L.	T	166	
STINSON, JORDAN B.	B	50 - 52	
STOKES, B.B.	U	14	
STONE, ELLENDER	C	26 - 28	
STONE, J.G.	I	361, 362	
STOUGH, MRS. LENA	D	385	
STREETMAN, M.S.	H	534, 607, 608	
STRICKLAND,IRENE COBB	Q	137, 591	
STRIEF, HARRY J.	E	60 - 90	
STRIEF, MABEL	E	41 - 59	
STRINGER, SALLIE MAE	M	763	
STRINGER, SALLIE MAE	N	100 - 103	
STRINGER, SALLIE MAE	N	874, 879 - 882	

STRINGER, ZOLLIE JR	O	411, 414 - 424	
STRIPLING, AARON	A	193 - 196	
STUBBS, DAN	G	530	
STUBBS, LEWIS	A	85	
STUDDARD, SAMUEL WALLACE	D	349	
SUGGS, KATIE L.	L	823	
SUGGS, KATIE L.	N	189 - 192	
SULLINS, BRADFORD	B	47 - 49	
SULLIVAN, CECIL J	G	578	
SULLIVAN, CECIL J.	H	306, 307	
SWAIN, WILLIAM J.	F	124	
SWIFT, SYDNEY	D	253 - 254	
SWISHER, RUTH DIXON	X	260 - 271	
SYNCO, JESSE ROY	H	367, 427, 428	
TALBOT, BAILEY M.	D	104 - 105	
TALBOT, HEZEKIAH	A	232	
TALBOT, MINNIE	D	330	
TALBOT, SUSIE	D	303	
TALBOT, SUSIE MAE	D	331	
TATE, ANNIE R.	C	170 - 171	
TATE, J.B.	D	232	
TATE, W.W.	C	160 - 162	
TAUNTON, THOMAS W.	J	456, 524 - 527	
TAYLOR, N. J.	G	424, 426 - 427	
TAYLOR, BESSIE LEE	I	89, 138 - 140	Trans. to Circuit Ct.
TAYLOR, GROVER PALMER	H	555	
TAYLOR, JEWELL G.	N	883 - 888	
TAYLOR, JOHN D.	Q	592	
TAYLOR, LENA MAE	J	91	
TAYLOR, LENA MAE	K	527 - 530	
TAYLOR, N.H.	I	280 - 282	final settlement
TAYLOR, OWEN CLARENCE	Q	749	
TAYLOR, SARAH J.	D	85	
TAYLOR, WENDELL K.	H	333, 429, 430	
TEAL, ROBERT BURNS	Q	339	
TEW, CLARA F.	M	749	
TEW, CLARA F.	N	108 - 111	
TEW, M.A.	E	157 - 159	
THERIOT, LEOLA	X	137 - 149	
THIGPEN, HELEN SANDERS	L	419, 619 - 622	
THOMAS, BESSIE KATE HERNER	L	694, 730 - 733	
THOMAS, HENRY T.	F	152	
THOMAS, JOHN SR.	A	21 - 22	

THOMAS, SARAH BETTY	U	267	
THOMAS, W. EMMITT	J	111, 240 - 242	
THOMASTON, WM. JEFFERSON	E	173 - 175	
THOMPSON, COLLIS D.	G	419, 422 - 423	
THOMPSON, A.W.	D	147 - 148	
THOMPSON, ANNIE MAE	I	443, 551 - 553	
THOMPSON, ARIOSTO WILEY	K	739, 740	
THOMPSON, ARIOSTO WILEY	L	56 - 60	
THOMPSON, HUGH	C	311 - 313	
THOMPSON, IRA A.	F	489	
THOMPSON, IRA A.	J	427 - 436	
THOMPSON, JAMES A.	I	141, 142	223, 224
THOMPSON, JULE	M	59, 172 - 175	
THOMPSON, LUCILLE J.	H	444	
THOMPSON, LUCILLE J.	I	221, 222	
THOMPSON, MARVIN B.	X	79 - 108	
THOMPSON, MATTIE LOU	O	310, 312 - 318	
THOMPSON, RHODIA ALICE	R	463	
THOMPSON, RHODIA ALICE	S	745	
THOMPSON, TINYE	L	357, 529 - 532	
THOMPSON, TOMMIE L.	Q	605	
THOMPSON, W.L. JR.	S	460	
THOMPSON, WYCHE	J	414 - 416	
THOMPSON, WYCHE W.	H	107	
THREADGILL, LUTHER ERNEST	K	92, 523 - 526	
THROWER, NELL	J	770	
THROWER, NELL	K	205 - 210	
TICER, ANIS	D	220	
TILLERY, JOHN FRANK	U	25	
TILLERY, MARTHA D.	X	552 - 567	
TILLMAN, B.D.	N	798 - 807	
TILLMAN, C.A.	H	521, 613, 614	
TISDALE, MARY JANE	J	283, 320, 321	324
TISDALE, MARY JANE	J	370, 847 - 849	
TOLBERT, ALMA	E	176 - 177	
TOLBERT, LILLIE MAE	M	622, 727 - 732	
TOWERY, EMMA L.	N	889 - 893	
TOWNSEND, ANDREW	G	428 - 430	
TOWNSEND, ARRIE V.	H	24, 131, 132	
TOWNSEND, ELIZABETH	D	21 - 22	
TOWNSEND, HOMER C.	L	182, 304 - 307	
TOWNSEND, JEFF	M	514, 610 - 613	
TOWNSEND, JOHN WILLIAM	H	535, 609, 610	

TOWNSEND, S.O.	F	499	
TOWNSEND, SUSIE S.	E	467	Recorded before death
TOWNSEND, WILLIE JAMES	Y	343 - 359	
TRANUM, LANDER D.	G	574, 597 - 598	
TRAPP, LEONARD Y.	R	156, 700	
TRICE, THOMAS C.	B	122 - 124	
TROTMAN, JOHN L.	C	223 - 226	
TROTMAN, JOHN P.	D	368	
TROTMAN, LOTTIE M.	K	610 - 613	
TROTMAN, LOTTIE MAE	E	165 - 166	
TROTMAN, LOTTIE MAE	J	554	
TROTTER, HELEN R.	G	481, 647 - 648	
TROTTER, NAPOLEON	G	625	
TROTTER, DOWLING W.	F	492	
TROTTER, EDWARD WAYNE	N	514-517, 696	610-613 Trans. Cir. Ct.
TROTTER, ELEANOR GARDNER	S	631	
TROTTER, ERNEST H.	H	9	
TROTTER, J. CALDWELL	F	497	
TROTTER, JEFF	E	325 - 327	& 459 - 463
TROTTER, MARY L.	Q	143	
TROTTER, NAPOLEON	H	91	final settlement
TROTTER, SAMUEL	C	114 - 115	
TROTTER, WHITFIELD	C	166 - 167	
TUCKER, CATHERINE	M	509, 733	
TUCKER, HIRAM	A	164 - 166	
TUCKER, WILLIE ESTELLE	F	493	
TULLIS, P.T.	C	4 - 6	
TURNER, MILDRED	G	392, 505 - 506	
TURNER, ANNA DUBOSE	D	335	
TURNER, EUNICE	K	765	
TURNER, FERNIE	N	193 - 198	
TURNER, FOY C.	J	593, 632 - 634	
TURNER, JAMES AUBREY	L	310, 525 - 528	
TURNER, NELSON BYRON	M	785	
TURNER, NELSON BYRON	N	104 - 107	
TURNER, PEARL	J	372, 423 - 426	
TURNIPSEED, FOX REYNOLDS	S	635	
TURNIPSEED, JOHN THOMAS	C	150 - 153	
TURNIPSEED, LAURA NADINE	R	276	
TURNIPSEED, SAMMIE CLARA	J	760	
TURNIPSEED, SAMMIE CLARA	M	176 - 179	
TWAY, DUANE CONVERSE	R	285	
TYNER, FRANK B.	H	544	

TYNER, FRANK BEAN	H	611, 612
TYNER, J.T.	E	96 - 102
TYNER, MARGENE V.	J	557
TYNER, MARGENE V.	K	211 - 214
TYNER, MATTIE PEARL	L	369, 521 - 524
VAN LEWEN, RICHARD	G	523, 601 - 602
VANN, JOE THOMAS	H	32, 135, 136
VARNER, DAVID M.	A	235 - 236
VAUGHAN, A. T.	G	589, 645 - 646
VINCENT, COLUMBUS P.	B	81 - 83
VINCENT, H.B.	X	169 - 189
VINCENT, HOUSTON BURROUGH	P	200, 201
VINCENT, HOUSTON BURROUGH	W	586 - 608
VINCENT, PENNINGTON	A	30 - 31
VINSON, WEST	A	47 - 49
WADE, ALVENA BRUNDIDGE	X	1 - 17
WADE, W.S.	C	178 - 179
WADOWICK, MARTHA	P	856 - 875
WADOWICK, MARTHA	Q	444
WAGONER, MILDRED PARSONS	K	226, 299 - 302
WALDEN, ARTHUR D.	I	143 - 162
WALDEN, ARTHUR D.	X	357 - 372
WALKER, WILLIAM J.	G	71, 434 - 436
WALKER, ALER	D	370 - 371
WALKER, ANNIE H.	C	469, 471, & 472
WALKER, FELIX	C	34 - 35
WALKER, HAROLD E.	I	288, 322, 323
WALKER, ROBBIE	F	149
WALKER, ROBERT H.	D	136 - 139
WALLACE, FRANCES C.	M	501, 614 - 617
WALLACE, PAULINE	M	760
WALLACE, PAULINE	N	112 - 115
WALLACE, REYNOLDS E. SR.	K	336
WALLACE, REYNOLDS E. SR.	L	175 - 179
WALLER, RUTH MORGAN	H	245
WALTERS, MRS. M. E.	G	431 - 433
WALTERS, JAMES	D	7
WALTERS, JOE FRANK SR.	N	551 - 554 614 - 622
WALTERS, JOHN C.	I	397
WALTERS, MRS. ETTA H.	D	324
WALTERS, W.O.	D	200
WARD, ANN SMITH	K	319
WARD, GRIFFIN C.	H	327, 435, 436

WARD, H.W.	D	317	
WARD, HENRY P.	R	471	
WARD, JAMES L.	F	523	
WARD, JAMES L.	I	243 - 245	
WARD, MINNIE I.	M	275	
WARREN, ANNA MCBRYDE	F	501	
WARREN, CECIL R.	Y	46 - 75	
WARREN, DANIEL	C	42 - 44	
WARREN, J.M.	D	20 - 21	
WARREN, LOURUE G.	S	279	
WARREN, LOURUE G.	T	289	
WARREN, O.D.	Q	634	
WARREN, RANDOLP G.	S	293	
WARREN, RANDOLPH G.	T	181	
WARREN, W.L.	I	471, 587 - 589	
WATERS, CLEVELAND	S	182	
WATERS, CLEVELAND O.	R	477	
WATERS, CLEVELAND O.	T	243	Estate
WATERS, HERBERT MEREDITH	N	733 - 737	
WATERS, J. CARSON	F	509	
WATERS, J.M.	C	444 - 447	
WATERS, JOHN H.	G	8, 447 - 448	
WATERS, LEE	Q	451	
WATERS, LEE	T	230	
WATERS, NELLIE F.	S	105	
WATKINS, J. HAROLD	G	15	
WATKINS, J.M.	D	124	
WATKINS, JAMES ABBIE	J	768	
WATKINS, JAMES ABBIE	K	215 - 218	
WATSON, DOROTHY M.	X	474 - 483	
WATSON, EUGENIE	D	149 - 150	
WATSON, VIRGINIA W.	V	484 - 497	
WEBB, ELOISE B.	G	21	
WEBBER, ELIZABETH PELZER	K	639	
WEBSTER, HAROLD C.	W	452 - 464	
WEEDON, H.M.	D	26	
WEEDON, JULIA HENDERSON	H	286	
WEEKS, ALICE JONES	D	274 - 275	
WELCH, H.A.	F	542	
WELCH, HELEN FAYE HOLLEY	W	240 - 249	
WELCH, JOHN O.	P	659 - 669	
WELDON, MYRA	P	782 - 791	
WELDON, MYRA	Q	465	

WELLS, MITTIE THURMAN	J	765	
WELLS, VALERIA G.	W	346 - 358	
WELLS, VALERIA G.	X	131 - 136	
WESLEY, H. C. JR.	G	662	
WESLEY, BERTHA ROSHELL	M	242, 244	476-481, 734-737 final
WESLEY, G.C.	M	257, 482 - 485	
WESLEY, H.C. JR.	H	214, 215	
WESLEY, MRS. THETIE	E	160 - 161	
WESSON, FORNIE H.	L	361, 415 - 418	
WEST, LUCIOUS	M	180 - 183	
WEST, MARY ELLA	N	684 - 691	
WHALEY, LESTER	G	100, 443 - 444	
WHALEY, ANNIE PEARL	H	523	
WHALEY, ANNIE PEARL	I	71 - 75	final settlement
WHALEY, ARCHIBALD	B	120 - 122	
WHALEY, ELIGER S.	C	182 - 183	
WHALEY, JAMES M.	C	82 - 83	
WHALEY, L.E.	D	409	
WHALEY, MARGARET G.	V	667 - 675	
WHALEY, SAM	D	310	
WHALEY, WILLIE DORA	H	566	
WHALEY, WILLIE DORA	I	240 - 242	
WHATLEY, ENOCH M.	F	520	
WHATLEY, JAMES THELMA	X	272 - 287	
WHATLEY, LABAN	C	13 - 14	
WHEELER, J.D.	I	11	
WHETSTONE, JOHN ASA	H	285, 433, 434	
WHIGHAM, MARY LUCILLE	I	254 - 260	
WHITE, CLIFFORD F.	O	578, 617, 632	626-630, 635, 638-641
WHITE, D.J.	D	210	
WHITE, JOHN SR.	A	148 - 151	116 - 118
WHITE, JOHN T.	A	233 - 234	
WHITE, LUCY A.	K	7, 219 - 222	
WHITE, MADELL B.	S	475	
WHITE, MADELL B.	T	393	
WHITE, MARY E.	D	379	
WHITE, MAZIE PARKER	R	805	
WHITE, MAZIE PARKER	S	761	
WHITE, OSCAR	F	198	
WHITE, ROSE KING	D	332	
WHITE, SYLVESTER	H	281, 431, 432	
WHITE, W. SHEP	F	506	
WHITEHEAD, NELL	N	504 - 509	

WHITEHURST, ALBERT C.	W	262 - 272	
WHITEHURST, ANNIE MYRTLE	I	82, 225, 226	
WHITEHURST, CARRIE LOIS	X	238 - 259	
WHITEHURST, HATTIE RUTH	U	365	
WHITEHURST, MATTIE RUTH	T		
WHITEHURST, W.W.	I	558, 590 - 592	
WHITESIDE, ELLA	I	163	
WHITESIDE, JOHN	W	497 - 517	
WHITMAN, W. T.	G	121, 445 - 446	
WHITTINGTON, CARLTON	R	825	
WHITTINGTON, MILDRED P.	Q	329	
WHITTLE, JAMES W.	F	567	
WIDDOWSON, DAVID CHARLES	L	533 - 536	
WIGGINS, MARGIE SCOTT	T	767 - 779	
WILCOXON, MRS. NANNIE BELL	E	3 - 4	
WILEY, GUSSIE M.	D	128	
WILEY, J.M.	D	66 - 67	
WILEY, MITTIE MURPHREE	D	154 - 155	
WILEY, OLIVER	C	374 - 376	
WILEY, OLIVER (final settlement)	G	69,537 - 539	
WILKERSON, HALBERT	O	319 - 328	
WILKERSON, HALBERT	P	792 - 808	
WILKERSON, HALBERT	Q	241	
WILKERSON, JOHN H.	E	295 - 297	
WILKERSON, MADGE A.	N	627, 628	692 - 695
WILKERSON, MADGE A.	P	191, 193	195 - 197, 236, 237
WILKERSON, NETTIE M.	F	512	
WILKERSON, T.E.	F	564	
WILKES, J. C.	G	440 -442	
WILKES, PEARL W.	S	372	
WILLIAMS, MAGGIE H.	G	437 -439	
WILLIAMS, ALBERT	Q	301	Estate
WILLIAMS, BURGESS D.	A	64	
WILLIAMS, DEKALB	C	103 - 106	
WILLIAMS, EVA	H	82, 260, 261	
WILLIAMS, HAZEL A.	L	754	
WILLIAMS, HORACE O.	H	438, 615 - 616	
WILLIAMS, JOHN W. JR.	Q	291	
WILLIAMS, LOUIS M.	S	487	
WILLIAMS, LOUTIE W.	D	283	
WILLIAMS, MYRTLE LEE	F	146	
WILLIAMS, R.J.	C	297 - 298	
WILLIAMS, S.J.	C	186 - 187 & 194	

WILLIAMS, SAM A.	D	189
WILLIAMS, SAM S.	P	490, 492 - 499
WILLIAMS, SIMEON	B	162 - 163
WILLIAMS, WM.	C	76 - 77
WILLIAMSON, ANDREW J.	H	309
WILLIAMSON, CHARLOTTE M.	D	245
WILLIAMSON, JAMES A.	K	636, 720 - 723
WILLIAMSON, JAMES P. JR.	H	169
WILLIAMSON, PETER	A	31 - 33
WILLIAMSON, ROBERT GEORGE JR.	O	425,428 - 435
WILLIFORD, LUTHER F.	G	449 - 451
WILLIFORD, CLEMENT	D	209
WILLIFORD, GUY R.	H	152, 229, 230
WILLIFORD, LEWIS HILL	D	391
WILLIFORD, LEWIS HILL	D	407
WILLIS, MOSES P.	B	92 - 96
WILSON, AVER GREEN	R	840
WILSON, AVER GREEN	S	502
WILSON, BEN R.	D	373
WILSON, CELIA BRAGG	V	197 - 211
WILSON, EDWARD C.	A	6 - 8
WILSON, FURNIE A.	F	515
WILSON, IDA HARRIS	M	626, 738 - 741
WILSON, JOE CHESTER	R	486
WILSON, JOE CHESTER	S	625	Estate
WILSON, LAURA JEAN	Q	237
WILSON, MACK S.	K	136, 143
WILSON, NORMAN	H	45, 119, 120
WILSON, WILLIE NELSON	S	505
WILSON, WILLIE NELSON	T	268
WILSON, WM. H.	C	309 - 310
WINDHAM, E.I.	D	210 - 240 - 241
WINDHAM, JOHN E.	D	221
WINDHAM, R.E.	N	354 - 357, 258
WINDHAM, ROBERT P.	X	497 - 508
WINDHAM, ZONA LEE	R	491
WINDHAM, ZONA LEE	T	67
WINFIELD, RUBY L.	M	676
WINFIELD, RUBY L.	N	120 - 123
WINFIELD, WESLEY HARVEY	M	63, 360 - 363
WINGARD, G.F.	D	351 - 353
WINGARD, HUEY	R	340
WINGARD, IDA LOU	K	307, 728 - 731

WINGARD, LOMAX	N	547, 548	623 - 626
WINGARD, SUSIE MAE	N	116 - 119	
WINGARD, T.B.	F	141	
WINGARD, W.L.	F	517	
WINGARD, WILLIE H.	L	805	
WINGARD, WILLIE H.	M	184 - 187	
WINSLETT, JOEL A.,	C	204 - 205	
WINSLETT, MARGARET A.	C	204 - 205	
WINSLETT, MARY C.	C	204 - 205	
WINSLETT, NANCY A.	C	204 - 205	
WINSLETT, SARAH J.	C	204 - 205	
WITHERINGTON, JOSEPH D.	W	880 - 891	
WITHERINGTON, MITTIE B.	L	742	
WITHERINGTON, MITTIE B.	M	32 - 35	
WITT, CHARLES	S	591	
WITT, CHARLES	U	409	
WOEST, THOMAS C.	X	484 - 496	
WOOD, J.P. SR.	D	25	
WOOD, JAMES	B	42 - 43	
WOOD, LEO HENDERSON	I	434, 554 - 557	
WOOD, LUCILLE M.	G	471, 473 - 474	
WOOD, W.F.	D	117 - 118	
WOODS, GRACE	L	734	
WOODS, GRACE	M	40 - 43	
WOODS, WILLIE A.	U	289	
WORTHINGTON, CRAVEN A.	C	394 - 398	
WRIGHT, ARKANSAS	D	143 - 144	
WRIGHT, E.M.	D	153	
WRIGHT, EDWARD N.	C	146 - 149	
WRIGHT, JAMES	F	504	
WRIGHT, MARY TALBOT	F	560	
WRIGHT, WALTER	N	518, 519	
WRIGHT, WALTER	O	165 -167	172 - 180, 182 - 193
WYLLIE, EMILY ELIZ. SMITH	L	751	
WYLLIE, EMMA ELIZABETH SMITH	M	36 - 39	
WYNN, BERTHA	J	856	
WYNN, BERTHA	L	61 - 64	
WYNN, OZONA D.	J	813, 850 - 853	
WYNN, S. BENNETT	J	247	
WYNNE, JAMES CURTIS	C	112 - 114	
WYNNE, NANETTE P.	N	520, 521	
WYNNE, NANNETTE P.	T	420	
WYNNE, STEPHEN L.	B	217 - 219	

WYROSDICK, ALEXANDER	B	117 - 119	
YATTAW, MARY ELIZ. CAMPBELL	P	315, 318	321 - 326
YOUNG, MRS. KATIE E.	E	225 - 227	
YOUNGBLOOD, C. EDWIN	N	808 -816	
YOUNGBLOOD, ELZIE	S	301	
YOUNGBLOOD, ELZIE	T	626 - 661	
YOUNGBLOOD, GEORGE W.	I	655	
YOUNGBLOOD, GEORGE W.	J	216 - 221	
YOUNGBLOOD, HERMAN	Q	474	
YOUNGBLOOD, MAE	X	298 - 313	
YOUNGBLOOD, THOMAS	B	14 - 16	
YOUNGBLOOD, ZERAH MOTES	S	317	
ZACHRY, LEVIN	C	93 - 95	
ZEIGLER, W.N.	D	50 - 51	

ABBITT, LUCY F. - DECD.	ABBITT, JAMES	112
ABERCROMBIE, JAMES A.	ABERCROMBIE, ALLEN F. - DECD.	99
ABERCROMBIE, M.E. - ETAL	BROWN, GANNO - GDN.	15
ABRAMS, HARRY - DECD.	ABRAMS, Herman & Cohn, M. - Admr	129
ADAIR, LENA (C)	EXPARTE - HOMESTEAD	71
ADAMS, Alice P., Wilbert, Tommie L.	First F & M Nat'l. Bank, Gdn	150
ADAMS, COLSON - WILL		15
ADAMS, ELIZA C. - DECD.	STURGEON, J. LOWRY - ADMR.	89
ADAMS, HARMON - DECD.	HAMIL, JOHN M. - EXEC.	1
ADAMS, JOHN - DECD.	ADMR. - Dock. Bk. 1, pg. 90	94
ADAMS, ROBERT LEE	ADAMS, T.W.	97
ADAMS, WM. W.	ADAMS, T.W. - EXEC. WILL	63
ALA. BROKERAGE CORP.	CORPORATION	89
ALA. ELECTRIC CO-OP - VS.	JOHNSON, IDA T.	151
ALA. ELECTRIC CO-OP - VS.	RICHBURG, H.H.	161
ALA. HARD LUMBER CO.	CORPORATION	61
ALA. LONG DISTANCE TEL. CO.	INCORPORATION	70
ALA. MID. R.R. CO. - VS.	HICKS, LUCINDA - Condemnation	57
ALA. MID. R.R. CO. - VS.	OWENS, REUBIN - Condemnation	57
ALA. MID. R.R. CO. - VS.	Wiley, A.A. & Tompkins, H.C. - Conde	57
ALA. MID. R.R. CO. - VS.	LAWSON, E.F. - Condemnation	57
ALA. MID. R.R. CO. - VS.	BLAIR, JANE P. - Condemnation	57
ALA. MID. R.R. CO. - VS.	EVANS, REBECCA - Condemnation	57
ALA. MID. R.R. CO. - VS.	GRIFFIN, IRVIN - Condemnation	57
ALA. MID. R.R. CO. - VS.	STEPHENS, FELIX - Condemnation	57
ALA. MID. R.R. CO. - VS.	BARNETT, M.H. - Condemnation	57
ALA. MID. R.R. CO. - VS.	CHAMPION, F.D. - Condemnation	57
ALA. MID. R.R. CO. - VS.	ZACHRY, L.A. - Condemnation	57
ALA. MID. RY. CO. - CONSTANCE	Smith & Sneed - Etals Condemnation	61
ALA. MID. RY. CO. - VS.	M. & R.R. CO. - Condemnation	57
ALA. MID. RY. CO. - VS.	TROTTER, A.A. - Condemnation	57
ALA. MID. RY. CO. - VS.	CU. R.R. & BKG. CO. - Condemnation	57
ALA. MID. RY. CO. - VS.	HICKS, J.P. - Condemnation	57
ALA. MID. RY. CO. - VS.	GRIFFIN, ELIZA C. - ETAL	59
ALA. MID. RY. CO. - VS.	WHITHURST, J.M. - ETAL	59
ALA. MID. RY. CO. - VS.	REGISTER, D.A. - Etal Condemnation	61
ALEXANDER, W.F.	EXPARTE - INSANITY	64
ALFORD, ALLEN - DECD.	ALFORD, ALMON - ADMR.	16
ALFORD, TABITHA - DECD.	ALFORD, A.A. & H.C. - ADMR.	16
ALFORD, TALMAGE - MINOR	NON AGE	86
ALLEN, C.A. & A.A.	AD QUOD DAMNUM	71
ALLEN, CHARLES L. - MINOR	SMITH, J. OWENS - GDN.	8
ALLEN, D.B. - DECD.	ALLEN, L.E. - ADMR.	50

ALLEN, D.B. - DECD.		66
ALLEN, J.F. - DECD.	ALLEN, S.E. - ADMR.	16
ALLEN, JAMES - DECD.	ALLEN, NANCY D. - EXEC.	1
ALLEN, JAMES - DECD.	ALLEN, NANCY D. - ADMR.	46
ALLEN, JOHN - DECD.	WINDHAM, R.D. - ADMR. WILL	62
ALLEN, M.G. - DECD.	LOCKARD, A.T. - ADMR.	15
ALLEN, MARY J. - DECD.	COOK, R.F. & J.G. - ADMR.	16
ALLEN, R.P. - Exempt from road duty	MINUTE BOOK O - PAGE 128	
ALLEN, SARAH E. - DECD.	SEAY, W.J. & FRENCH, J.E. - Exec.	54
ALLISON, M.O. - DECD.	WORTHY, A.C. - ADMR.	73
ALLOWAY, Addie Ruth - Etal Minors	ALLOWAY, ELIZA - GDN. Doc. Bk. 1,	92
ALLOWAY, BENNIE JAMES - Decd.	MCCULLOUGH, MAGGIE LUE	148
ALLRED, AVIS - DECD.	Wilkerson, Madge; McPherson, Sarah	156
ALLRED, J.P. - DECD.	ALLRED, J.S. - ADMR.	66
ALLRED, MRS. ELLA - DECD.	ALLRED, O.B. - GDNSHIP.	63
AMMONS, J.D. - ETAL MINORS	AMMONS, E.E. - GDN.	87
AMMONS, JOHN - DECD.	AMMONS, MARGARET - ADMR.	50
AMMONS, KANNIE - ETAL	TENANTS IN COMMON	87
AMMONS, RANDALL B. - DECD.	AMMONS, ROY S. - ADMR.	120
AMMONS, W.J.R. - ETAL	TENANTS IN COMMON	58
AMOS, BEVERLY - DECD.	EVERETT, JOHN J.	1
AMOS, J.T. - DECD.	JOHNSON, M.F. - ADMR.	83
AMOS, J.W.B. - DECD.	AMOS, IDA - ADMR.	114
ANDERSON, A.M. - DECD.	ANDERSON, MYRTLE S.; Exec. Will	167
ANDERSON, BAMA - DECD.	ANDERSON, SHELLY D.; Exec. Will	154
ANDERSON, C.P. - DECD.	ANDERSON, JOHN - WILL	88
ANDERSON, F.E. - ETAL MINOR	ANDERSON, J.A. - GDN.	56
ANDERSON, GRADY C. - DECD.	ANDERSON, CALLIE M. - ADMR.	162
ANDERSON, JACKSON - DECD.	PROBATE OF WILL	68
ANDERSON, JAMES - DECD.	ANDERSON, W.C. - ADMR.	1
ANDERSON, JAMES W.	VETERAN	136
ANDERSON, JAMES W. - DECD.	ANDERSON, GLADYS L.; Exec. Will	137
ANDERSON, JOSEPH	DISABILITIES - NON AGE	90
ANDERSON, L.K.	WATSON, W.E. - APPRENTICESHIP	77
ANDERSON, REBECCA J. - minor	TRANSCRIPT	15
ANDERSON, Rebecca J. Williams	WILLIAMS, BENJ. D. - GDN.	97
ANDERSON, ROBERT - DECD.	BARNHILL, L.E. - ADMR.	57
ANDERSON, Robt. & Eliza - Minors	MURPHREE, JOEL D. - GDN.	57
ANDERSON, ROBT. - Etal Minors	JONES, J.D. - GDN.	62
ANDERSON, SARAH		1
ANDERSON, SARAH F. - ETAL	Tenants in Common doc bk 1, pg 152	97
ANDERSON, T.J.	WATSON, E.W. - APPRENTICESHIP	77
ANDERSON, W.C. - ETAL	TENANTS IN COMMON	1

ANDRESS, COLLIE E. - DECD.	ANDRESS, ROBERT L. - WILL	82
ANDRESS, DOROTHY	ANDRESS, J.W. - ADMR.	105
ANDRESS, FRANK P. - DECD.	ANDRESS, I.N. & M.F. - EXEC. WILL	53
ANDRESS, ISAAC - DECD.	ANDRESS, MARY J. - ADMR.	15
ANDRESS, JAMES - MINOR	PEARSON, THOMAS J. - GDN.	15
ANDRESS, JOSEPH M. - DECD.	CARROLL, F.M. - ETAL EXEC.	53
ANDRESS, JOSEPH M. - DECD.	ANDRESS, J.B. - EXEC.	78
ANDRESS, M.T. - DECD.	HARRIS, W.H. - ADMR.	50
ANDRESS, MAGGIE B. - DECD.	ANDRESS, R.L. - WILL	77
ANDRESS, PEARLIE - Etal Minors	HARRIS, W.W. - GDNSHIP.	67
ANDRESS, PEARLY - Etal Minors	ANDRESS, S.F. - ADMR.	51
ANDRESS, SARAH J. - DECD.	ANDRESS, JAMES G. - ADMR.	1
ANDREWS, EDGAR - ETAL	TENANTS IN COMMON	99
ANDREWS, J.W. - ETALS	TENANTS IN COMMON	129
ANDREWS, WM. - DECD.	ANDREWS, JAMES - ADMR.	16
ANGLIN, JOHN M. - DECD.	COPE, THOMAS - ADMR.	16
ANSLEY, WILLIE & LOIS - MINORS	ANSLEY, W.W. - GDNSHIP.	64
ARMSTRONG, A.J. - IDIOT	DOWNING, THOMAS - GDN.	15
ARMSTRONG, CLEM - ETAL	TENANTS IN COMMON	7
ARMSTRONG, H.P. - DECD.	DOWNING, THOMAS - ETAL ADMR.	16
ARMSTRONG, M.F. & H.P. - Minors	BEAN, DORCUS - GDN.	15
ARMSTRONG, ROBERT - DECD.	ARMSTRONG, CHARLES - EXEC.	55
ARMSTRONG, SALLY - DECD.	DOWNING, THOMAS - EXEC.	15
ARNOLD, MARY E. - ETAL	TENANTS IN COMMON	1
ARNOLD, MARY E. - ETAL	TENANTS IN COMMON	53
ARNOLD, SIMPSON - DECD.	ARNOLD, SIMEON C. - ADMR.	16
ASBILL, SOLOMON - DECD.	HILL, H. - ADMR.	16
ASHE, ANNA - DECD.	MANLEY, BERTHA W. - Exec. Will	117
ASHE, MARGARET - MINOR	MANLEY, BERTHA W. - GDN.	122
ASHLEY, WILLIAM - MINOR	COLLEY, J.O. - GDN.	129
ASHWORTH, Johnny Edward - Decd	ASHWORTH, IRENE C. - Exec. Will	151
ATHEY, HENRY - DECD.	ATHEY, WM. - ADMR.	15
ATKINSON, P.W. - DECD.	ATKINSON, C.E. - ADMR.	1
AUERBACK, ANNIE T. - WILL	Auerback, Frederic S. - Exec. d. bk. 1	99
AUSTIN, TINIE	MCBRYDE, W.A. - SHERIFF ADMR.	87
AVANT, MARY - MINOR	Prestwood, Noah J. - Apprenticed	82
AVANT, W.B. - ETAL	TENANTS IN COMMON	75
BABB, E.E. - DECD.	EARNEST, S.D. - ADMR.	91
BABCOCK, H.T. - DECD.	Babcock, Jimmie Glenn - Exec. Will	150
BAILEY, DAVID E. - DECD.	BAILEY, MARY A. - ADMR.	78
BAILEY, H.C. (?) - DECD.	BAILEY, MARY E. - ADMR.	61
BAILEY, JAMES - DECD.	LOVE, WM. M. - ADMR.	2
BAILEY, LUCINDA - IDIOT	BAILEY, D.E. - GDN.	25

BAILEY, MARY A. - DECD.	STEVENS, R.H. - WILL	80
BAKER, J.M.	Thompson, A.W. - Admr.. (Circuit Ct.)	134
BAKER, J.M.B. - DECD.	BAKER, ELIZABETH - ADMR.	17
BAKER, J.T. - DECD.	BAKER, MRS. J.T. - ADMR.	143
BALAKO, JIMMY - DECD.	BALAKO, MARY - ADMR.	145
BALDWIN, GEO. O. - DECD.	BALDWIN, SARA C. - ADMR.	1
BALDWIN, GUSSIE A. - MINOR	THWEATT, HIRAM - GDN.	52
BALDWIN, LENA - MINOR	HENDRICK, W.L. - GDN.	50
BALDWIN, WILLIAM - DECD.	BALDWIN, CALEB - ADMR.	16
BALLARD, E.F.	TRANS. TO CIRCUIT CT.	166
BALLARD, EDIE ANN - DECD.	FLOWERS, JOHN - ADMR.	117
BALLARD, EMMETT - ETAL	TENANTS IN COMMON	94
BALLARD, J.C. - DECD.	BALLARD, SARAH A. - ADMR.	59
BALLARD, J.E.	DORRILL, EMMA - EXEC. WILL	164
BALLARD, JNO. J. - MINORS	BALLARD, NANCY - GDN.	25
BALLARD, JOHN - VS.	STATE OF ALA.	141
BALLARD, NANCY - DECD.	CARPENTER, C.N. - ADMR.	1
BALLARD, T.M. - DECD.	BALLARD, C.R. - ADMR.	83
BALLARD, T.V. - DECD.	BALLARD, ADA E. - ETAL EXEC.	110
BANKS - VS.	JORDAN, J.J. - CONDEMNATION	73
BANKS CANNING COMPANY	INCORPORATION	22
BANKS, TOWN OF	INCORPORATION	63
BAPTIST CHURCH OF BANKS	INCORPORATION	88
BARBAREE, GLADYS	BARBAREE, W.B. - GDN.	108
BARBAREE, JAMES L. - MINOR	THOMPSON, W.L. - GDN.	115
BARBAREE, ROY J. - DECD.	THOMPSON, W.L. - ADMR.	113
BARBAREE, ROY JR. - DECD.	THOMPSON, W.L. - ADMR.	113
BARBAREE, W.E. - DECD.	BARBAREE, ANNIE - ADMR.	133
BARBAREE, W.T. - DECD.	BARBAREE, J.G. - EXEC.	91
BAREFOOT, ARAMINTA	BAREFOOT - GDNSHIP	66
BAREFOOT, ARAMINTA	REEVES, S.M. - ADMR.	66
BAREFOOT, J.P. - DECD.	MIDDLEBROOKS, W.T. - ADMR.	66
BARFIELD, NANCY - DECD.	FRENCH, J.M. - ADMR.	88
BARFIELD, Walter & Foster - Minors	BARFIELD, VIRGINIA - GDN.	88
BARKER, CHARLIE - MINOR	WILLIAMS, M.M. - Apprenticeship	65
BARKER, G.W. - DECD.	BARKER, CLARA A.M. - ADMR.	67
BARNES, ED S. - DECD	BARNES, ANNIE G. - EXEC. WILL	140
BARNES, JAMES - MINORS	SIMMONS, DANIEL - GDN.	23
BARNES, JOHN - DECD.	SMITH, SARAH A. - ADMR.	18
BARNES, W.G. - DECD.	WILSON, W.E. - ADMR.	75
BARNETT, ASA - DECD.	JACKSON, ROBERT L. - ADMR.	1
BARNETT, J.J. - DECD.	BARNETT, B.W. - ADMR.	2
BARNETT, M.H. - DECD.	BARNETT, W.H. - EXEC.	58

BARNETT, M.J. - DECD.	DAVIS, J.D. - ADMR.	16
BARNETT, M.M. - DECD.	BARNETT, B.W. - ADMR.	18
BARNETT, M.M.A. - ETAL MINORS	BARNETT, M. FRANCIS - GDN.	23
BARNETT, WEDDON - DECD.	BARNETT. KATHARINE - EXEC.	17
BARNEY, GINCY - DECD.	LOVE, A.P. - ADMR.	18
BARNEYCASTLE, GINCY - MINORS	LOVE, A.P. - GDN.	24
BARR, ANNIE M. - DECD.	BARR, ANNIE H. - ADMR.	154
BARR, DOVIE E. - MINOR	BARR, ELLA E. - GDN.	107
BARR, J.T. - ETAL MINORS	BARR, MOLLIE V.	73
BARR, J.W. & J.B. JAMES	AD QUOD DAMNUM	2
BARR, J.W. - DECD.	BARR, R.A.E. - ADMR.	53
BARR, J.W. - ETAL	TENANTS IN COMMON	85
BARR, J.W. - ETAL VS.	Barr, Willis T.; Etal Tenants in Comm(	130
BARR, LELA - NON COMP. MEN.	BARR, W.C. - GDN.	90
BARR, MORRIS RAY - DECD.	BARR, CHARLIE D.	148
BARR, R.J. - DECD.	Barr, Annie Mae - Admr. doc. bk. 1, 5{	93
BARR, WILL - ETAL	TENANTS IN COMMON	90
BARR, WILLIAM C.J. - MINOR	WINDHAM, W.C. - GDN.	85
BARR, WM. L. - DECD.	BARR, J.H. & W.C. - WILL	76
BARR. MARY E. - DECD.	BARR, T.A. - EXEC.	94
BARRON, CHARLES - DECD.	BARRON, WILLIAM - ADMR.	17
BARRON, CLAUD L.	PET. FOR LETTER OF GDN.	67
BARRON, HENRY C.	BARRON, W.L. - ADMR.	105
BARRON, J.C. - DECD.	REEVES, BEN - ADMR.	156
BARRON, JAMES - DECD.	BARRON, CHARLES - ADMR.	18
BARRON, THOMAS - DECD.	BRADSHAW, W.J. - ADMR.	18
BARTLETT, ANNIE G. - MINOR	HAYGOOD, J.W. - GDN.	16
BARTLETT, MINNOA - Etal Minors	BARTLETT, JOHN - GDN.	25
BASHINSKY, L.M. - DECD.	BASHINSKY, LEO L.; Etal Exec. Will	143
BASHINSKY, L.M. - ETAL	INCORPORATION	70
BASS, F.C. - DECD.	BASS, SALLIE C. - ADMR.	131
BASS, SALLIE C. - DECD.	Bass, Walter & Ann Cloud - Exec.	146
BASS, URIAH - DECD.	JONES, D.B. - ADMR.	48
BASS, WILLIS	DIVISION OF CROPS	63
BASSETT, JOHN H. - DECD.	BASSETT, E.C. - EXEC	122
BATEMAN, MOSES	TOMPKINS, J.A. - Master Apprentice	62
BATIE, ALEX - DECD.	HEARD, BESSIE - ADMR.	163
BATIE, JULIA - VS.	BATIE, ALEX - Div. of Per. Property	114
BATTLE, ELIZABETH A. - MINORS	ROWELL, E.H. - GDN.	24
BATTLE, JOHN M. - DECD.	BATTLE, N.A. - EXEC.	16
BATTLE, MINNIE - DECD.	HARRIS, JOHN - EXEC. WILL	155
BATTLE, TIMOTHY - DECD.	BATTLE, MINNIE - ADMR.	139
BAYGENTS, JOHN D. - DECD.	BAYGENTS, JAMES - ADMR.	18

BAYLEY, SARAH - DECD.	DUKE, A.P. - ADMR.	17
BEAMAN, A. - DECD.	BEAMAN, URIAH - ADMR.	4
BEAN, ALEXANDER - DECD.	BEAN, DORCAS - ADMR.	18
BEAN, ALONZO L. - ETAL	SALE OF LAND	76
BEAN, DR. J.F. - DECD.	BEAN, SUE MC. - ETAL ADMR.	103
BEAN, JAMES F. - DECD.		1
BEAN, JAMES FRANK - DECD.	BEAN, SUE MCE. - ADMR.	117
BEAN, MAJOR	DAVIS, J.M. - ADMR.	72
BEAN, MOLLIE H. - DECD.	TYNER, JANIE BEAN - ADMR. WILL	162
BEAN, S. - DECD.	YOUNGBLOOD, J.B. - ADMR.	18
BEAN, SUE MCE. - ETAL	TENANTS IN COMMON	122
BEAN, WM. MCEACHERN - MINOR	F & M NAT'L. BANK - GDN.	110
BEAN, WM. MCEACHERN - MINOR	F & M NAT'L. BANK - GDN.	111
BEARD, BOWDEN - ETAL MINORS	BEARD, J.S. - GDN.	59
BEARD, DR. J.S. - DECD.	BEARD, DR. R.B. - EXEC. WILL	139
BEARD, JAMES WILEY - DECD.	BEARD, J.S.	98
BEARD, LOIS A. - DECD.	BEARD, ROBERT B. - EXEC. WILL	158
BEARD, MRS. IDA W.	BEARD, R.B. - EXEC. WILL	137
BEARD, W.F. - ETAL	TENANTS IN COMMON	85
BEARMAN, OLIVER - DECD.	COLLINSWORTH, E. - GDN.	13
BEASLEY, B.B. - DECD.	BEASLEY, MARY FRANCES - Admr.	123
BEASLEY, ELIZABETH - MINORS	JACKSON, RANDALL - GDN.	23
BEASLEY, H.T.E.V.B. - MINORS	BEASLEY, ROBERT - GDN.	6
BEASLEY, JAMES - DECD.	THODES, JOHN F. - ADMR.	17
BEASLEY, LLOYD - MINOR	WILLIAMS, MRS. E.D. - GDN.	96
BEASLEY, Mrs. Martha A. - Decd	STEPHENS, OTIS - EXEC. WILL	156
BEASLEY, W.L. - DECD.	BEASLEY, ED - EXEC. WILL	164
BEASLEY, WILLIAM - DECD		18
BECK, JOHN B.	BECK, MARTHA A. - HOMESTEAD	90
BECK, JORDAN - DECD.	BECK, J.J. - EXEC.	4
BECKWITH, ELIZABETH - DECD.	MORGAN, JOHN H. - ADMR.	51
BECKWITH, H.C. - ETALS	TENANTS IN COMMON	2
BEECHER, MANAH - DECD.	SEGARS, H.R. - ADMR.	18
BELL, Easter, Ramer, Essie, Terry	SHIELDS, ABE - Apprenticed To:	83
BELL, EMANUEL - DECD.	BELL, HARRIETT - ADMR.	18
BELL, JOSEPH	DUCK, THOMAS - EXEC	109
BELL, L.L. & MALACHI - DECD.		95
BELL, LAURA W.	DUCK, THOMAS - EXEC	109
BELL, LOUISA - DECD.	HARRIS, GEORGE L. - ADMR.	129
BELL, Mary's children - Minors	SHIELDS, ABE - Apprenticed To:	83
BELL, SAMUEL - DECD.	BELL, MALACHI - EXEC.	18
BELL, SARAH - DECD.	HARRIS, GEORGE L. - ADMR.	121
BELSER, MATTIE		166

BLAIR, HENRY O. - MINOR	DURDEN, W.B. - GDN.	61
BLAIR, JANE P. - DECD.	Bryan, Oscar L.; Exec. doc. bk. 1, 189	101
BLAIR, JOHN - DECD.	MURPHREE, JOEL D. - ADMR.	51
BLAIR, JOHN L. - MINORS	BLAIR, M.C. - GDN.	25
BLAIR, L.L. - DECD.	BLAIR, MRS. ANNIE - ADMR.	77
BLAIR, L.M. - DECD.	BLAIR, JOHN - ADMR.	17
BLAIR, MARY ALICE - ETAL	Tenants in Common - doc. bk. 1, 157	97
BLAIR, MARY ALICE - ETAL	TENANTS IN COMMON	119
BLAIR, MARY ALICE - ETAL	TENANTS IN COMMON	119
BLAIR, MARY C. - INSANE	BLAIR, J.C. - GDN.	63
BLAIR, S.D. - ETAL	TENANTS IN COMMON	56
BLAIR, W.S. - DECD.	TENANTS IN COMMON	56
BLAKE, BUCK - DECD.	FRYER, DICK - ADMR.	137
BLANCHARD, AMOS	LOURY, R.A. - APPRENTICESHIP	76
BLANN, FRANCIS J. - MINORS	COADY, GREEN - GDN.	24
BLANTON, J.B. - DECD.	Blanton, Mrs. S.E.; Gordon R.; Ex. Wi	143
BLANTON, J.B. - ETAL	TENANTS IN COMMON	88
BLEDSOE, WM. - DECD.	OGBORNE, W.H. - ADMR.	2
BLUE, DANIEL - DECD.	BLUE, HECTOR - ADMR.	17
BLUE, FLORA E. - ETAL MINORS	BLUE, MARY - GDN.	25
BLUE, JOHN - DECD.	FINLAYSON, N. - ADMR.	17
BLUE, M.M. - DECD.	BLUE, M.P. - ADMR.	17
BLUE, PETER - DECD.	BLUE, JOHN - ADMR.	17
BOATNER, JOHN F. - DECD.	BOATNER, JUANITA T. - ADMR.	108
BOATWRIGHT, JAMES - DECD.	SCARBROUGH, JAS. W. - ADMR.	49
BODDIE, J.F. - ETAL	TENANTS IN COMMON	67
BODIFORD, GEORGE J.	EXPARTE	76
BOND, ALFRED C.		1
BOND, WM. B. - DECD.	BOND, SARAH - ADMR.	1
BOND, WM. M. - DECD.	BOND, CHARLOTTE R. - ADMR.	1
BONE, P.H. JR.	CARROLL, M.W. - ADMR.	64
BOONE, LAURA S. - DECD.	Boone, Edgar L. - Exec. Will Etal	109
BOOSE, JAMES - DECD.	BOOSE, WILLIE BELL - ADMR.	141
BOOTHE, PERRY LEE & MINNIE C.	GRANT, MINNIE - NON AGE	75
BOROUGHS, STEPHEN - ETAL	Tenants in Common - Land Sale	81
BOSWELL, JOHN - DECD.	BOSWELL, FRANCIS A. - ADMR.	17
BOSWELL, JOHN W. - DECD.	BOSWELL, FRANCIS M. - ADMR.	16
BOSWELL, M.A. - ETAL MINORS	BOSWELL, F.A. - GDN.	25
BOSWELL, M.V. - MINOR	POWELL, G.C. - GDN.	13
Boswell, Marcellous - Etal Minor	CARGILE, JASON - GDN.	13
BOSWELL, S.F. - DECD.	BOSWELL, WILSON - ADMR.	17
BOSWELL, SANBORN - DECD.	BOSWELL, BETHANY - WILL	76
BOSWELL, THOMAS C. - DECD.	BOSWELL, MARTHA & F.A. - Admr.	16

BOSWELL, WACO HOBSON	BOSWELL, W.B. - GDNSHIP.	80
BOSWELL, WACO HOBSON	DISABILITIES NON AGE	91
BOUTWELL, CHARLOTTE - MINOR	JOHNSON, J.M. - GDN.	61
BOUTWELL, ISAAC	Boutwell, Fannie Caroline; Ex. (Cir. Cl	118
BOUTWELL, ISAAC - ETAL - VS.	THOMPSON, EMMA - Lis Pendens	91
BOUTWELL, JANE - DECD.	BOUTWELL, J. - ADMR.	17
BOUTWELL, MARTHA J. - DECD.	BOUTWELL, CLAUDE - ADMR.	148
BOUTWELL, NOEL - MINOR	BOUTWELL, JENNY - GDN.	13
BOUTWELL, THOMAS - DECD.	CARROLL, M.J. - ADMR.	52
BOUTWELL, THOS. - DECD.	FRAZIER, ALLEN - ADMR.	18
BOUTWELL, W.C. - VS.	GOODSON, WILL - CROP DIVISION	136
BOUTWELL, WM. - DECD.	BOUTWELL, DELANEY - ADMR.	2
BOUTWELL, WOODROW W. - ETAL	Boutwell, Clara E. gdn. doc. bk. 1, 19	101
BOWDEN, I.T. - DECD.	BOWDEN, W.H. - ADMR.	119
BOWDEN, MRS. WILLIE, ETAL - VS.	Flowers, Robert, Etal - Sale of land	141
BOWERS, BENJAMIN - DECD.	SEGARS, H.R.	1
BOWERS, JOHN W. - DECD.	BOWERS, TINIE J. - ADMR.	123
BOWERS, TINIE J.	1ST F & M NAT'L. BK. - GDNSHIP.	156
BOWERS, TINIE J. - DECD.	1ST F & M NAT'L. BK. - EXEC. WILL	159
BOYD PLAT	PLAT OF LANDS	76
BOYD, ALICE - ETAL	TENANTS IN COMMON	1
BOYD, ANNIE MELL - DECD.	BOYD, JAMES T. - EXEC. WILL	154
BOYD, C.L.R. - DECD.	L.R. & B.H. - EXEC.	73
BOYD, C.W. - DECD.	BOYD, CAROLINE - ADMR.	18
BOYD, FRANCES ALLEN	BOYD, L.A. - ADMR.	96
BOYD, JAKE - ETAL MINORS	Boyd, Mrs. Bettie; Gdn. Dk. Bk. 1, 29	104
BOYD, MELL - EXPARTE	DISABILITIES - NON AGE	75
BOYETT, HENRY - ETAL MINORS	BOYETT, DAVID - GDN.	23
BOYETT, M.A. & CHAS. - MINORS	BOYETT, HENRY - GDN.	13
BRABHAM, MARTIN - MINOR	BRABHAM, J.G. - GDN.	13
BRABHAM, REBECCA - DECD.	MCCALL, D.A. - ADMR.	2
BRADBERRY, ERNEST	APPRENTICE	73
BRADLEY, A.L. - DECD.	WINDHAM, EULA - ADMR.	150
BRADLEY, AMY WILKINSON; minor	APPRENTICE	72
BRADLEY, ANNIE F. - DECD.	BRADLEY, W.A. - EXEC. WILL	108
BRADLEY, FLORA B. - DECD.	BRADLEY, JOSEPH M. - ADMR.	144
BRADLEY, HENRY T. - DECD.	FINLEY, J.N. - ADMR.	73
BRADLEY, HUGH	BRADLEY, SARA MILLER - ADMR.	138
BRADLEY, J.P. - ETAL	TENANTS IN COMMON	68
BRADLEY, J.W. - DECD.	BRADLEY, LILLIE H. - ADMR.	156
Bradley, Joann, Janie M., Willowdean	BRADLEY, MRS. ANNA - GDN.	151
BRADLEY, John & Buna Mae - minors	WILLIAMS, J.W. - GDN.	85
BRADLEY, M.F. - DECD.	BRADLEY, J.W. - ADMR. ETAL	115

BRADLEY, M.F. - ETAL	TENANTS IN COMMON	65
BRADLEY, M.F. - ETAL	TENANTS IN COMMON	85
BRADLEY, MARY - ETAL MINORS	DOCK. BK. 1, PG. 44	82
BRADLEY, RHODA C. - ETAL	TENANTS IN COMMON	1
BRADLEY, T.H. - ETAL	TENANTS IN COMMON	80
BRADLEY, TATE - ETAL MINORS	BRADLEY, W.A. - GDNSHIP.	82
BRADLEY, W.F. - DECD.	BRADLEY, F.E. - ADMR.	123
BRADLEY, W.T.	DISABILITIES NON AGE	89
BRADSHAW, ELIZA & H.J. - Minors	DAVIS, E. - GDN.	23
BRADSHAW, JOHN - DECD.	DAVIS, EDWARD - ETAL ADMR.	16
BRADSHAW, JOHN J. - MINOR	DUNN, URIAH - GDN.	13
BRADSHAW, LIZZIE - MINORS	BRADSHAW, FRANCIS - GDN.	25
BRADSHAW, SARAH - MINORS	JONES, H.S. - GDN.	23
BRADY, JAS. T. - DECD.	BRADY, SARAH R. - EXEC.	2
BRADY, MARY C. - DECD.	WHITESIDE, D.D. - EXEC.	17
BRAGG, G.A. - ETAL	TENANTS IN COMMON	74
BRAGG, JOSEPH W. - DECD.	ROSS, AGNES E. - ADMR.	51
BRANDIS, E.A. - DECD.	Brandis, Esther Lunette - Exec. Will	162
BRANNEN, C.C. - DECD.	BRANNEN, Annette M. - Exec. Will	160
BRANNEN, E.R. - DECD.	BRANNEN, IDA MILLER - Exec. Will	90
BRANNEN, MRS. S.E.	Brannen, E.R.; C.C.; Ex. doc. bk. 1, 8:	94
BRANNOCK, M.D. - MINORS	COLLEY, J.O. - GDN.	120
BRANSCOMBE, BERRY	EXPARTE	59
BRANTLEY, EMMA MARY - DECD.	BRANTLEY, J.G. - EXEC. WILL	115
BRANTLEY, H.L. - DECD.	BRANTLEY, K.M. - ADMR.	139
BRANTLEY, J.A. - DECD.	BRANTLEY, FLAVIA O. - EXEC.	100
BRANTLEY, J.G.	1ST F & M NAT'L. BK. - EXEC. WILL	160
BRANTLEY, J.T. & W.H. - VS.	Boswell, Jack - Etal to Sell Lands	88
BRANTLEY, JAMES T.	Brantley, Julia W. & Thomas K., Exec	161
BRANTLEY, JOS. T. - DECD.	BRANTLEY, CARRIE E. - ADMR.	91
Brantley, Joseph Thomas - Decd.	BRANTLEY, JOCK - ADMR.	97
BRANTLEY, MARY - ETAL MINORS	BRANTLEY, MILDRED T. - GDN.	119
Brantley, Mary Henderson - Decd.	CONRAD, MADGE B. - EXEC. WILL	166
BRANTLEY, T.K. & SON - ETAL	TENANTS IN COMMON	59
BRANTLEY, T.K. - DECD.	BRANTLEY, J.T. & W.H. - Exec. Will	87
BRANTLEY, W.H. - DECD.	BRANTLEY, W.H. JR. - ETAL	102
BRANTLY, FLAVIA O'NEAL - DECD.	Brantley, James Thomas - Exec. Will	149
BRASWELL, JOS. W. - DECD.	BRASWELL, BLANY - EXEC.	16
BRAY, JAMES - MINOR	WEAMS, WILCE - GDN.	85
BRAZIL, WILLIAM - DECD.	HAMILTON, S.R. - ETAL EXEC.	16
BREWER, J.A. - ETAL	Sorrel, J.F.; sale land; Doc. bk. 1, 61	93
BREWER, LAURA - ETAL MINORS	BREWER, WINFIELD - GDN.	88
BRIGHTWELL, J.F. - DECD.	HOMESTEAD	71

BRISTOW, MARY W. - DECD.	BRISTOW, JNO. T. - ADMR.	18
BRISTOW, WM. F. - MINORS	BRISTOW, JOHN T. - GDN.	23
BROOKS, ANNA - MINOR	WILEY, H.C. - APPRENTICESHIP	50
BROOKS, C.S. - DECD.	BROOKS, JAS. T. - ADMR.	16
BROOKS, DOUGLASS - MINOR	Ray, Millie, & Jones, W.S. - Gdnship	77
BROOKS, E.D. - DECD.	KEY, JOHN - ADMR.	16
BROOKS, J.M. - VS.	JONES, SNIDY - TO SELL LANDS	91
BROOKS, JAMES A. - DECD.	BROOKS, LUCY R. - ADMR.	18
BROOKS, JOSEPH - DECD.	PATRICK, D.A. - ADMR.	17
BROOKS, JOSEPH C.	PROPERTY APPRAISEMENT	24
BROOKS, JOSIAH - DECD.	BROOKS, LYDIA - ADMR.	16
BROOKS, L.D. - DECD.	BROOKS, SARAH M. - ADMR.	2
BROOKS, LELA - DECD.	COPELAND, J.L. - ADMR.	114
BROOKS, M.M.	MCGILVRAY, H.T. - ADMR.	107
BROOKS, M.M. - DECD.	MCGILVARY, H.M. - ESTATE	97
BROOKS, ROBERT - DECD.	BROOKS, SAMUEL - ADMR.	18
BROOKS, WINNIE D. - DECD.	PATTERSON, MARY B. - Exec. Will	153
BROOKS, WM. C. - DECD.	LANE, R.H. - ADMR.	1
BROWDER, HARDY - DECD.	MURPHREE, JOEL D. - ADMR.	18
BROWDER, Henry Harrell - Decd.	ANDERSON, BEULAH A. - ADMR.	147
BROWN, ARIOSTA H. - DECD.	HOMESTEAD TO WIDOW	164
BROWN, B.G. - DECD.	BROWN, NANCY - ETAL EXEC.	1
BROWN, CAROLINE - MINORS	BOYD, SARAH - GDN.	25
BROWN, CHARLES G. - DECD.	BROWN, EUNICE C. - EXEC. WILL	132
BROWN, CHARLES K. - DECD.	PUGH, GRACE BROWN - Exec. Will	166
BROWN, COLUMBUS - DECD.	1ST F & M NAT'L. BK. - ADMR.	118
BROWN, DR. P.H.	BROWN, PUGH U. - Pet. for Admr.	74
BROWN, E.J. - DECD.	BROWN, C.G. - ADMR.	84
BROWN, ELSA E. - ETAL MINORS	BROWN, W.W. - GDN.	121
BROWN, FANNIE C. - DECD.	JONES, GEORGE W. - EXEC. WILL	115
Brown, Frank Bean & Virginia Frances	BROWN, SALLIE - GDN.	144
BROWN, FRED REYNOLDS - Minor	REYNOLDS, FRED D. - GDN.	147
BROWN, HATTIE E. - DECD.	BROWN, W.W. - ADMR.	121
BROWN, IDA - ETAL	TENANTS IN COMMON	68
BROWN, J. RANDOLPH - DECD.	BROWN, MRS. L.J. - EXEC. WILL	89
BROWN, J.T. - DECD.	BROWN, W.A. - ADMR.	155
BROWN, JESSE - DECD.	SCARBROUGH, J.W. - ADMR.	49
BROWN, JOHN - DECD.	BROWN, INTIA - ADMR.	18
BROWN, JOHN G. - DECD.	BROWN, J. RANDOLPH - WILL	66
BROWN, JOHN H. - ETAL MINORS	BROWN, W.L. - GDN	59
BROWN, JONATHAN - DECD.	BROWN, JOHN O. - ADMR.	2
Brown, Lucy Knox & Helen M., minors	DOCK. BK. 1 PG. 60	93
BROWN, M. ANDERSON - DECD.	Reynolds, Drs. Fred D., Grover C., Ex	147

BRYAN, J.B. - ETAL	TENANTS IN COMMON	78
BRYAN, JAMES - VS.	Baker, Henry, Lampley; Geo., Rich'd.	155
BRYAN, LUCY A.F. - MINORS	CHANCEY, WM. J. - GDN.	25
BRYAN, M.P.	Bryan, Julia - Dower doc. bk. 1, 59	93
BRYAN, MILDRED E. - ETAL	TENANTS IN COMMON	62
BRYAN, OSCAR - ETAL MINOR	BRYAN, ELIZA - GDN.	57
BRYAN, S.L. - DECD.	LOVE, A.P. - ADMR.	17
BRYAN, SANFORD - ETAL	BRYAN, J.F. - GDN.	93
BRYAN, YANCEY L. - DECD.	BRYAN, LEILA & CLAUDE - WILL	123
BRYANT, JOHN COLLINS - DECD.	WILL	95
BRYANT, STONEWALL - Etal Minor	APPRENTICE	73
BUCHAN, D.T. & WM. A.S. - DECD.	BUCHAN, M.B. - ADMR.	2
BULLARD, JAS. R. - MINOR	HEAD, RICHARD - GDN.	18
Bullock, Andrew Jackson - Decd.	Bullock, Mattie Green; Homestead Pe	149
BUNDRICK, WILLIAM J. - DECD.	Bundrick, Robert B. - Exec. Will	107
BUNDY, JOHN L. - DECD.	BUNDY, MARY	2
BUNDY, W.M. - DECD.	BUNDY, MRS. ELLA - ADMR.	90
BURDEN, WILL - DECD.	CEPHAS, ANNIE JO - EXEC. WILL	154
BURGESS, ESQUIRE - Etal Minors	Clayton, J.B. & Pruitt, J.W. - Gdn.	23
BURGESS, JAS. M. - DECD.	BURGESS, S.H. - ADMR.	2
BURGESS, W.M. - DECD.	BURGESS, S.L. - ADMR.	2
Burgess, William, Heirs of - Minor	TRANSCRIPT	12
BURGESS, WM. - DECD.	PITTS, J.W. - ADMR.	17
BURKS, C.J. - DECD.	BURKS, CLYDE G. - ADMR.	144
BURKS, MARILYN - MINOR	BURKS, CLYDE G. - ADMR.	144
BURKS, WILLIS - DECD.	EDGE, O.N. - ADMR.	?
BURNEY, LILLIE A. - ETAL	BURNEY, REBECCA J. - GDN.	57
BURROUGHS, Fannie Ines Lawson	Exparte/Delayed Birth Certificate	164
BUSH, HENRY - DECD.	BUSH, MRS. M.C. - WILL	81
BUSH, M.C. - DECD. WILL	BEARD, J.S. - EXEC.	84
BUSH, VIOLA E. - MINOR	FAULKNER, M.A.L. - GDN.	53
BUTLER, MYRA G. - DECD.	HIGHTOWER, Harold F. - Exec. Will	153
BUTLER, ROBT. A. - DECD.	BUTLER, ELIZABETH - ADMR.	18
BUTTS, SUSIE PHILLIPS - DECD.	PHILLIPS, ANNIE - EXEC. WILL	143
BYRD, CLEVE - DECD.	GIDDENS, J.L. - ADMR.	143
CADE, CALVIN A. - MINOR	RICHARDSON, A. - GDN.	51
CADE, IGNATIUS - DECD.	CADE, JANE C. - EXEC.	2
CADE, JAMES C. - DECD.	MURPHREE, JOEL D. - ADMR.	51
CADENHEAD, Willis E. - Etal Minors	EXPARTE	52
CAISON, F.J. - MINOR	CODY, G.W. - GDN.	3
CALFEE, LAURENCE C. JR. - Decd.	TROY BANK & TRUST CO. - ADMR.	161
CALFEE, LAWRENCE C. - DECD.	CALFEE, SALLIE	95
CALLOWAY, JEWELL - ETAL	TENANTS IN COMMON	94

CALLOWAY, MATTIE	CALLOWAY, Thomas C. - Exec. Will	136
CALLOWAY, WILLIS M. - MINOR	CALLOWAY, EMILY - ETAL GDN.	27
CAMERON, A.M. - DECD.	CAMERON, LOUISA - ADMR.	3
CAMERON, GEORGIA S. - DECD.	CAMERON, FRED - EXEC. WILL	153
CAMERON, SUSIE	CAMERON, FRED - ADMR.	145
CAMERON, W.C.	CAMERON, FRED - EXEC. WILL	136
CAMERON, W.K. - DECD.	CAMERON, Florence - Exemption	66
CAMERON, W.K. - ETAL	TENANTS IN COMMON	63
CAMP, JOS. M. SR. - DECD.	CAMP, J.M. - ADMR.	98
CAMPBELL, A.B. - DECD.	CAMPBELL, Sarah A. - Wid. & Admr.	79
CAMPBELL, ABNER - DECD.	Bradley, W.A. & Key Murphree, Exec.	95
CAMPBELL, ALEX'D. - DECD.	CAMPBELL, HUGH - ADMR.	3
CAMPBELL, BENJ. W. - DECD.	LIVINGSTON, S.B. - ETAL ADMR.	19
CAMPBELL, H.A. - DECD.	CAMPBELL, Chas. A. - Admr. Cir. Ct.	140
CAMPBELL, HORACE	EXPARTE - APPRENTICE	66
CANADY, ELIZABETH - MINORS	POOL, KEENAN - GDN.	24
CANADY, ELIZABETH - MINORS	FARNELL, ROBT. J. - FINAL GDN.	24
CANNON, JOHN F.		29
CANTY, ASBURY - DECD.	CANTY, Alice - Homestead Exempt.	110
CANTY, G.N. - DECD.	CANTY, Lamon Parker - Exec. Will	163
CAPPS, GEO. F. - DECD.	PERDUE, J.S. - ADMR.	2
CARAWAY, EUGENE - ETAL	LOFLIN, GEO. A. - GDN.	100
Carey, Margarette, Violet McComb	ANDERSON, W.M. - GDN.	96
CARGILE, C.M. - DECD.	KIRKLAN, JAS. L. - ADMR.	2
CARGILE, F.P. - DECD.	CARGILE, CHAS. B. - EXEC. WILL	139
CARGILE, H.C. & F.P. - MINORS	HILL, W.S. - GDN.	3
CARGILE, JASON - MINOR	HURLEY, NOAH - GDN.	3
CARGILE, M.M. & A.D. - MINORS	CARGILE, W.A. - GDN.	3
CARGILE, Margaret - Etal Minors	HOOKS, D.M. - GDN.	24
CARGILE, WM. A, - ETAL MINORS	CARGILE, CHARLES M. - GDN.	3
CARGILL, JASON - DECD.	TOWNSEND, ELI - EXEC.	19
CARLISLE, ARCUS & LILLIE	CARLISLE, L.A. - GDN.	79
CARLISLE, CARO - MINOR	COPELAND, E.A. - GDN.	67
CARLISLE, E.L. - DECD.	CARLISLE, G.W. - ADMR.	3
CARLISLE, FRED - ETAL MINORS	CARLISLE, M.A. - GDN.	65
CARLISLE, G.W. - DECD.	CARLISLE, T.J. & M.N. - ADMR.	48
CARLISLE, JAMES	CARLISLE, J.P. & W.M. - ADMR.	144
CARLISLE, JOHN - DECD.	CARLISLE, CAROLINE - ADMR.	18
CARLISLE, JOHN - MINOR	FOLMAR, ISAAC S. - GDN.	27
CARLISLE, JOHN - MINORS	CARLISLE, GRACY C. - GDN.	24
CARLISLE, L.A. - ETAL	TENANTS IN COMMON	65
CARLISLE, LILLIE	CARLISLE, R.A. - GDN.	76
CARLISLE, Lillie & Arcus - Minors	LAW, T.W. - GDN.	71

CARLISLE, LILLIE - ETAL	TENANTS IN COMMON	79
CARLISLE, LILLIE - MINOR	CARLISLE, R.A. - GDN.	76
CARLISLE, LILLIE - MINOR	DISABILITIES OF NON AGE	84
CARLISLE, R.A. - MINOR	DISABILITIES	72
CARLISLE, REX, MAX - Etal Minors	CARLISLE, MARY - GDN.	145
CARLISLE, ROBERT - Etal Minors	CARLISLE, MARY - GDN.	145
CARLTON, JUGERTHA - DECD.	SMITH, EDITH - ADMR.	157
CARNLEY, GEORGE - MINORS	LEE, JESSE	27
CARNLEY, LEWIS - DECD.	SNIDER, NATHAN - ADMR.	18
CARNLEY, Sarah Ann - Etal Minors	HENDRICKS, A.R. - GDN.	24
CARNLEY, VICY - DECD.	CARNLEY, LEWIS - ADMR.	18
CARPENTER, ELIZA - DECD.	CARPENTER, C.N. - ADMR.	33
CARPENTER, IDA L. - MINOR	HILL, B.A. - GDN.	2
CARPENTER, JESSE	ROSS, R.A. - ADMR.	52
CARPENTER, JESSE - DECD.	CARPENTER, C.N. - ADMR.	19
CARPENTER, W.A. - DECD.	CARPENTER, C.N. - ADMR.	59
CARPENTER, WM. A. - DECD.	CARPENTER, C.N. - ADMR.	33
CARR, ANSLEY - DECD.	DICKINSON, LAURA - ADMR.	2
CARR, DANIEL - DECD.	Carr, Catharine & Gibson, E.L. - Admr	3
CARR, ISAAC - MINORS	DARBY, JEFF - GDN.	26
CARR, ROSANNA P. - DECD.	CARR, DANIEL - ADMR.	3
CARR, SAMUEL - DECD.	GIBSON, E.L. - ADMR.	19
CARR, T.J.	TENANTS IN COMMON	63
CARROLL, ALLIE M. - DECD.	MURPHREE, T.E. & J.D. - Exec Will	137
CARROLL, AMANDA - ETAL	TENANTS IN COMMON	2
CARROLL, C.G. - DECD.	CARROLL, LAWRENCE - Exec Will	150
CARROLL, CLAUDINE - MINOR	CARROLL, M.E. - GDN.	19
CARROLL, D.L. - DECD.	CARROLL, A.E. - ADMR.	3
CARROLL, D.M. - DECD.	CARROLL, MARY C. - ADMR.	93
CARROLL, D.S. - DECD.	CARROLL, W.C. - ADMR.	94
CARROLL, ERVIN E. - DECD.	CARROLL, GENIE - ADMR.	85
CARROLL, FRANCES M.	Carroll, Sallie A. - Non Age Decree	75
CARROLL, J.S. - DECD.	CARROLL, ALMIRA - WILL	81
CARROLL, J.S. - ETAL	TENANTS IN COMMON	66
CARROLL, J.S. - ETAL	COLLIER, A.A. - Tenants in Common	78
CARROLL, J.S. MERCANTILE	INCORPORATION	81
CARROLL, JOHN - DECD.	CARROLL, M.J.	2
CARROLL, JUNIUS GARRY	Carroll, Sallie A. - Non Age Decree	74
CARROLL, M.E. & G.W. - MINORS	CARROLL, C.J. - GDN.	3
CARROLL, M.J. - DECD.	CARROLL, CHARITY - ADMR.	2
CARROLL, MARTHA B. - DECD.	CARROLL, NATHAN - ADMR.	3
CARROLL, MRS. MARY C. - DECD.	CARROLL, G.B. - ADMR.	146
CARROLL, N.A. - ETAL	TENANTS IN COMMON	79

CARROLL, NORA - DECD.	CARROLL, JOE - EXEC. WILL	146
CARROLL, OSCAR F. - Etal Minors	CARROLL, SALLIE A. - GDN.	58
CARROLL, S.B. - DECD.	CARROLL, CAROLINE - ADMR.	19
CARROLL, S.J. - ETAL	TENANTS IN COMMON	3
CARROLL, S.M. - ETAL MINOR	GIBSON, E.L. - GDN.	3
CARROLL, SARAH J. - Etal Minors	CARROLL, C.I. - GDN.	54
CARROLL, W.C. - DECD.	Carroll, Nora Youngblood - Exec.	132
CARTER, B.J. - DECD.	CARTER, W.J. - ADMR.	154
CARTER, CHARLES A. - MINOR	CARTER, J.P. - GDN.	3
CARTER, CINTHIA - LUNATIC	CARTER, JOHN E. - GDN.	3
CARTER, D.T. - DECD.	PET. FOR EXEMPT FROM ADMR.	93
CARTER, DARLING - DECD.	CARTER, DRUCILLA - ADMR.	19
CARTER, FRANCIS - MINOR	HARRIS, W.H. - GDN.	3
CARTER, GUS (COL.)	HOMESTEAD BY WIDOW	66
CARTER, HENRY S. - MINOR	BRAGG, W.D. - GDN.	3
CARTER, HENRY S. - MINOR	BRAGG, WM. - GDN.	24
CARTER, HETTIE	CARTER, J.A. - GDN.	71
CARTER, J.A. - DECD.	CARTER, NATTIE - EXEC. WILL	151
CARTER, J.P. - DECD	CARTER, S.E. - ADMR.	76
CARTER, JAS. PRICE - Etal Minors	CARTER, T.S. - GDNSHIP.	72
CARTER, JOHN - DECD.	CARTER, JOEL - ADMR.	18
CARTER, LEE - MINORS	CARTER, WM. - GDN.	24
CARTER, LENA (C) NONA ADAIR	EXPARTE - HOMESTEAD	71
CARTER, LILLY ETHEL - ADMR.	CARTER, A.M. - ADMR.	163
CARTER, MARVIN H. - DECD.	Blumentritt, Rudolph - Exec. Will	163
CARTER, PATRICIA - DECD.	CARTER, ROY H. - ADMR.	160
CARTER, S.F. - MINORS	WHITEHURST, F.W.T. - GDN.	26
CARTER, SELLERS - DECD.	CARTER, CAROLYN	167
CARTER, THOMAS R.	Carter, Thos. E. - Non Age Decree	75
CARTER, W.W. & C.F. - Etals vs.	Pike County - Land Condemnation	166
CASEY, J.D. - ETAL MINOR	PEACOCK, JOE H. - PETITIONER	95
CASON, EMALINE - MINORS	CASON, HENRY - GDN.	24
CASON, FRANCIS - MINORS	Cody, G.W. & Davis Presley - Gdn.	24
CASON, FRANCIS J. - MINOR	DAVIS, PRESSLEY - GDN.	3
CASON, HENRY - DECD.	FRAZIER, ALLEN - GDN.	19
CASON, HENRY - MINORS	CASON, JOHN - GDN.	24
Castleberry, Drucilla - Etal Minor	BYRD, JOHN R. - GDN.	3
CASTLEBERRY, ISAAC - DECD.	BIRD, JOHN R. - ADMR.	19
CATRETT, JOHN - DECD.	FOWLER, N.S. - ADMR.	50
CATRETT, JOHN J. - DECD.	FOWLER, N.S. - ADMR.	19
CATRETT, LACEY - ETAL.	TENANTS IN COMMON	87
CATRETT, LOUISA - ETAL MINOR	CATRETT, W.J. - GDN.	3
CATRETT, MARY J. - ETAL MINORS	FOWLER, N.S. - GDN.	4

CATRETT, THOMAS - DECD.	CATRETT, WILLIS - ADMR.	3
CEAWFORD, W.M. - DECD.	CRAWFORD, J.T. - ADMR.	2
CHAFFIN, E.G. SR. - DECD.	CHAFFIN, E.G. JR. - ADMR.	109
CHAFFIN, S.A. - ETAL	CONDEMNATION	61
CHAFFIN, WILLIAM H. - DECD.	CHAFFIN, E.G. - ADMR.	158
CHANCELLOR, J.E.	WOOD, J.P. - ADMR. (CIR. COURT)	121
CHANCELLOR, LOUELLA - MINOR	FAULKNER, W.J. - Apprenticeship	51
CHANCELLOR, W.W. - DECD.	CHANCELLOR, M.J. - ADMR.	19
CHANCEY, ALEX	CHANCEY, ERIE - Homestead for	149
CHANCEY, DAVID - DECD.	CHANCEY, A.E. & I.D. - WILL	63
CHANCEY, FRANCIS	RHODES, M.A. - ADMR.	99
CHANCEY, J.I. - DECD.	CHANCEY, WILLIAM H. - ADMR.	132
CHANCEY, JOHN A. - MINOR	CHANCEY, W.J. - GDN.	3
CHANCEY, LUOISA - MINOR	LAWSON, MINERVA - GDN.	58
CHANCEY, SAMUEL E. - DECD.	CHANCEY, JOHN A. - ADMR.	83
CHANCEY, WILLIE G. - DECD.	CHANCEY, LAURA J. - EXEC. WILL	137
CHAPMAN, E.H. - DECD.	CHAPMAN, SADIE E. - EXEC. WILL	146
CHESSER, JOHN C. - DECD.	WARREN, BENJ. - ADMR.	19
CHESSER, REBECCA - DECD.	CHESSER, LENA - ADMR.	71
CHIAS, LYDIA - DECD.	JENKINS, G.A. - ADMR.	88
CHILDERS, CAROLINE E. - DECD.	WATSON, JOHN M. - ADMR.	58
CHILDERS, J.H. - DECD.	CHILDERS, BEULAH	150
CHILDS, G.L. - DECD.	HARRIS, W.T. - ADMR.	19
CHILDS, RAIBON - ETAL MINORS	CHILDS, A.S. - GDN.	24
CHILDS, REBECCA	CHILDS, H.C. - ADMR.	97
CHILDS, RUBIN - ETAL MINOR	CHILDS, ALFRED - GDN.	3
CHILDS, WILLIAM - DECD.	OWENS, WILLIAM - ADMR.	3
CHILDS, WM. P. - DECD.	CHILDS, FLOYD D. - ADMR.	97
CHRISTIAN, W.T., Susan A. - Minors	Rainer, J.H. & Harris, J.W. - Admr.	26
CHRISTIAN, WM. F. - MINORS	WILLIAMS, WM. B. - GDN.	24
CITIZENS BANK GOSHEN	CORPORATION	81
CITY BOARD OF EDUCATION - VS.	GRANDE LODGE K OF P	142
CLARK, BETHANY - ETAL MINORS	SMITH, ALEX & JOHN WOOD - Gdn.	24
CLARK, D.W. - ETAL	EXPARTE	67
Clark, Donald & Harold Donaldson	CLARK, AMOS - GDN.	152
CLARK, ELIZABETH - DECD.	WILL	81
CLARK, HOSEA - DECD.		19
CLARK, HOSEA W. - DECD.	CLARK, JAMES W. - ADMR.	19
CLARK, JOHN - DECD.	CLARK, JAS. - EXEC.	19
CLARK, JOHN J. - DECD.	MCLENDON, JAS. - ADMR.	19
CLARK, SARAH MARTHA - Minors	GRAVES, SARAH - GDN.	26
CLARKE, JOHN T. - MINORS	DISABILITIES	72
CLARY, W.S. - MINORS	CLARY, ELIZA J. - GDN.	26

CLAYTON, J.B. - DECD.	CLAYTON, H.W. - ADMR.	2
CLAYTON, REBECCA - ETAL	TENANTS IN COMMON	100
CLEVELAND, J.A. - CONSTABLE	CITATION TO	58
COBB, Eula & C.A. Petty - Minors	PETTY, W.B. - GDN.	89
COBLER, SAM - FREEDMAN	FAULKNER, JAMES - GDN.	24
COCHRAN, H.R. - DECD.	COCHRAN, CARRIE B. - Exec. Will	154
COCHRAN, T.G. & L.L. - MINORS	STEWART, R.C. - GDN.	3
COCHRAN, T.G. & L.L. - MINORS	STEWART, R.C. - GDN.	24
COCKRAFT, HENRY - DECD.	HEAD, D.J. - ADMR.	19
COGBURN, CYNTHIA - DECD.	SHIRLEY, J.S. - ADMR.	19
COGBURN, MARTHA - Etal Minor	COGBURN, SAMUEL - GDN.	3
COHN, ABE - DECD.	COHN, MRS. DORA - ADMR.	135
COHN, JOE - MINORS	COHN, MRS. DORA - GDN.	132
COHN, MRS. DORA - DECD.	1ST F & M NAT'L. BANK - EXEC.	147
COKER, JOHN - MINORS	JACKSON, DAN'L. S. - GDN.	24
COKER, THOS. - DECD.	THOMPSON, J.M. - ADMR.	18
COLE, CELIA - ETAL MINORS	COLE, RANSOM - GDN.	24
COLE, JOHN EDWARD		?
COLEMAN, FRANK	WOOD, J.P. - ADMR.	?
COLEMAN, FRANK - DECD.	WOOD, J.P. - ADMR.	132
COLEMAN, P.J. - MINORS	COLEMAN, MARY A. - GDN.	26
COLEMAN, Sylvester & Samuel	MCNEAL, HENRY - GDNSHIP.	75
COLEMAN, W.S. - MINORS	HIGGINS, R.J. - GDN.	24
COLEMAN, WHEELER	MCNEAL, HENRY - GDNSHIP.	75
COLES, MASON - DECD.		19
COLLEY, Katherine M. Reid - Minor	COLLEY, J.H. - GDN.	166
COLLIER, ALLIE - DECD.	DICKINSON, LENA - WILL	91
COLLIER, AMANDA A.	EXEMPTION	90
COLLIER, BENJ. - MINOR	COLLINS, J.B. - GDN.	27
COLLIER, DR. J.M. - DECD.	Pace, M.D. & Smith, P.F. - Exec. Will	83
COLLIER, G.C. - DECD.	COLLIER, T.A. - ADMR.	61
COLLIER, KATE MARSHALL - Decd.	PACE, M.D. - ADMR.	74
COLLIER, MARY DEAN - MINOR	BARNES, SARAH C. - GDN.	147
COLLINS, EMMA - MINOR	McPherson, J.M. - Gdn. Sale of Land	83
COLLINS, G.W. - DECD.	BROOKS, W.C. - ADMR.	18
COLLINS, GEO. W. - MINORS	ORR, ELIZABETH - GDN.	24
COLLINS, JOHN J.	COLLINS, W.J. - Pet. for Letters	67
COLLINS, N.M.	EXPARTE	58
COLLINS, R.F. - DECD.	COLLINS, E.H. - ADMR.	73
COLLINS, W.F.	EXEMPTION	88
COLLINS, WM. B. - DECD.	COLLINS, A.L. - ADMR.	2
Collinsworth, Zachariah - Decd.	COLLINSWORTH, ELIJAH - ADMR.	19
COLQUITT, W.B. - MINORS	COLQUITT, W.B. - GDN.	24

COWART, Albert Hansford - Decd.	COWART, F. JOY - ADMR.	138
COWART, BERNICE - DECD.	DOSTER, MABEL C. - ADMR.	135
COWART, BESSIE C. - DECD.	COPELAND, JOSH S. - EXEC. WILL	167
COWART, CLARENCE H. - DECD.	COWART, BESSIE O. - ADMR.	84
COWART, F.J. - DECD.	COWART, BERNICE - ADMR.	101
COWART, F.J. - ETAL	PARTITION & DIVISION	81
COWART, JAMES - DECD.	COWART, HANSFORD D. - ADMR.	3
COWART, JOHN W. - DECD.	BRUNSON, E.H. & I.J. - ADMR.	2
COWART, JOSEPH	COWART, D.A. - ADMR.	109
COWART, MABEL - ETAL	COWART, F.J. - GDN.	66
COWART, MATTIE J. - DECD.	COWART, F.J. - ADMR.	66
COWART, MRS. N.L. - DECD.	REDDOCH, H.A. - ADMR.	92
COWART, NATHANIEL - LUNATIC	INQUISITION	3
COWART, Spotswood G. & Ira G.	COWART, NANCY L. - NON AGE	83
COWART, STEPHEN - MINOR	MURPHREE, JOEL D.	47
COX, IRA P. - ETAL MINORS	COX, H.W. - GDN.	58
COX, J.D.	EXPARTE	59
COX, S.P. - DECD.	HENDERSON, L. - ADMR.	62
COX, WILLIAM - DECD.	COX, E.R. - ADMR.	51
COX, WILLIAM R. - DECD.	SMITH, GEORGE W. - ADMR.	20
COX, WM. SR. - DECD.	COX, JAMES B. - ADMR.	67
CRAIG, DAVID - DECD.	CRAIG, MARTHA - ADMR.	19
CRAIG, MARTHA - DECD.	STEWART, G.W. - ADMR.	3
CRANSWELL, ADA - MINOR	Lassiter, R.D. & Jeter, Franklin, Gdn.	3
CRANSWELL, EMMA - MINOR	CARGILE, F.P. - GDN.	3
CRANSWELL, JAMES S. - DECD.	CRANSWELL, WM. - ADMR.	19
CRANSWELL, WESLEY - DECD.	WILL	71
CRASWELL, REBECCA - DECD.	WILSON, E. - ETAL ADMR.	19
CRAWFORD, EDWARD A. - MINOR	CRAWFORD, WM. H. - GDN.	3
CRAWFORD, MARY A. - DECD.	CRAWFORD, W.H.	3
CRAWFORD, WILLIAM M. - DECD.	CRAWFORD, J.T. - ADMR.	49
CRIBB, THOMAS - DECD.	GIBSON, WM. A. - ADMR.	19
CRITTENDEN, SARAH E.	BOYD, LILLIE C. - ETAL EXEC.	117
CROSBY, ROBERT - DECD.	BURNETT, A.B. - ADMR.	61
CROSWELL, ELI - DECD.	SELLERS, LUTHER - ADMR.	18
CROSWELL, EMMA - MINOR	CARGILE, F.P.	49
CROSWELL, WILLIAM - DECD.	CROSWELL, WESLEY - ADMR.	2
CROSWELL, WILLIAM - DECD.	CROSWELL, J.W. - ADMR.	49
CROUCH, J. GLENN - DECD.	BALLARD, ERIC - ADMR.	145
CROW, & C.A. PETTY - MINORS	PETTY, W.B. - GDN.	89
CROW, DAVID F. - MINOR	LIVINGSTON, J.B. - GDN.	62
CROW, F.B. - DECD.	WIIL - CIRCUIT COURT	139
CROW, HENRY C. - ETAL MINOR	CROW, C.C. - GDN.	68

CROW, JOHN - ETAL	TENANTS IN COMMON	2
CROW, JOHN - ETAL	TENANTS IN COMMON	3
CROWDER, JOHN M. - DECD.	CROWDER, JAS. H. - ADMR.	18
CROWDER, R.P. - DECD.	Crowder, Mary L.; Ex. (Tucker, Vester	159
CROWE, F.B. - DECD.	MAY, W.H. - SPEC. ADMR.	140
CULPEPPER, CHARLIE	WRIT OF HABEOUS CORPUS	93
CULPEPPER, E.C. - DECD.	CULPEPPER, L.A. - ADMR.	58
CULPEPPER, G.H. - DECD.	JOINER, GUSSIE C. - ADMR.	161
CULPEPPER, Y.M. - DECD.	Pet. for Exemption Before Admr.	87
CUMMING, JOHN - DECD.	CUMMING, RICHARD - EXEC.	2
CURETON, MARY - ETAL MINORS	CURETON, JOHN - GDN.	4
CURRY, CLARINDA - ETAL MINOR	CURRY, I.W. - GDN.	3
CURRY, J.C.	CURRY, MARY C. - ETAL ADMR.	101
CURRY, MATTIE - ETAL	TENANTS IN COMMON	61
CURRY, S.C. - DECD.	CURRY, MRS. I.M. - ADMR.	82
CURTIS, J.R. - DECD.	Curtis, J. Aubrey & W.D. - Exec. Will	91
CURTIS, JOHN D. - DECD.	White, Wyly & Thompson, J.M. - Adm	3
CURTIS, P.C. - DECD.	Curtis, Ora C. - Widow Homestead	164
DABY, Jas. Caroline - Minor Etal	STEWART, C.P. - GDN.	24
DANIEL, ISAAC B. - DECD.	DANIELS, ELIZABETH - ADMR.	21
DANIELS, A.M. - DECD.	DANIELS, J.J. - ADMR.	118
DANIELS, ISAAC - DECD.	HIGHTOWER, J.F.	94
DANIELS, J.J. - DECD.	ARMSTEAD, MARY A. - ADMR.	143
DANIELS, MARY - DECD.	WICKER, B.J. - ADMR. WILL	92
DANIELS, THOS. J. - DECD.	DANIELS, ROSANNA - EXEC. WILL	90
DARBY, B.F. - ETAL	TENANTS IN COMMON	21
DARBY, CELESTE - DECD.	Gardner, Henriette W. - Admr. Will	159
DARBY, JAMES - DECD.	DARBY, B. & B. - EXEC.	20
DARBY, M.E.	HOLLIS, MOSE - EXEC.	102
DARBY, MAY		159
DARBY, MCLEOD - DECD.	DARBY, JULIA J. - EXEC. WILL	102
DARBY, Oscar & Ross Freeman	MCLEOD, ELIJAH - Apprenticeship	82
DARBY, SUSAN - DECD.		21
DARBY, WILLIS - MINOR	HENDERSON, ELI - GDN.	14
DASSINGER, JOSEPH - DECD.	DASSINGER, ERASMUS - ADMR.	21
DAUGHTRY, H.C. - DECD.	DAUGHTRY, W.E. - ADMR.	111
DAVENPORT, ELIZABETH - DECD.	DAVENPORT, J.W. - ETAL	20
DAVENPORT, JIM	GREEN, COY - EXEC. WILL	160
DAVIE, MARY E. - MINOR ETAL	ROSS, C.J. ROSS - GDN.	64
Davis Knowles Dry Goods Co.	Knowles Henderson, etal - Art. of Inc.	75
DAVIS, ALVIN C. - DECD.	DAVIS, ODESSA J. - ADMR.	160
DAVIS, C.C. - VS.	DAVIS, T.J. - ETAL SALE OF LAND	135
DAVIS, ELIZABETH - DECD.	RAINER, Y.W. - ADMR.	20

DAVIS, ENOCH - ETAL	TENANTS IN COMMON	21
DAVIS, GEORGE F. - ETAL	TENANTS IN COMMON	21
DAVIS, J. ED. - DECD.	DAVIS, MARY B. - ADMR.	149
DAVIS, J.E. - ETAL	TENANTS IN COMMON	122
DAVIS, J.E.F. - MINOR	DAVIS, T.L.M. - GDN.	57
DAVIS, J.G. & PUGH - MINORS	CASTLEBERRY, S.F. - GDN.	148
DAVIS, J.G. & PUGH - MINORS	CASTLEBERRY, S.F. - GDN.	149
DAVIS, J.M. - DECD.	HOOD, W.M.	107
DAVIS, J.M. - ESTATE	HOOD, W.M. - ADMR.	102
DAVIS, JAMES E. - ETAL	CASTLEBERRY, MRS. S.F. - GDN.	110
DAVIS, JAMES E. - ETAL	CASTLEBERRY, MRS. S.F. - GDN.	148
DAVIS, JAMES EASON - DECD.	DAVIS, ROBERTA P. - ADMR.	151
DAVIS, JAMES ORIN - Minors Etal	Hood, W.M. & Castleberry, Mrs. S.F.	110
DAVIS, JAS. D. - DECD.	COLLIER, J.B. - ADMR.	21
DAVIS, JOHN P. - LUNATIC	HUDGENS, JOHN - GDN.	14
DAVIS, JOHN P. - LUNATIC	HUDGENS, JOHN - GDN.	20
DAVIS, JOSIAH - DECD.	BRYAN, W.W.	4
DAVIS, M.S. - ETAL	Davis, Foster Lawford; Tenants in Cor	79
DAVIS, MATTIE P.	Copeland, Mrs. N.B.; Assmt. of Dower	77
DAVIS, MATTIE P. - Name Change	MINUTE BOOK 0, PAGE 100	84
DAVIS, MERLE W.	DAVIS, PRESLEY - ADMR.	167
DAVIS, MRS. J.D. - DECD.	EDGE, DR. O.N. - ADMR.	167
DAVIS, PRESSLEY - DECD.	WOOD, DANIEL - ADMR. WILL	20
DAVIS, R.F. - DECD.	Davis, Ellender J.; appt. of dower int.	4
DAVIS, ROBERT W.	NON AGE REMOVED	77
DAVIS, S.C. - DECD.	JORDAN, BETTIE - EXEC.	112
DAVIS, SANDRA - MINOR	DAVIS, H.O. - GDN.	166
DAVIS, T.J. - DECD.	DAVIS, MINNIE CLYDE - Exec. Will	139
DAVIS, WILLIAM - DECD.	RAINER, YOUNG - ADMR.	21
DAVIS, WILLIAM - DECD.	HARRIS, LESTER - ADMR.	148
DAVIS, WILLIAM DOUGLAS - Decd.	DAVIS, MRS. PEARLIE - ADMR.	143
DAVISON, ANN A. - DECD.	ECHOLS, H.J. - ADMR.	50
DAVISON, J.A.	DAVISON, JOHN - EXEC. WILL	149
DAVISON, J.L. - DECD.	DAVISON, MRS. J.L. - ADMR.	117
DAWKINS, A.T. - DECD.	DAWKINS, R.H. - ADMR.	21
DAWKINS, D.J.	LIFFORD, W.E. - ADMR.	97
DAWKINS, M.A.C. - DECD.	HENDRICK, G. - ADMR.	4
DAWSON COMPANY, THE	Dawson Henderson, etal - Art. of Inc.	75
DAWSON, GEORGE - DECD.	DICKINSON, A.S. - ADMR.	114
DAWSON, PIT PAT	EXPARTE - HABEAS CORPUS	52
DAY, GEORGE W. - DECD.	WALTERS, JOHN C. - ADMR.	130
DAY, MARTIN H. - DECD.	FORD, ELI N. - ADMR. ETAL	21
DEAN, AS. L. - MINOR	BIGHAM, JOHN - GDN.	5

DOWNING, A.J. - DECD.	DOWNING, DUNCAN - ADMR.	21
DOWNING, REBECCA F. - DECD.	DOWNING, THOS. - ADMR.	13
DOWNING, THOMAS - DECD.	WELDON, W.A. - ADMR. ETAL	20
DOZIER, MRS. NETTIE - DECD.	TOWNSEND, S.A. - EXEC. WILL	142
DRIGGERS, ANZA - DECD. ETAL	DRIGGERS, J.W. - GDN.	14
DRIGGERS, VIRGINIA - MINOR	DRIGGERS, W.B. - GDN.	120
DRINKARD, IDA - VS.	HARVILL, THOMAS - Etal Land Sale	135
DRINKARD, W.C. - ETAL	TENANTS IN COMMON	86
DUBOSE, BETSY - DECD.	BEARD, J.S. - ADMR.	78
DUBOSE, DAN'L. - ETAL MINOR	DUBOSE, WADE H. - GDN.	14
DUBOSE, F.H. - ADMR.	DUBOSE, W.H. - EXEC. ETAL WILL	115
DUBOSE, GERTIE - MINOR	DUBOSE, W.H. - GDN.	66
DUBOSE, JEREMIAH - DECD.	WILL	21
DUBOSE, R.W. - ETAL	TENANTS IN COMMON	86
DUBOSE, SHERMAN	APPRENTICESHIP	63
DUBOSE, W.H. - DECD., HEIRS OF	DUBOSE, SAMUEL - GDN.	14
DUKE, DAVID - DECD.	RADFORD, J.W. - ADMR.	50
DUKE, MARTHA E.	STEVENS, J.P. - ADMR.	96
DUKES, M.C. & M.F. - DECD.	REYNOLDS, J.H. - GDN.	14
DUNCAN, Patrick & Daisey - Decd.	DUNCAN, JULIUS - GDN.	58
DUNCAN,. J.M. - DECD.	DUNCAN, J.C. - ADMR.	4
DUNN, A.B.	DUNN, W.B. - ADMR.	101
DUNN, DAVID A. - DECD.	RUTHERFORD, F.A. - ADMR.	20
DUNN, ETHEL - MINORS		92
DUNN, J.T. - EXPARTE	TO CORRECT MISTAKE IN LAND	61
DUNN, MARION J. - MINORS ETAL	MURPHREE, JOEL D. - GDN.	65
DUNN, SARAH E. - DECD.	KNOX, C.J. - ADMR.	54
DUNN, WILLIE BENTON - DECD.	DUNN, ELIZABETH ANN - ADMR.	138
DYER, JOHN F. - DECD.		21
DYKES, ALVA HELEN - ETAL	TENANTS IN COMMON	77
DYKES, LIZZIE - DECD.	LEE, DOCK - EXEC. WILL	118
EAGAN, W.V.	EAGAN, ETHEL P. - ADMR.	103
EAGERTON, CALLIE E.	Pet. sell land of Wm. W. Eagerton dec	128
EAGERTON, WILLIAM E. - DECD.	EAGERTON, CALLIE E. - ADMR.	123
EAST VIEW (PARK PROPERTY)	TUTWILER, C.S. - PLAT OF LAND	76
EAST, W.A. - DECD.	EAST, MRS. W.A. SR. - ADMR.	123
EASTERLING, HENRY - DECD.	FRAZIER, ALLEN - ADMR.	21
EASTERS, ERNSLEY - DECD.	MAYBERRY, JOEL - ADMR.	22
EASTERS, WM. M. - MINOR	EASTERS, CLARINDA - GDN.	4
EAVES, JANE B. - DECD.	MAY, T.L. - EXEC.	4
ECHOLS, MISS MAY R.	HAMIL, GEO. W. - EXEC. WILL	95
EDDINS, JOHN S. - DECD.	EDDINS, MARTHA L. - EXEC.	4
EDDINS, JOSEPH - MINOR ETAL	GIBSON, J.M. - GDN.	14

EDDINS, R.C. - EXPARTE	CERT. OF DISABILITY	65
EDMONSON, A.C. - DECD.	EDMONSON, ELLA - EXEC. WILL	90
EDMONSON, ELLA A. - DECD.	CHAPMAN, SADIE E. EXEC.	137
EDWARDS, BENJAMIN - DECD.	BOSWELL, F.A. - ADMR.	22
EDWARDS, CHAS. O. - DECD.	RUSHING, W.E. - ADMR.	67
EDWARDS, DORA BELLE	HABEAS CORPUS	92
EDWARDS, JAS. H. - DECD.	EDWARDS, SINA - ADMR.	21
EDWARDS, JOHN - DECD.	EDWARDS, SUSAN J. - EXEC.	4
EDWARDS, JOHN - ETAL	TENANTS IN COMMON	87
EDWARDS, JOHN - Exparte Lunacy	EDWARDS, ABIGILL	85
EDWARDS, JOSEPH - DECD.	EDWARDS, WM. S. - ADMR.	21
EDWARDS, LOU & F. - MINORS	EDWARDS, J.J. - GDN.	4
EDWARDS, LUCINDA S. - DECD.	EDWARDS, J.I. - GDN.	4
ELLIS, DELL LEE - DECD.	CAWTHON, LOUISE - ADMR.	144
ELLIS, ELIZABETH - DECD.	ELLIS, W.J. - ADMR.	90
ELLIS, JOE SEAFAS	ELLIS, ELLA - GDN.	98
ELLIS, MILDRED LEE - ETAL	ELLIS, VICTORIA - GDN.	95
ELLIS, W.B. - DECD.	GDNSHIP.	96
ELLIS, WM. S. - DECD.	ELLIS, NATHAN J. - ADMR.	22
ELLITT, DAVIS - DECD.	PYLES, ROBERT - ADMR.	21
EMFINGER, H.W. - DECD.	MCEACHERN, J.A. - ADMR. WILL	67
EMFINGER, M.C. - DECD.	Emfinger, W.O. & Dickinson, R.C.	68
EMMERSON, F.M. - DECD.	RHODES, JOHN F.	4
EMMERSON, JOHN - DECD.	HEAD, A.S. - ADMR.	21
ENGLISH, J.M. - DECD.	SAVAGE, SARAH M. - ADMR.	120
ENGRAM, B.H. - DECD.	ENGRAM, J.A. - ADMR.	111
ENZOR, ELENOR A. - DECD.	ENZOR, CYNTHIS - EXEC. WILL	118
ENZOR, HENRY C. - DECD.	ENZOR, NONIE M. - ADMR.	145
ENZOR, J.N. - DECD.	ENZOR, F.L. - ADMR.	57
ENZOR, MARY E.	ENZOR, H.C. & LANE - ADMR.	99
ENZOR, TOY F. - DECD.	TRANS. TO CIRCUIT COURT	166
ETHERIDGE, JIM - ETAL EXPARTE	HENDERSON, GEO. - DECD.	81
ETHRIDGE, GEO. - MINOR ETAL	ETHRIDGE, MALACHI - GDN.	14
ETHRIDGE, P.Z. - DECD.	ETHRIDGE, M. - ADMR.	22
EUBANKS, JOHN - DECD.		22
EUBANKS, M.F. & GEO. - MINORS	JONES, LITTLETON - GDN.	14
EUSTACE, JUDITH S. - DECD.	GRAVES, J.E. - ADMR.	73
EVANS, RICK - DECD.	MCBRYDE, W.A. - ADMR.	81
EVANS, WILLIS J. - DECD.	CINNINGHAM, C. - ADMR.	22
EVANS, WM. P. - DECD.	DICKSON, J.J. - ADMR.	21
EVANS, WM. T. - DECD.	LAWSON, JOHN R. - ADMR.	54
EVERETT, D.J. - DECD.	EVERETT, LOUISA A. - ADMR.	21
EVERHART, SUSAN - DECD.	RAMAGE, G.W. - ADMR.	4

FLOWERS, SILAS R. - DECD.	FLEMING, J.M. - ADMR.	5
FLOWERS, SILAS W. -Etal Minor	FLEMING, J.M. - GDN.	23
FLOWERS, TALMAGE JR. - MINOR	FLOWERS, MRS. VELA - GDNSHIP.	109
FLOWERS, TEMPE H. - DECD.	FLOWERS, W.C. - ADMR.	67
FLOWERS, W.C. - ETAL	TENANTS IN COMMON	67
FLOWERS, W.S.	HILLIARD, W.J. - GDN.	68
FLOWERS, W.S. - DECD.	COLEMAN, W.S. - ADMR.	49
FLOWERS, W.S. - MINOR	FLOWERS, V.C. - GDNSHIP.	66
FLOWERS, WILLIAM - DECD.	PARISH, A.S. - ADMR.	115
FLOWERS, WINGATE - DECD.	FLOWERS, WRIGHT - ADMR.	5
FLOWERS, WM. W. - DECD.	FLOWERS, MARY C. - ADMR.	3
FLOWERS, Z.E. - DECD.	FLOWERS, MRS. IDA - EXEC. WILL	146
FLOYD, ANN E. - ETAL	TENANTS IN COMMON	50
FLOYD, ELI F. - ETAL	TENANTS IN COMMON	56
FLOYD, JAS. H. or JOS. H. - Minors	FLOYD, N.E. - GDN.	58
FLOYD, JETHRO - DECD.		23
FLOYD, JOSEPH PETTUS - DECD.	FLOYD, YOUNG - ADMR.	150
FLOYD, LEWIS J. - DECD.	FLOYD, J.L.C. - GDN.	26
FLOYD, MRS. LAURA M. - DECD.	VEAL, F.D. - ADMR. (Equity Ct.)	133
FLOYD, O.D. - DECD.	FLOYD, OLA LEE - EXEC. WILL	159
FLOYD, OSBURN J. - DECD.	BEASLEY, WM. L. - ADMR.	94
FLOYD, SAM'L. - DECD.	FLOYD, SUSAN - ADMR.	22
FLOYD, SAM'L. O. - MINOR	HIGHTOWER, J.E. - GDN.	4
FLOYD, TEMPA - MINOR	FLOYD, D. - GDN.	4
FLOYD, WILLIAM - DECD.	FLOYD, FANNY M. - GDN.	58
FLOYD, WM. - DECD.	FLOYD, SAMUEL - ADMR.	22
FLYNN, MATTIE	TATE, M.F. - WILL	77
FOLKES, Ida F. & Ona Belle - Minors	MCLURE, R.N. - GDN.	56
FOLMAR, A.J. - MINOR	FOLMAR, JAMES - GDN.	4
FOLMAR, ANN AUGUSTA - MINOR	FOLMAR, WILSON BIBB - GDN.	119
FOLMAR, BENJ. F. - MINOR	FOLMAR, JAMES - GDN.	23
FOLMAR, DAN'L. - DECD.	FOLMAR, ELIZA - ADMR.	23
FOLMAR, DANIEL - MINOR	FOLMAR, ISAC S. - GDN.	23
FOLMAR, HELEN H. - DECD.	FOLMAR, Emory - Exec (Equity Ct.)	131
FOLMAR, ISAAC S. - DECD.	FLOWERS, J.N. & MARY - ADMR.	25
FOLMAR, JACOB - DECD.	SIMMS, JACOB L. - ADMR.	25
FOLMAR, JAMES M. - MINOR	FOLMAR, M.B. - GDN.	119
FOLMAR, JNO. N. - ETAL	TENANTS IN COMMON	73
FOLMAR, JOEL - MINOR	FOLMAR, ISAAC S. - GDN.	23
FOLMAR, JULIA KNOX - DECD.	HENDERSON, KNOX - EXEC. WILL	114
FOLMAR, MALISSA - ETAL MINOR	FOLMAR, ABRAM - GDN.	23
FOLMAR, MARY - DECD.	FOLMAR, J.N. - ADMR.	73
FOLMAR, MARY - MINOR	Colley, Annette Folmar; Gdn. Equity Ct.	

FOLMAR, MAX - DECD.	RHODES, HELEN L. - ADMR.	99
FOLMAR, OSCAR P. - DECD.	FOLMAR, SAM D. - ADMR.	160
FOLMAR, PINKNEY L. - VS.	Folmar Ins. Co.; Tenants in Common	105
FOLMAR, PINKNEY L. - VS.	Folmar, W.B. & Sons - Ten. in Comm	105
FOLMAR, R.E.L. - DECD.	FOLMAR, W.R. - EXEC. WILL	111
FOLMAR, R.E.L. - DECD.	FOLMAR - SPECIAL ADMR.	109
FOLMAR, SEALY - DECD.	WILL	121
FOLMAR, W.B. - ETAL	TENANTS IN COMMON	81
FOLMAR, WALTER D. SR. - DECD.	FOLMAR, SARAH T. - ADMR.	97
FORD, E.N. - DECD.		56
FORD, J.C. - ETAL	TENANTS IN COMMON	112
FOREMAN, JACOB O. - DECD.	GRIFFIN, WM. A. - ADMR.	5
FOREMAN, JEFF T. - MINOR	FOREMAN, H. - GDN.	4
FOREMAN, LILA - DECD.	NEWBY, LUCILE - EXEC. WILL	155
FORTUNE, JOSHUA - DECD.	LEE, WILLIAM - EXEC.	25
FOSTER, ANNIE - DECD.	FOSTER, S.A. - ADMR.	61
FOSTER, JOHN L. - DECD.	FOSTER, ROBT. A. - ETAL	49
FOWLER, BURRELL - DECD.	FOWLER, LYDIA - ADMR.	22
FOWLER, J.L.	BOROM, T.L. - ADMR.	92
Fowler, Margaret Carey - Etal		96
FOXWORHT, W.A. - DECD.	TRAWICK, P.B. - ADMR.	100
FRANKLIN, BARNETT - DECD.	FRANKLIN, Martha & John B. - Admr.	25
FRANKLIN, Barnett - Minors Heirs of	FRANKLIN, MARTHA - GDN.	23
FRANKLIN, H.D. - DECD.	FRANKLIN, J.R. - ADMR.	22
FRANKLIN, JOHN - DECD.	BOYD, T.G. - ADMR. ETAL	25
FRAZER, WM. - DECD.	FRAZER, ALLEN - ADMR.	25
FRAZIER, FRANCIS - MINOR	FRAZIER, ALLEN - GDN.	4
FRAZIER, MARTHA - DECD.	FRAZIER, GUS - EXEC. WILL	98
FRAZIER, MODINA - MINOR	FRAZIER, MARGARETT - GDN.	23
FREEMAN, EARNEST	FREEMAN, FANNIE D.	?
FREEMAN, IRENE P. - DECD.	FREEMAN, PINK - EXEC. WILL	166
FREEMAN, J.C. - ETAL	TENANTS IN COMMON	48
FREEMAN, J.T. - DECD.	FREEMAN, G.B. - ADMR.	113
FREEMAN, JOHN - DECD.	FREEMAN, R.C. - ADMR.	63
FREEMAN, MARY KING - DECD.	FOLMAR, M.B. - ADMR.	121
FREEMAN, Mrs. Fannie D. - Decd.	Freeman, George Miles - Exec. Will	147
FREEMAN, W.C. - Special Coroner	REEVES, L. - PETITIONER	74
FRENCH, A.J.M. - ETAL	TENANTS IN COMMON	48
FRENCH, J.E.	FRENCH, FOX - ADMR.	95
FRIZEL, JASON - DECD.	FRIZLE, CLARK - ADMR.	22
FRIZLE, ELIZABETH J. - DECD.	O'NEAL, WM. - ADMR.	25
FRIZLE, EPHRAIM - DECD.	O'NEAL, B.F. - ADMR.	25
FRIZLE, JASON - DECD.	FRIZLE, CLARK - ADMR.	25

FRIZZLE, E.E. - ETAL MINORS	O'NEAL, B.F. - GDN.	4
FRIZZLE, ELZANA - MINOR	FRIZZLE, EPHRAIM - GDN.	23
FRIZZLE, TEMPERANCE - DECD.	FRIZZLE, JACKSON - ADMR.	5
FRIZZLE, THOMAS - DECD.	FRIZZLE, JASON - ADMR.	25
FRYER, A. & J. - MINORS	FRYER, GILLIA - GDN.	23
FRYER, ALEXANDER - DECD.	FRYER, THOMAS S. - ADMR.	25
FRYER, DICK - DECD.	FRYER, VELMA - EXEC. WILL	156
FRYER, JEFF - MINOR	SCARBROUGH - GDN.	4
FRYER, JOHN - DECD.	FRYER, JOHN LUDE - EXEC. WILL	151
FRYER, LEWIS A. - ETAL	TENANTS IN COMMON	5
FRYER, S.A.	FRYER, JOHN - EXEC. WILL	97
FRYER, THOS. L. - DECD.	FRYER, W.H. - ADMR.	11
FRYER, WM. - MINOR	CROSWELL, WM. - GDN.	4
FRYER, WM. Y. - DECD.	LEE, HAMILTON - ADMR.	25
FULLER, HARRIET - DECD.	BROWDER, MARY - WILL	82
FULLER, JESSE FRANK	1ST F. & M. BK., Troy; Gdn. Doc bk 2	
FULLER, MARSHALL MAY - MINOR	REDDOCH, W.M. - GDN.	87
FULLER, MRS. RUTH - DECD.	LAWSON, WM. - ADMR.	88
FULLER, RALPH - ETAL MINORS	STRINGER, JEFF - ETAL GDNSHIP.	128
FUQUA, JAS. M. - DECD.	SEGARS, H.R. - ADMR.	5
FURLOW, J.S.	FURLOW, G.C. - ADMR.	95
GAFFORD, VETURIA - DECD.	MCBRYDE, VALLIE - Etal Exec. Will	120
GALA AMUSEMENTS	INCORPORATION	88
GALLOWAY, FANNY S. - MINOR	GALLOWAY, R.F. - GDN.	6
GALLOWAY, H.H. - DECD.	GALLOWAY, R.A. - Etal Exec. Will	118
GALLOWAY, JAMES - DECD.	GALLOWAY, N.W. - ADMR.	38
GALLOWAY, MARY A. - MINOR	HIX, CHAS. W. - GDN.	5
GALLOWAY, Mary Frances - Decd.	GALLOWAY, W.L. - ADMR.	129
GALLOWAY, R.A. - DECD.	GALLOWAY, MARY E. - ADMR.	133
GALLOWAY, W.L. - DECD.	GALLOWAY, Mary Mark - Exec. Will	147
GALLOWAY, WILEY - DECD.	PERKINS, W.L. - ADMR.	123
GAMBLE, JOHN - DECD.	COPELAND, J.L. - ADMR.	118
GAMBLE, SALLIE A. - ETAL	TENANTS IN COMMON	5
GANEY, R.E. - DECD.	BRUNSON, D.A.F. - ADMR.	26
GANEY, STEPHEN - DECD.	SPEAR, H.K. - ADMR.	26
GARDNER, F. & S.H. - MINOR	GARDNER, BENJ. - GDN.	23
Gardner, J.D., Phillip, Phieffer - Etal	EXPARTE	59
GARDNER, JAMES C. - MINOR	FURLOW, JAMES M. - GDN.	4
GARDNER, JOHN D. - DECD.	HENDERSON, J.C. - ADMR.	64
GARNER, C.M. - ETAL	Tenants in Common - Pet. to sell land	83
GARNER, J.L. - DECD.	TUCKER, J.M. - ADMR.	6
GARNER, THEO - DECD.	GARNER, MATTIE - ADMR.	117
GARRETT, S.L. - DECD.	FORD, ELI N. - ADMR.	5

GLAWSON, JAMES - DECD.	GLAWSON, CINDERILLA - EXEC.	5
GLENN, HENRY	EXPARTE	58
GLOVER, MRS. ADDIE G. - DECD.	BARNES, MRS. ED S. - Exec. Will	139
GODDIN, EPHRAIM - DECD.	GODDIN, GODDIN - ADMR.	25
GODDIN, NATHAN - DECD.	GODDIN, JORDAN - ADMR.	25
GODWIN, JORDAN - DECD.	GODWIN, EPHRAIM E. - ADMR.	50
GODWIN, LEILA	FRENCH, J.H. - NON AGE	75
GODWIN, S.P. - DECD.	WHITE, GEORGE - GDN.	23
GODWIN, WILEY - DECD.	SMITH, JOHN R. - ADMR.	26
GODWIN, WILLIAM J.	GODWIN, LELA - ADMR.	74
GOFF, DAN'L. A. - DECD.	CARTER, A.J. - ADMR.	5
GOFF, J.W.	TAYLOR, J.P. - N.C.M. & GDNSHIP.	82
GOFF, J.W. - DECD.	FOSTER, A.B. - ADMR.	87
GOFF, SARAH J.	JOHNSTON, ARTHUR G. - EXEC.	116
GOINS, MINNIE LEE - ETAL	GOINS, WM. D. - Letters of Gdnship.	74
GOLDEN, ELIZABETH - DECD.	CONNOR, THOMAS - ADMR.	5
GOLDEN, LEILA	DIS NON AGE - MIN. BK. O pg. 117	88
GOLDTHWAITE, JOHN R. - DECD.	Goldthwaite, Julia & C.B. - Exec. Will	55
GOLSON, C.O.	PET. TO SELL LAND	93
GOMMILLON, HENRY - MINOR	GOMMILLON, JOS. H.	23
GOODE, BETTIE	EXPARTE	5
GOODMAN, JOHN - DECD.	CARMICHAEL, A. - ADMR.	5
GOODWIN, LEILA LAW - DECD.	GOODWIN, ALFONZO - ADMR.	150
GOOLSBY, J.J. - DECD.	LEVERETTE, J.E. - ADMR.	90
GOOLSBY, MARY E.	TENANTS IN COMMON	75
GOOLSBY, MICAJAH - DECD.	BROWN, JAMES H. ADMR.	25
GOOLSBY, WOOTSON - DECD.	GOOLSBY, EPSY C. - ADMR.	26
GORDON, SUSIE - ETAL	TENANTS IN COMMON	49
GOSHEN, TOWN OF	INCORPORATION	75
GOSS, JULIUS C. - DECD.	BATES, ALLEN - ADMR.	38
GRACE, MONROE - N.C.M.	LASSITER, J.M. JR. - EQUITY CT.	96
GRADY, H.M. - MINORS	RHODES, J.F. - ADMR.	6
GRAHAM, EMMA J. - ETAL MINORS	GRAHAM, DUNCAN - GDN.	6
GRANGER, JOHN - MINOR	GRANGER, J.R. - GDN.	23
GRANGER, JOHN C. - LUNATIC	GRANGER, JAMES R. - PET.	26
GRANT, C.W. - ETAL	TENANTS IN COMMON	68
GRANT, DR. C.A. - DECD.	GRANT, MATTIE K. - EXEC. WILL	153
GRANT, I.W. or J.W. - ETAL	TENANTS IN COMMON	73
GRANT, J.O. SR. - DECD.	GRANT, I,W, - ETAL EXEC.	118
GRANT, LAURA I. - DECD.	Turnipseed, Maurice - Exec. Will	156
GRANT, MATTIE K. - DECD.	KYZAR, ANNIE - EXEC. WILL	157
GRANT, SARAH - DECD.	GRANT, WILSON - ADMR.	6
GRANT, WILSON - DECD.	GRAVES, J.O. & Carlisle, J.J. - Will	61

GRANTHAM, ANNA MAY - MINOR	GRANTHAM, H.C. - GDN.	85
GRANTHAM, SUSAN	CHANGE OF NAME	63
GRAVES, A.L. - DECD.	GRAVES, A.A. - EXEC.	53
GRAVES, ARCH'D. - DECD.	GRAVES, HARRIETT - ADMR.	6
GRAVES, D.P. - DECD.	CARROLL, M.W. - SHERIFF	67
GRAVES, DAVID - DECD.	WILLIAMS, DEKALB - EXEC.	5
GRAVES, Edward Malcomb - Decd.	THRASH, HILLIARY D. - ADMR.	94
GRAVES, ELIJAH D. - DECD.	MILES, ELIZA - ADMR.	26
GRAVES, EMMA	WILL - NOT PROBATED	109
GRAVES, EMMA - DECD.	SPIVEY, J.C. - PROBATE OF WILL	109
GRAVES, GEO. W. - MINORS	GRAVES, CHARLES - GDN.	6
GRAVES, HARDY - DECD.	GRAVES, CHARLES - ADMR.	26
GRAVES, J.C. - DECD.	BATES, ALLEN - ADMR.	26
GRAVES, JAMES - DECD.	GRAVES, CHARLES - ADMR.	38
GRAVES, JAMES - DECD.	GRIFFIN, G.A. - ADMR.	77
GRAVES, JOHN - DECD.	GRAVES, CHARLES - ADMR.	26
GRAVES, JOHN J. - MINORS	MILES, D.D. - GDN.	6
GRAVES, M.E. & J.W. - MINORS	SNIDER, ELIZA - GDN.	6
GRAVES, SUSANNAH - DECD.	JACKSON, SARAH - EXEC. WILL	106
GRAVES, THOMAS - DECD.	YOUNGBLOOD, J.B. - ADMR.	5
GRAVES, Z.H. - ETAL	TENANTS IN COMMON	38
GRAY, ELI B. - MINORS	GRAY, PARK - GDN.	6
GRAY, J.V. - DECD.	GRAY, M.L. - ADMR.	54
GRAY, MARY - DECD.	GRAY, PARKER - EXEC.	11
GREATHOUSE, JOHN - DECD.	GREATHOUSE, Martha. - Exemption	87
GREATHOUSE, MARTHA S. - Decd.	GREATHOUSE, D.L. - ADMR.	114
GREATHOUSE, Z.B. - DECD.	DUBOSE, SAM - ADMR.	114
GREEN, CARL - ETAL	MINORS	93
GREEN, EMMA - ETAL	TENANTS IN COMMON	122
GREEN, HENRY BROOKS - DECD.	GREEN, JOHN WESLEY - ADMR.	145
GREEN, JNO. T. - ETAL MINORS	GREEN, WM. T. - GDN.	6
GREEN, JNO. WOODSON - DECD.	GREEN, NANCE - ADMR.	112
GREEN, JOHN O. - DECD.	GREEN, PETER M. - ADMR.	91
GREEN, MARY E. - ETAL	TENANTS IN COMMON	72
GREEN, N.C. - DECD.	GREEN, R.H. - ADMR.	103
GREEN, N.F. JR. - MINOR	TROY BANK & TRUST CO. - GDN.	155
GREEN, N.F. SR. - DECD.	GREEN, BRADLEY - EXEC. WILL	154
GREEN, NANCY B. - ETAL	TENANTS IN COMMON	5
GREEN, NATHAN C. - DECD.	GREEN, HENRY L. SR. - ADMR.	159
GREEN, RILEY P.	GREEN, Mamie Louise - Exec. Will	162
GREEN, RILEY P. JR. - MINOR	GREEN, MAMIE LOUISE - GDN.	164
GREEN, W.C. - DECD.	GREEN, MAGGIE P. - ADMR.	155
GREEN, W.H. - VS.	HARDEN, G.W. - Partition of Property	134

GRIMMER, T.J.	GRIMMER, IRENE - ADMR.	93
GRUBBS, EMMIE C. - DECD.	WATKINS, KATIE - ESTATE WILL	100
GRUBBS, JASPER & GILMORE, J.L.	EXPARTE	66
GRUBBS, MARY	KINDRED, CORINE - EXEC. WILL	150
GUILFORD, HOWARD - Etal Minors	CARROLL, W.C. - GDN.	110
GUNNELS, J.H. - DECD.	GUNNELS, DELPHIA - EXEC. WILL	156
GUNTER, ADDIE M. - ETAL	MULKEY, W.G. - GDNSHIP.	75
GUNTER, MAE	JONES, BRITTON - PRO ANNI	23
HAIL, D. - DECD.	FOLMAR, I.S. - ADMR.	27
HAINES, J.D. - MINOR	MCLANE, J.H. - GDN.	6
HAIR, JOHN C. - ETAL MINOR	CANNON, JOHN F. - GDN.	23
HAIR, PETER - DECD.	CANNON, JNO. - ADMR.	29
HAISTEN, BERTHA E. - Etal Minors	HAISTEN, SALLIE E. - GDN.	74
HAISTEN, ELBERT RAY - MINOR	HAISTEN, F.A. - GDN.	71
HAISTEN, ELBERT ROY - MINOR	HAISTEN, JAMES N. - GDN.	71
HAISTEN, J.N. - DECD.	HAISTEN, LUCY A. - ADMR.	151
HAISTEN, J.W.	FOLMAR, W.B. - ADMR.	92
HAISTEN, JOHN T. - ETAL MINORS	HAISTEN, T.W. - GDN.	65
HAISTEN, MARY E. - DECD.	HAISTEN, J.C. & W.H. - ADMR.	142
HAISTEN, ROY - MINOR	HAISTEN, F.A. - GDN.	71
HAISTEN, T.W. VS. BASS, WILLIS	DIVISION OF CROPS	63
HAISTEN, THOS. W. - DECD.	HAISTEN, H.S. - ADMR.	71
HAISTEN, THOS. W. - ETAL	WILL	71
HAISTEN, WILLIE - MINOR	HARDIN, G.W. - GDN.	65
HALL, ELLA - DECD.	HALL, L.D. - ADMR.	113
HALL, ISAAC N. - DECD.	JONES, JOS. D. - ADMR.	7
HALL, W.S. - DECD.	HALL, LULA - Pet. for Allotment	86
HAM, B.A. - DECD.	HAM, ANNA J. - EXEC.	81
HAMIL, ELLEN - DECD.	MCLURE, JOHN R. - ADMR.	128
HAMIL, GEORGE W. - DECD.	HAMIL, LIZZIE K.	102
HAMIL, JENNINGS	NON AGE	87
Hamil, John, Geo. & Marjorie - Minors	HAMIL, MRS. MARIE - GDN.	132
HAMILTON, DANIEL - DECD.	BUNDRICK, A.M. - ADMR.	27
HAMILTON, J.A. - DECD.	CUNNINGHAM, Y.L. - ADMR.	29
HAMM, THOMAS - DECD.	HAMM, WM. - EXEC. ETAL	28
HAMM, THOMAS - DECD.	HAMM, WM. - ETAL EXEC.	30
HAMMERLY, EDWIN TERRY - Decd.	Murphree, Elizabeth Barton - Exec.	165
HAMMERLY, PEARL ROSS - DECD.	Murphree, Lizzie Barton - Exec.	161
HAMMONDS, JOHN - DECD.	LOVE, A.P. - ADMR.	28
HANCHEY, JOHN - DECD.	HANCHEY, WILLIAM - ADMR.	28
HANCHEY, JOHN W. - MINOR	SEGARS, H.R. - GDN.	23
HANCHEY, L.A. - ETAL	TENANTS IN COMMON	65
HANCHEY, LOTTIE G. - Etal Minors	HANCHEY, L.A. - GDNSHIP.	67

HENSTISS, VIRGINIA - MINOR	HENSTISS, D.M. - GDN.	50
HERALD PUBLISHING CO.	CORP.	85
HERIN, HENRY - DECD.	HERRIN, WM. - ADMR.	27
HERM, VALENTINE - DECD.	HERM, VALENTINE - ADMR.	28
HERNDEN, JOHN P. - DECD.	LIVINGSTON, S.B. - ETAL EXEC.	30
HERNDON, J.J.	NON COMPUS MENTIS	66
HERNDON, J.J. - DECD.	REEVES, S.M. - SHFF. ADMR.	66
HERNDON, J.P. - DECD.	LIVINGSTON, S.B. - ETAL EXEC.	7
HERNDON, SYLVIA - DECD.	HERNDON, J.J. - ADMR.	28
HERNSON, BURRELL - DECD.	CROSWELL, WM. - ADMR.	28
HERREN, CLEOPATRA - DECD.	MCEACHERN, C.P. - ADMR.	99
HERRIN, MICHAEL - DECD.	HERRIN, M.C. - ADMR.	29
HERRIN, SARAH - DECD.	HERRIN, M.W. - ETAL EXEC.	28
HERRING, J.H. - VS.	WHATLEY, FELIX - CERTIORARI	73
HERRING, W.M. - DECD.	HOMESTEAD - CIR. CT.	95
HERRINGTON, ARTHUR C. - Decd.	HERRINGTON, W.H. - ADMR.	110
HERRINGTON, W.H. - DECD.	Herrington, Lilla Belle - Exec. Will	152
HERRINS, PHILLIP R. - DECD.	TALBOT, JAS. - ETAL ADMR.	27
Hickman, Ewell O., Robbie L.; Minors	HICKMAN, J.P. - GDN.	95
HICKMAN, MRS. JULIA - DECD.	HICKMAN, A.E. - ADMR. ETAL	143
HICKMAN, S.R. - DECD.	HICKMAN, JULIA A. - ADMR.	109
HICKS, CARRIE - MINOR	HICKS, D.M. - GDN.	77
HICKS, F.A. - DECD.	HICKS, CARRIE W. - ADMR.	54
HICKS, JAMES M. - DECD.	ROSS, R.A. - ADMR.	52
HICKS, JAMES M. - DECD.	ROSS, R.A. - ADMR.	81
HICKS, T.J. - ETAL	TENANTS IN COMMON	63
HICKS, W.G. - ETAL	TENANTS IN COMMON	70
HICKS, W.H. - DECD.	HICKS, JAMES A. - ADMR.	28
HICKS, WILLIE M. - DECD.	HICKS, W.G. - ADMR.	89
HICKS, WILLIE MAVIS	PET. TO SET ASIDE REAL ESTATE	83
HIGDEN, TERRILL - DECD.	HIGDON, EZEKIEL - ADMR.	27
HIGGS, M.A.U. - DECD.	ROSS, R.A. - ADMR.	54
HIGH, DOROTHY - ETAL MINORS	GREEN, AGNES - GDN.	119
HIGH, ERNEST L.	GREEN, L.S. - ADMR.	101
HIGH, JIMMIE	GREEN, AGNES HIGH - GDN.	108
Highland Farmers Alliance Store Co.	INCORPORATION	58
HIGHTOWER, C.W.	Hightower, Oscar E.; exec. trans equit	98
HIGHTOWER, HAROLD F. - DECD.	HIGHTOWER, JULIA B. - Exec. Will	156
HIGHTOWER, LUCINDA R. - DECD.	FLOYD, SUSAN E. - ADMR.	6
HIGHTOWER, MRS. O.E.	PARTITION	97
HIGHTOWER, O.E. - ETAL	TENANTS IN COMMON	86
HIGHTOWER, WM. R. - DECD.	PARKS, WM. W. - ADMR.	68
HILL, CEPH K. - DECD.	HILL, JEPP	132

HILL, HILAMORE	GDN.	15
HILL, JAMES - MINOR	BRAY, JEFFERSON - GDN.	6
HILL, Mark W. & Martha Johnson	EXPARTE - MINORS	57
HILL, R.H. - DECD.	SKINNER, W.R. - ADMR.	6
HILLIARD, ANNIE V. & L.L. - Minor	HENDRICK, G. - GDN.	6
HILLIARD, FRED - N.C.M.	Hilliard, Elizabeth - Gdn. (Cir. Ct.)	130
HILLIARD, G.W. - DECD.	HILLIARD, W.J.A.J. - ADMR.	47
HILLIARD, J.B. - DECD.	WALTERS, Joe Frank - Exec. Will	134
HILLIARD, KATE H. - DECD.	Hilliard, W.L. & Charles - Exec. Will	129
HILLIARD, W.L. - DECD.	HILLIARD, ELIZABETH - Exec. Will	153
HILLIARD, WILLIAM - DECD.	HILLIARD, W.J.A.J. - ADMR.	7
HIMBERG, A.A.	HIMBERG, JOSEPHA	70
HIXON, DAN'L. A. - ETAL MINORS	BAXTER, CATHARINE - GDN.	7
HIXON, J.M. - DECD.	Troy Bank & Trust Co. - Exec. Will	154
HIXON, SAMUEL - DECD.	HALL, DANIEL M. - ETAL ADMR.	6
HIXON, W.L. - DECD.	FINLAYSON, M.A. - EXEC.	29
HIXON, WM. L. - DECD.	MCCALL, DAVID - ADMR.	6
HOBDY, BEULAH EMMA - MINOR	GELLERSTEDT, L.E. - GDN.	65
HOBDY, CHARLOTTE	GDN.	96
HOBDY, EDMUND - DECD.	HOBDY, HARRELL - ADMR.	29
HOBDY, H. - DECD.	HOBDY, J.M. - ADMR.	29
HOBDY, IRA - DECD.	WELDON, W.A. - ADMR.	47
HOBDY, IVEY - DECD.	HOBDY, IRA - ADMR.	28
HOBDY, JANE A. - DECD.	WHITE, REBECCA A. - EXEC.	56
HOBDY, JOHN & C. - MINOR	ARMSTRONG, JAS. F. - GDN.	23
HOBDY, JOHN - ETAL DECD.	TENANTS IN COMMON	7
HOBDY, JOHN - ETAL MINORS	HOBDY, IVEY - GDN.	28
HOBDY, JOHN E. - ETAL MINORS	MURPHREE, D.B. - GDN.	6
HOBDY, JOHN R. - ETAL MINOR	HOBDY, IRA - GDN.	23
HOBDY, MARY E. - MINOR	HOBDY, JAMES M. - GDN.	23
HOBDY, WILL - ETAL	TENANTS IN COMMON	133
HODGES, B.W. - DECD.	HODGES, J.M. - ADMR.	27
HOLENHEAD, A.P. - MINOR	SMITH, J.A. - GDN.	6
HOLLAND, T.J. - DECD.	YOUNGBLOOD, J.B. - ADMR.	6
HOLLEY, BEASANT - DECD.	LOCKEY, G.W. - ADMR.	29
HOLLEY, J.C. - DECD.	FLOWERS, LESTER - ADMR.	139
HOLLEY, JULIA K. - DECD.	LESLIE, MOLLIE J. - ADMR.	167
HOLLINGSWORTH, M.E. - DECD.	REEVES, S.M. - SHFF. ADMR.	64
HOLLINGSWORTH, Sam F. - Decd.	HOLLINGSWORTH, Claudie - Admr.	118
HOLLIS, Thomas & Oscar - Minors	NON AGE REMOVED	61
HOLLOWAY GEORGE F. - DECD.	COTTON, SAM'L. R. - ADMR.	53
HOLLOWAY, M.E. - ETAL MINOR	BLOXOM, HENRY - GDN.	23
HOLLOWAY, Marvin - Etal Minors	THOMAS, J.C. - GDN.	58

HOLLOWAY, WM. F. - DECD.	HOLLOWAY, REBECCA - ADMR.	50
Holmes, Bertie May & Tupsie; minors	AVANT, W.G. - GDN.	77
HOLMES, R.H.	HOLMES, GROVER MAE - ADMR.	104
HOLMES, SALLIE - DECD.	WILSON, J.M. - ADMR.	86
HOMER, THOMAS H.	EXPARTE	51
HOOK, HILLERY SR. - DECD.	HOOK, HILLERY JR. - ADMR.	27
HOOKS, C.G. - DECD.	HOOKS, WILLIE C. - ADMR. WILL	142
HOOKS, CHARLES - DECD.	HOOKS, DANIEL - ADMR.	28
HOOKS, DANIEL - DECD.	HOOKS, SARAH J. - ADMR.	27
HOOKS, FRANCIS M. - MINOR	HOOKS, CHARLES A. - GDN.	6
HOOKS, GEORGE - DECD.	GRANT, WILSON - ADMR.	29
HOOKS, J.T. - DECD.	HOOKS, C.G. - ADMR.	133
HOOKS, JAMES - MINOR	TAYLOR, R.E. - GDN.	14
HOOKS, RACHAEL - MINOR	BRUCE, JACOB - GDN.	14
HOOKS, ROBERT M. - DECD.	GRANT, WILSON - ADMR.	7
HOOKS, TAMAR - DECD.	COLEMAN, AMANDA - ADMR.	52
HOOKS, THOMAS J. - DECD.	HOOKS, FRANCES E. - ADMR.	27
HOOKS, VONCILE - ETAL MINORS	HOOKS, BEULAH B. - GDN.	111
HOOTEN, MARCUS - DECD.	Homestead Exemption to Widow	155
HORN, ISAAC - DECD.	HORN, ISAAC - ADMR.	28
HORN, MICHAEL - DECD.	HORN, ISAAC H. - ADMR.	30
HORTON, WM. - DECD.	MCEACHERN, J.D. - ADMR.	29
HOSMER, MARGARET A. - DECD.	Sessions, Fannie H. - exec. (Cir. Ct.)	119
HOSMER, S.M. - DECD.	BAXLEY, J.W. - EXEC. WILL	89
HOUGH, JOS. D. - MINOR	COLLINGSWORTH, Z.W. - GDN.	14
HOUGH, MARGARET F. - DECD.	THOMPSON, JOB - ADMR.	29
HOUGH, NANCY - DECD.	HOUGH, J.B. - ADMR.	28
HOUGHTON, F.R. - DECD.	HOUGHTON, MARY E. - ADMR.	28
HOUSTON, H.L.	DECLARATION OF RESIDENCE	81
HOWARD, G.B. - DECD.	LAWSON, CLIFFORD - ADMR.	134
HOWARD, HARRIS	HOWARD, J.W. - EXEC WILL	108
HOWARD, HARRIS A. - EST.	HOMESTEAD EXEMPTION	137
HOWARD, J.H. - DECD.	HOWARD, NANCY A. - WILL	102
HOWARD, JNO. A. - DECD.	PARKS, WM. H. - ADMR.	7
HOWELL, Nora Mae & Lou - minors		149
HUBBARD, A.G. - ETAL	TENANTS IN COMMON	71
HUBBARD, ANN G.	WILL	91
HUBBARD, JNO. P. - DECD.	HUBBARD, ANN G. - EXEC.	73
HUBBARD, JOHN P. - DECD.	HUBBARD, G.J. - ETAL ADMR.	91
HUBBARD, Laura Gaines - Minor	HUBBARD, G.J. - GDN.	89
HUDNALL, Ida & Willie Johnston	DARBY, JNO. R. - GDN.	81
HUDSON, A.R. - MINOR	HUDSON, DAVID - GDN.	24
HUDSON, ELIZABETH A. - MINOR	HUDSON, DAVID - GDN.	14

HUEY, R.E. & S.S. - DECD.	HUEY, G.W. - Etal Ten. in Common	72
HUEY, ROBERT E. - DECD.	HUEY, S.S. - ADMR.	47
HUFF, J.V. - DECD.	HUFF, KATE - ADMR.	99
HUGGINS, MARCUS A. - DECD.	HUGGINS, L.A. - ADMR.	61
HUGGINS, REBBECA - DECD.	STEWART, U.A. - ADMR.	89
HUGGINS, WILLIAM - DECD.	WILL	89
HUGGINS, WILLIE - ETAL	Tenants in Common - Pet. for Sale	75
HUGHES, CAWTHON - ETAL	Hughes, Mrs. M.A.; Magnolia Cawthoi	84
HUGHES, DANIEL B. - DECD.	COSKREY, DAVID B. - ADMR.	49
HUGHES, FOX - DECD.	HUGHES, LENA - ADMR.	149
HUGHES, JOHN - DECD.	Hughes, Gussie Mae; homestead exe	122
HUGHES, WILLIAM S. - DECD.	WALLACE, ALLEN - ADMR.	27
HULEN, DOCK - DECD.	EARNEST, S.D. - ADMR.	95
HULEN, ODIS R. - ETAL	HAISTEN, W.H. - GDN.	102
HULL, K.U. - DECD.	HULL, J.B. - ADMR.	159
HUME, WILLIAM H. - DECD.	HUME, H. - ADMR.	77
Huner, Hubert E. & Stanley Jr. minors	STANLEY, H. HUNER - GDN.	167
HURLEY, FREEMAN B. - DECD.	HURLEY, RHODA - ADMR.	27
HURLEY, JOEL - DECD.	TILLERY, V.H. - ADMR.	28
HURLEY, L.J.G. - DECD.	HURLEY, ISABELLA - ADMR.	6
HURLEY, W.F. - ETAL	TENANTS IN COMMON	54
HURLEY, W.F. - MINOR	HURLEY, J.G. - GDN.	13
HURLEY, W.P. - Minors Heirs of	HURLEY, ELIZABETH F. - GDN.	53
HURST, HOLLIS - ETAL MINOR	HURST, ISAAC - GDN.	24
HURST, James - Slaves of - Decd.	WORTHY, A.N.	29
HURST, PRISCILLA - DECD.	HURST, JOHN	29
HURST, WILLIAM - DECD.	KING, BERRY H. - ADMR.	6
HURST, WILLIAM - DECD.	KING, BERRY H. - ADMR.	61
HURSTON, ORPAH	HURSTON, J.M. - ADMR.	96
HURT, JOHN - DECD.	HURT, K.A. - ADMR.	28
HURY, RICHARD - MINOR	WORTHY, A.N. - GDN.	23
HUSSEY, JOS. F. - DECD.	ROLING, A.V. - Widow Exemption	72
HUSSEY, L.L. - DECD.	HUSSEY, L.M. - ADMR.	90
HUSSEY, MINNIE - ETAL MINORS	HUSSEY, M.B. - GDN.	84
HUSSEY, WILLIE - ETAL	ROLING, A.V. - GDNSHIP.	72
HUSSEY, WILLIE - ETAL MINOR	HUSSEY, J.R. - GDN.	72
HUTCHISON, J.B. - DECD.	HORN, ISAAC H. - ADMR.	28
HUTCHISON, JAMES - DECD.	HUTCHISON, J.B. - ADMR.	28
HUTCHISON, JOHN - DECD.	WILLIS, T.L. - ADMR.	28
HUTCHISON, KATHERINE - ETAL	BROCK, S.H. - GDN.	99
HUTCHISON, N.B. - ETAL MINOR	COCHRAN, D.S. - GDN.	6
HUTCHISON, W.W. - DECD.	HUTCHISON, J.B. - ADMR.	28
HUTCHISON, WM. B. - DECD.	HUTCHISON, J.B. - ADMR.	27

HUTTO, CHARLES - DECD.	MCKERLEY, WM. - ADMR.	28
HUTTO, NANCY A. - MINOR	GILMORE, WILLIAM - GDN.	6
HYATT, MARY M. - MINOR	HOBDY, JAMES M. - GDN.	6
HYBART, J.H. - ETAL	TENANTS IN COMMON	76
HYBERT, J.H. - DECD.	HYBERT, Susan & J.H. Jr. - Admr.	51
HYSMITH, MARIENE - MINOR	HYSMITH, THAD - GDN.	147
Independent King David Temple	CORP.	67
INGRAM, H.R.	EXEMPTION	89
INGRAM, LILLA	COLE, JAMES - EXEC.	149
INGRAM, THADEUS A. - DECD.	TATOM, J.P. - ADMR.	131
INGRAM, W.S. - DECD.	ADMR. & SALE OF LAND	159
INNIS, S. BUFORD - DECD.	INNIS, FANNIE M. - ADMR.	153
ISHMAELITES OF AMERICA	CORP.	86
ISRAEL, CORA SMITH	WALKER, GERTRUDE - Exec. Will	140
IVEY, IDA F. - DECD.	WILLIAMS, STEPHEN B. - ADMR.	119
IVEY, M.C.	HARPER, P.O. - ADMR.	62
IVEY, THOMAS E. - DECD.	IVEY, MAUDE - ADMR.	165
JACKSON, A.A. - MINOR	BERRY, JOHN - GDN.	7
JACKSON, A.L. - ETAL MINOR	JACKSON, J.H. - GDN.	7
Jackson, A.L., F.M., & N.E.; Minors	JACKSON, J.H. - GDN.	50
JACKSON, A.M. - ETAL	TENANTS IN COMMON	63
JACKSON, ALEXANDER - DECD.	JACKSON, A.M.	29
JACKSON, ARENA - Etal Minors	WELDON, M.A. - GDN.	49
JACKSON, BOB - DECD.	GRIFFIN, H.P. - ADMR.	133
JACKSON, CHARLIE - ETAL	TENANTS IN COMMON	53
Jackson, D.F. vs. Folmar, W.B.; Etal	TENANTS IN COMMON	95
JACKSON, DANIEL - DECD.	JACKSON, ELIZABETH	29
JACKSON, ELLEN	HOMESTEAD EXEMPTION	137
JACKSON, ETTIE & H.V. - MINORS	JACKSON, MARY E. - GDN.	58
JACKSON, F.A. - DECD.	JACKSON, Mrs. Collie H. - Exempt	61
JACKSON, H.G.	LAND SALE	97
JACKSON, H.J.	Choice of Residence; County to Coun	77
JACKSON, HOLLIS - Etal Minors	HURST, ISAAC - GDN.	7
JACKSON, J.H.		7
JACKSON, J.H. - ETAL	TENANTS IN COMMON	57
JACKSON, J.T. - DECD.	WILLIAMS, R.J. - ADMR.	7
JACKSON, J.W.W. - DECD.	CHANCEY, J.I. - ADMR.	67
JACKSON, JAMES - DECD.	JACKSON, L.V. - EXEC.	57
JACKSON, JNO. T. - DECD.	HUGGINS, WM.	30
JACKSON, JOHN B. - DECD.	JACKSON, CLEM - ADMR.	152
JACKSON, L.	BASHINSKY, L.M. - ADMR.	80
JACKSON, L. SYLVESTER - Decd.	JACKSON, EASTER - ADMR.	85
JACKSON, MARY - ETAL MINORS	JACKSON, JAMES E. - GDN.	15

JINRIGHT, JESSE - DECD.	JINRIGHT, J.D. - ADMR.	96
JOHNS, L.J. - DECD.	JOHNS, T.M. - ADMR.	29
JOHNS, LEROY B.	JOHNS, THELMA - ADMR.	29
JOHNS, LEWIS	JOHNS, THOMAS - ADMR.	29
JOHNS, MARY - ETAL MINOR	JOHNS, LUCINDA - GDN.	7
JOHNS, Motier & Lewis - Minors	JOHNS, THOS. M. - GDN.	7
JOHNS, SHERMAN - DECD.	JOHNS, C.W. - ADMR.	99
JOHNSON, A.D. - DECD.	JOHNSON, L.A. - ADMR.	8
JOHNSON, ALEX	WALTERS, A.D. - ADMR.	90
JOHNSON, ALEX - ETAL	JOHNSON, ADA A.M. - GDNSHIP.	62
JOHNSON, ARTHUR LEE - DECD.	Johnson, Estelle Kimbell - Exec. Will	155
JOHNSON, BOB - MINORS	JOHNSON, ISAAC - GDN.	30
JOHNSON, DELILAH - DECD.	JOHNSON, G.M. - ADMR.	74
Johnson, Dempsey, Oscar, Chancery	JOHNSON, DELILAH - Dis Non Age	75
JOHNSON, E.H. - DECD.	JOHNSON, ROBERT E. - ADMR.	77
JOHNSON, ELIAS - DECD.	BEECHER, JOHN F. - ADMR.	7
JOHNSON, ELMA - VS.	Whitehead, Aubrey - Sale of Land	134
JOHNSON, F.B. - DECD.	DANIELS, T.J. - EXEC.	90
JOHNSON, FELDER B. - DECD.	JOHNSON, CLARENCE C. - ADMR.	135
JOHNSON, G. MONROE - DECD.	JOHNSON, ANNIE F. - ADMR.	115
JOHNSON, G.M. - ETAL	TENANTS IN COMMON	75
JOHNSON, GEO. S.	JOHNSON, J.I. - ADMR.	74
JOHNSON, IDA T.	ALA. ELECTRIC CORP.	151
JOHNSON, IDA T.	LUNACY INQUISITION	88
JOHNSON, J.A. - DECD.	JOHNSON, JASPER	29
JOHNSON, J.P. - DECD.	JOHNSON, G.M. - ADMR.	77
JOHNSON, J.W. - DECD.	WEED, MINNIE - ADMR.	163
JOHNSON, JAMES - DECD.	JOHNSON, MRS. MOLLIE - EXEC.	84
JOHNSON, JARREL - DECD.	SCARBROUGH, J.W. - ADMR.	7
JOHNSON, JIM (COL.) - DECD.	JOHNSON, ALICE - ADMR.	154
JOHNSON, John Irvin - Etal Minors	HARDY, RUBY MAE - GDN.	149
JOHNSON, JOHN LEPPIE - DECD.	GALLOWAY, R.A. - ADMR.	103
JOHNSON, JOSEPH Z. - MINOR	JOHNSON, T.E. - GDN.	56
JOHNSON, L.N. - DECD.	JOHNSON, JOHN MONROE - Admr.	161
JOHNSON, MARTHA S. - DECD.	JOHNSON, WM. M.	29
JOHNSON, MATTIE B.	JOHNSON, J.W. - EXEC. WILL	160
JOHNSON, Mrs. Florrie B. - Decd.	CONRAD, MADGE B. - ADMR.	151
JOHNSON, MRS. M.C. - DECD.	WILL	95
JOHNSON, NANCY A.	WALTERS, A.D. - ADMR.	90
JOHNSON, O.S. - DECD.	JOHNSON, MARTHA G. - ADMR.	8
JOHNSON, S.D. - DECD.	YOUNGBLOOD, J.B.	29
JOHNSON, SOLOMON - DECD.	SESSIONS, JASPER - ADMR.	29
JOHNSON, SQUIRE	LEGITIMACY	67

Jones, Juanita & Sikes, James David	TROY BANK & TRUST CO. - GDN.	160
JONES, L.S. - ETAL	TENANTS IN COMMON	93
JONES, LIVIA - ETAL MINORS	JONES, LEROY - GDN.	50
JONES, LIVIA - MINOR	WESTCOAT, E.J. - GDN.	53
JONES, LOU OLIVE	JONES, MRS. V.O. - NON AGE	75
JONES, LOU OLIVE - ETAL	TENANTS IN COMMON	91
JONES, M.J. - ETAL MINORS	YOUNGBLOOD, JNO. B. - GDN.	15
JONES, MARGARET E. - DECD.	MCLURE, JOHN W. - ADMR.	54
JONES, MARY - DECD.	JONES, L.F. - Admr. & Sale of Land	86
JONES, MIKE - DECD.	JONES, Moriah - Homestead Exempt.	90
JONES, MURRAY - MINOR	JONES, W.B. - GDN.	121
Jones, Nettie, Annie Laurie - Etal	JONES, V.D. - GDN.	74
JONES, PETER - DECD.	ROSS, R.A. - ADMR.	52
JONES, RICHARD - DECD.	JONES, JENNIE - ADMR.	87
JONES, ROBERT - ETAL	JONES, J.A.	62
JONES, ROBERT A. - ADMR.	JONES, MRS. SUSIE C. - ADMR.	106
JONES, S.B.	SIKES, NELL JONES - EXEC. WILL	160
JONES, S.F., B.M. & M.A. - Minors	JONES, U.L. - GDN.	16
JONES, S.L. - DECD.	JONES, MRS. HENRY - ADMR.	151
JONES, SALLY - DECD.	JONES, SANDERS	140
JONES, SANDERS - MINOR	JONES, JENNIE - GDN.	87
JONES, SHELBY E.	N.C.M. & GDN.	131
JONES, SUSIE C. - DECD.	JONES, HAMILTON - EXEC. WILL	162
JONES, URBAN L. - MINORS	BOYD, ALFRED - GDN.	15
JONES, V.D. - DECD.	JONES, W.A. - EXEC.	106
JONES, VICTORIA O. - DECD.	JONES, T.J. - ADMR.	75
JONES, VICTORIA O. - DECD.	JONES, T.J. - ADMR.	87
JONES, W.W. - DECD.	EVANS, J.C. & JONES, V.O. - Admr.	61
JONES, W.W.D. - DECD.	WILL	97
JONES, WILLIAM OSCAR - DECD.	JONES, WILLIAM H. - ADMR.	151
JONES, WM. A. - DECD.	YOUNGBLOOD, JACOB B. - ADMR.	8
JONES, Wm. W. L.J. M.E.; Minors	MORRIS, M.M. - GDN.	7
JORDAN, A.J.	BASTARDY BOND	67
JORDAN, CHARLES	HUTCHISON, ROBERT - GDN.	7
JORDAN, FRANK - MINOR	GDNSHIP.	92
Jordan, Hamilton, Wm., & Thos; decd	WELDON, W.A.	71
JORDAN, HENRY - DECD.	WELDON, W.A. - ADMR.	48
JORDAN, J.J. - DECD.	PARTIN, NORA F. - EXEC. WILL	115
JORDAN, J.J. - ETAL	TENANTS IN COMMON	91
JORDAN, J.T. - DECD.	PARTRIDGE, E.R. - ADMR.	107
JORDAN, JAS. H. - DECD.	STRICKLAN, W.H. - ADMR.	7
JORDAN, JOEL - DECD.	BAILEY, D.E. - ADMR.	7
JORDAN, JOSIAH - MINORS	JORDAN, Richard & James - Admr.	29

JORDAN, L.T. - ETAL	Tenants in Common; Wm. Taylor Lan	84
JORDAN, M.F. - DECD.	JORDAN, W.H. - ADMR.	110
JORDAN, MARY E. - DECD.	JORDAN, J.J. SR. - EXEC. WILL	106
JORDAN, MINNIE - MINOR	JORDAN, JENNIE BELLE - GDN.	97
JORDAN, ROSS - ETAL	TENANTS IN COMMON	7
JORDAN, SAMUEL B. - DECD.	HUGHLY, JOSEPH - ETAL	29
JORDAN, T.L. - ADMR.	BOTTOMS, CASTILAR	158
JUSTICE, H.N. - DECD.	1ST F & M NAT'L. BANK - WILL	163
KEELS, ISAAC - DECD.	KEELS, NICY - ADMR.	30
KEENER, JAS. M. - DECD.	CLAYTON, ISHAM B. - EXEC.	8
KELLEY, B.F. - ETAL	TENANTS IN COMMON	91
KELLEY, James Harris - Etal Minors	KELLEY, J.Z. - GDN.	131
KELLEY, Thomas Madison - Decd.	ENZOR, LANE - EXEC. WILL	133
KELLY, ANDREW J.	KELLY, D.L. - ADMR.	105
KELLY, BONNIE R. - MINOR	BAXLEY, W.M. - GDN. (91 or 92)	92
KELLY, ELIAS - DECD.	KELLY, JOHN J. - ADMR.	30
KELLY, ELINOR - ETAL MINORS	KNIGHT, NORA R. - GDN.	97
KELLY, G.J. - ETAL MINORS	Howard, James - Gdn. (Est. Bk. 9)	?
KELLY, J.M. - MINORS	KELLY, JAS. - GDN.	14
KELLY, J.M. - VS.	Howard, John D. - Partition of crops	105
KELLY, JAMES - DECD.	KELLY, Elias - Admr. (Box 56 or 58)	?
KELLY, JAMES M. - MINORS	BROOKS, M.M. - GDN.	8
KELLY, MARY A.		92
KENDRICK, SARAH E. - DECD.	SANDERS, W.S. - Etal Exec. Will	115
KENEDY, ELIZABETH - MINORS	Farnell, Robert J.; Gdn. (in Est. bk. 11	?
Kennedy, Jas, Bennie, Mary, Frank	KENNEDY, MRS. N.W. - GDN.	76
KENNEDY, MARTHA A. - DECD.	KENNEDY, ROBERT B. - EXEC.	79
KENNEDY, MYRTLE - VS.	PHILLIPS, J.D. - HABEAS CORPUS	104
KENT, KERCIE M. - ETAL MINORS	KENT, J.H. - GDN.	89
KENT, KESSIE	KENT, J.H.	98
KERCH, JOHN D. - MINOR	KERCH, L.C. - GDNSHIP.	95
KERSEY, JOHN - SLAVE	To Become Gdn. (in Est. Bk. 11)	?
KEY, Drucilla Steverson - Decd.	SENN, MATTIE LEE - ADMR.	138
KEY, JOHN - DECD.	DARBY, JEFF - ADMR.	30
KEY, SARAH E. - DECD.	HILLIARD, J.B. - ADMR.	100
KILGORE, GEO. W.	BELL, JOS. - ADMR.	68
KILGORE, T.L. - DECD.	BORUM, B.F. - ADMR.	56
KILLINGSWORTH, J.A. - DECD.	JORDAN, IONE K. - ADMR.	98
Killingsworth, Rosanna D. - Decd.	BASHINSKY, L.M. - EXEC. WILL	116
KILPATRICK, DAVID D. - DECD.	KILPATRICK, H.E. - ADMR.	86
KILPATRICK, RUFUS - Etal Minors	KILPATRICK, H.E. - GDN.	86
KILPATRICK, THOS. J. - DECD.	KILPATRICK, LILLIE J. - EXEC.	101
KIMBELL, JEWELL	Leverette, Annie T. - Dis Non Age	84

KIMBELL, MINNIE CLAUDE	KIMBELL, ANNIE T. - DIS NON AGE	82
KIMBELL, Minnie Claude & Jewell	KIMBELL, ANNIE T. - GDN.	81
KIMBER, DID - DECD.	KIMBER, ARCHIE - ADMR.	155
KINARD, EULA B. - DECD.	MCNEIL, MAMIE K. - EXEC. WILL	145
KINDRED, AVER B. - DECD.	McFaden, Ethel; will of G.A. Kindred	163
KINDRED, F.L. & J.H. - MINOR	KINDRED, HENRY - GDN.	30
KINDRED, G.A.	BROOKS, DOUGLAS & MRS. RAY	74
KINDRED, G.A. - DECD.	KINDRED, AVER M. - EXEC.	116
KINDRED, HOMER F. - MINOR	GREEN, A.U. - GDN.	103
KINDRED, HOMER F. - MINOR	GREEN, A.N. - GDN.	103
KINDRED, James Samuel - Minor	KINDRED, H.F. - GDN.	148
KINDRED, JOHN B. - DECD.	KINDRED, THRESA EPSA - WILL	136
KINDRED, MARY ANN - MINOR	COSTON, G.C. - GDN.	167
Kindred, Nolen & John A.; etal minors	GREEN, A.N. - GDN. Docket bk. 2	103
KINDRICK, JOHN M. - DECD.	KINDRICK, SAMUEL C.	82
KING, CHARLES		161
KING, CLARENCE E. - Etal Minors	KING, C.C. - GDNSHIP.	62
KING, CYNTHIA - ETAL MINORS	LINDSAY, W.P. - GDNSHIP.	62
KING, FRANKLIN E. - DECD.	Lightfoot, Bascom H. - Exec. Will	154
KING, G.N. - DECD.	CARLISLE, MARY - ADMR.	161
KING, GEO. W. - DECD.	MOXLEY, D.N. - ADMR.	53
KING, J.D.		161
KING, J.F. & D.W. - ETAL	TENANTS IN COMMON	91
KING, JOHN F. - DECD.	KING, GEO. W. - EXEC.	8
KING, L.C. - ETAL	HOMESTEAD	72
KING, L.C. - ETAL	TENANTS IN COMMON	73
KING, LUCY J. - DECD.	KING, J.F. & D.W. - ADMR.	91
KING, MARY W. - ETAL MINORS	WOOD, DAN'L. S. - GDN.	8
KING, NORMAN - DECD.	KING, LARKIE - ADMR.	143
KING, ROBERT - DECD.	GUADE, HINES H. - ADMR.	8
KING, ROY - ETAL MINORS	KING, FLORENCE - GDN.	91
KING, RUTH ELIZABETH	KING, MAGGIE L. - GDN.	98
KING, SUSAN - ETAL MINORS	KING, GEO. W. - GDN.	8
KING, T.B.	KING, O.A. - EXEC. WILL	97
KING, VERNON - DECD.	KING, MRS. VERNON - ADMR.	129
KING, W.E. - DECD.	KING, HENRY P. - EXEC. WILL	85
KING, WALKER - ETAL MINORS	KING, W.W. - GDN.	92
KING, WILLIE JOE - MINOR	ROUSE, J.J. - GDN.	66
KING, WM. R. & N.D. - MINORS	KING, C.B. - GDN.	14
KIRKSEY, I.C. - ETAL	TENANTS IN COMMON	93
KLASING, MRS. N.A.	RAMSEY, MRS. H.K. - ETAL EXEC.	105
KNIGHT, A.J. - DECD.	KNIGHT, LULA - ADMR.	71
KNIGHT, ABIGAIL - ETAL	TENANTS IN COMMON	80

LAW, MRS. S.A. - DECD.	DOZIER, EVELYN - ADMR.	153
LAW, W.H. - DECD.	NIXON, L.C. - ADMR. WILL	140
LAW, WILSON P.	POPE, W.B. - ADMR.	106
LAWHORN, JOHN - MINOR	LAWHORN, SPIAS - GDN.	14
LAWRENCE, E.Y. - ETAL	TENANTS IN COMMON	76
LAWRENCE, J.S. - DECD.	Lawrence, Mattie L.; Homestead to	157
LAWRENCE, JESSE - DECD.	REEVES, B.R. - ADMR.	132
Lawrence, Jessie & Raymond; Minors	ANDERSON, F.S. - GDN.	132
LAWRENCE, M.J. - ETAL MINORS	MITCHELL, E.F. - GDN.	56
LAWRENCE, R.O. - DECD.	LAWRENCE, CARROLL - ADMR.	123
LAWRENCE, SARAH - DECD.	LAWRENCE, WM. - ADMR.	8
LAWRENCE, STEPHEN	EXPARTE	51
LAWRENCE, WM. - DECD.	ROSS, R.A. - ADMR.	52
LAWSON, BOOKER - ETAL	HARRIS, JOS. W. - GDN.	60
LAWSON, BOOKER - ETAL MINOR	HARRIS, M.J. - GDN.	56
LAWSON, D.H. - ETAL GDN.	TO CONVEY LAND	100
LAWSON, ELIZA	EXPARTE HABEAS CORPUS	14
LAWSON, ELIZABETH - DECD.	REDDOCH, W.M. - ADMR.	72
LAWSON, FRANCES LAW	LAWSON, D.H. - EXEC.	100
LAWSON, JOHN R. - DECD.	LAWSON, M.J. - PETITIONER	49
LAWSON, JOHN R. - DECD.	LAWSON, M.J. - ADMR.	74
LAWSON, JOHN R. - ETAL	TENANTS IN COMMON	59
LAWSON, LAURA A. - DECD.	LAWSON, V.D. - ADMR.	116
LAWSON, LUCILE - ETAL	LAWSON, D.H. - GDN.	100
LAWSON, MINIOLA - ETAL	LAWSON, A.L. - GDN.	61
LAWSON, MINNIE E. - ETAL	LAWSON, JAMES - GDN.	100
LAWSON, MRS. M.J. (WILL)	LAWSON, BOOKER - EXEC.	104
LAWSON, MRS. M.J. - ETAL	TENANTS IN COMMON	84
LAWSON, WM. (C) - DECD.	MCEACHERN, J.A. - ADMR.	58
LEACH, JAS. M. - DECD.	WATSON, N.C. - ADMR.	8
LEAKE, WM. B. - DECD.	MCQUEEN, D.M. - ADMR.	31
LECROY, WM. M. - DECD.	Lecroy, Eliza - Widow's Exemption	94
LEDBETTER, ALONZA M. - DECD.	REYNOLDS, FANNIE E. - ADMR.	79
LEDBETTER, GEORGE A. - DECD.	LEDBETTER, RUTH - ADMR.	111
LEDBETTER, Georgia Ruth - Minor	LEDBETTER, RUTH - GDN.	149
LEE, B.H. - ETAL MINOR	LEE, W.W. & MRS. C.E. - GDN.	72
LEE, B.H. - ETAL MINOR	REEVES, J.M. - GDN.	70
LEE, BETSY - ETAL DECD.	TENANTS IN COMMON	8
LEE, EMMA - ETAL MINOR	LEE, R.E. - GDN.	68
LEE, EVAN - DECD.	LEE, CHARLOTTE E. - ADMR.	70
LEE, GEORGE	NELMS, WILL	148
LEE, GRADY - DECD.	REEVES, BEN - ADMR.	166
LEE, HENRIETTA - MINOR	HIGHTOWER, J.F. - GDN.	101

LEE, JAMES - DECD.	RAINER, C.W. - ADMR.	31
LEE, MATILDA E. - MINOR	LEE, BENJAMIN - GDN.	8
LEE, MINNIE	LEE, W.W. - ADMR.	71
LEE, MRS. LENA PRICE	CITY OF TROY - CONDEMNATION	142
LEE, SAM'L. P. - ETAL MINORS	FAULK, T.S. - GDN.	70
LEE, SILAS - DECD.	BRANTLEY, T.K. - GDN.	51
LEE, W.P. - DECD.	HENDRICK, W.L. - ADMR.	31
LEE, WILLIAM - DECD.	LEE, MARTHA A. - EXEC.	8
LEE, WILLIE E. - DECD.	HIGHTOWER, J.W. - ADMR. WILL	144
LEHMAN BROS. - ETAL	TENANTS IN COMMON	57
LEHMAN BROS. - VS.	SMITH, C.C. - Petition for Partitioner	57
LEIGHTON, JOHN W. - DECD.	LEIGHTON, MARY A. - WILL	90
LESLIE, FELIX W. - DECD.	LESLIE, Mollie Jones - Exec. Will	159
LEVERETT, HIRAM J. - DECD.	REEVES, M.J. - ADMR.	31
LEVERETTE, J.E. - DECD.	LEVERETTE, W.W. - ADMR.	122
LEVERETTE, Mrs. Mattie P. - Decd.	LEVERETTE, W.W. - ADMR.	141
LEWIS, ELISHA - DECD.	CHAPMAN, JAS. A. - ADMR.	8
LEWIS, JAMES - ETAL MINOR	LEWIS, L.L. - GDN.	8
LEWIS, JAS. L.	EXPARTE - AD QUO DAMMN	8
LEWIS, JOHN F. - DECD.	LEWIS, CARO - EXEC. WILL	152
LEWIS, MOSES W. - DECD.	LEWIS, GEORGIA ANN - ADMR.	81
LEWIS, PINKIE LEE - MINOR	BEAN, ALTARA - GDN.	122
LEWIS, R.H. - ETAL	TENANTS IN COMMON	71
LIDDON, J.J. - LUNATIC	LIDDON, A.M. - GDN.	8
LIGHTFOOT, JOSEPH I. - DECD.	LIGHTFOOT, R.M. - Exec. Etal Will	155
LIGHTFOOT, M. - DECD.	LIGHTFOOT, TUPPER - ADMR.	113
LIGHTFOOT, SUSIE P. - DECD.	LIGHTFOOT, B.H. - ADMR.	146
Lignoski, Mrs. B.G.; F.B. Lignoski, dec	EXPARTE	67
LIGON, D.W. - ETAL MINOR	LIGON, REBECCA - GDN.	8
Lindsay, Robt. L. & Julio O. - Minors	WRIGHT, R.G. - GDN.	90
LINDSEY, JOHN H. - DECD.	FOLMAR, M.C. - ADMR.	89
LINDSEY, JORDAN	BOSWELL, F.A. - GDN.	8
LINDSEY, NATHAN H. - DECD.	LINDSEY, LEWIS - ADMR.	8
LINDSEY, WM. - DECD.	CLOUD, WM. - ADMR.	31
LINTON, BUSTER - MINOR	OWENS, T.A. - GDN.	94
LINTON, CELESTIA P. - MINOR	SATCHER, J.W. - GDN.	8
LINTON, J.A. - ETAL	PET. FOR DIVISION	82
LINTON, JOHN & WINNIE - MINOR	SANDERS, JERE - GDN.	8
LINTON, MALINDA - ETAL	TENANTS IN COMMON - PET.	75
LINTON, WM. - ETAL MINOR	LINTON, J.M. - GDN.	24
LINZEY, SALTER - ETAL	TENANTS IN COMMON	100
LIPTROT, JOHN - DECD.	SCARBROUGH, JAS. W. - ADMR.	49
LIPTROT, WILLIE - MINOR	FAULK, LAURANIE - GDN.	49

LIPTROTT, K. - ETAL MINOR	FAULK, LURANA - GDN.	8
LIPTROTT, WM. A. - DECD.	FAULK, LURANN - ADMR.	31
LITTLE, JOHN N. - DECD.	CATRETT, W.J. - ADMR.	31
LITTLEJOHN, THOMAS P. - DECD.	SMITH, A.E. - ADMR.	140
LIVINGS, T.S. - DECD.	Livings, Mrs. Tinie - Pet. for Exemptio	85
LIVINGSTON, EMILY - ETAL	TENANTS IN COMMON	53
LIVINGSTON, W.A. - EXPARTE	PET. FOR WRIT OF LUNACY	81
LLOYD, LEROY - DECD.	LOYD, C. & E. - ADMR.	31
LOCK, RICHARD - DECD.	LOCK, JESSE - ADMR.	31
LOCKARD, A.T. - DECD.	ZACHRY, MITTIE E. - ADMR.	62
LOCKARD, MRS. M.J. - DECD.	BASHINSKY, L.M. - EXEC.	101
LOCKARD, PHOEBE J. - MINOR	LOCKARD, A.J. - GDN.	24
LOCKART, RICHARD M. - DECD.	LOCKART, WINAFRED - ADMR.	31
LOCKE, E.H. & R.D. - MINORS	JONES, U.L. - GDN.	8
LOCKE, E.H. - DECD.	WILL	97
LOFTIN, ANNIE JANE - DECD.	LOFTIN, H.D. - ADMR.	139
LOGUE, HUBERT LAMAR	LOGUE, HATTIE A. - ADMR.	105
LONG, DAVID A. - DECD.	LONG, WM. A. - ADMR.	31
LONG, J.T.	THOMPSON, W.L. - ADMR.	94
LONG, JAMES B. - DECD.	LONG, MARY J. - ADMR.	31
LONG, MARY A. - LUNATIC	LONG, WM. A. - PET.	8
LORD, JUDSON - ETAL	TENANTS IN COMMON	11
LOTT, ARIE LEE - ETAL	TENANTS IN COMMON	116
LOTT, George Washington - Decd.	TROY BANK & TRUST CO. - Admr.	140
LOTT, L.L. - DECD.	LOTT, C.L. - ADMR.	132
LOTT, WILLIAM HOWARD - MINOR	LOTT, JAMES H. - GDN.	109
LOVE, WM. M. - DECD.	MURPHREE, JOEL D. - Admr. Will	71
LOVELESS, D.J. - MINOR	GRIGGS, SARAH H. - GDN.	8
LOW, WM. & JOHN A. - MINORS	LOW, JESSE - GDN.	31
LOWE, WM. - DECD.	LOWE, MARY R. - ADMR.	8
LOWERY, R.A. - DECD.	LOWERY, SARAH - EXEC. WILL	152
LOYD, LEROY - ETAL MINOR	LOYD, J.T. - GDN.	14
LUCKIE, E.I. - MINOR	LUCKIE, JAS. B. - GDN.	8
LUCKIE, ELIZA - MINOR	FIELDER, J.H. - GDN.	15
LUCUS, WM. H. - MINOR	WATTS, ASBERRY - GDN.	24
LUDLAM, SAMUEL - DECD.	OLIVER, WILLIAM - ADMR.	31
Ludlow, Jeremiah - Decd. (Ludlam?)	RHODES, JOHN F. - ADMR.	31
LUDLOW, John - Decd. (Ludlum?)	SELF, DAVID - ADMR.	31
LUDLOW, Martha - Minor (Ludlam?)	Ludlow, Jeremiah - Gdn. (Ludlam?)	14
LUDLOW, WM. - MINOR	LUDLOW, ELIZA - GDN.	8
LUVERNE TELEPHONE CO.	CENTRAL OF GA..R.R. CO.	71
LYNN, LEROY W. - DECD.	PERDUE, J.S. - ADMR.	8
LYONS, ROBERT R. - DECD.	LYONS, MARY S. - ADMR.	162

MACON, AMANDA - ETAL	TENANTS IN COMMON	86
MACON, BETTIE - DIS. NON AGE	MIN. BOOK O	86
Macon, George C. - Dis. of Non Age	MIN. BOOK O, PAGE 100	86
MACON, L.W. - DECD.	MACON, MOLLIE - EXEC. WILL	137
MACON, T.H. - ETAL	TENANTS IN COMMON	116
MADISON, JAMES - MINOR	HOBDY, IRA - ETAL GDN.	24
MADISON, LOTTIE - Etal Minors	MADISON, THOMAS - GDN.	77
MAHONEY, C.T. - DECD.	MAHONEY, M.M. - ADMR.	33
MAHONEY, M.M. - ETAL	TENANTS IN COMMON	53
MAHONEY, MARTHA - Etal Minors	MAHONEY, ELIZABETH - GDN.	9
MALLETT, CHARLES N. - DECD.	LOFLIN, LORENA R. - EXEC. WILL	137
MALPRESS, LYDIA - DECD.	HENDERSON, J.E.W. - ADMR.	49
MAN, LEWIS - DECD.	MAN, J.W. - ETAL ADMR.	32/3
MANCILL, C.C. - ETAL MINOR	FAULK, JOS. F. - GDN.	9
MANN, or Marr, LEWIS - DECD.	MANN, or Marr, J.M. - ETAL ADMR.	32
MANN, ROBT. - LUNATIC	THOMAS, JOHN F. - ETAL GDN.	24
MANNING, LUCY LORAIN	HABEOUS CORPUS	92
MANNING, W.H. - DECD.	GIBSON, WM. A. - ADMR.	35
MANNING, W.H. - Heirs of, Minor	GIBSON, WM. A. - GDN.	24
MANSEL, G.W.	EXPARTE	58
MANSELL, ELISHA - Non Compos	MANSELL, WM. - GDN.	33
MANSELL, JOHN - DECD.	MANSEL, ELIZA - ADMR.	33
MANSELL, SAM'L. J. - ETAL	MANSELL, ELIZABETH - GDN.	24
MARK, HAROLD D. & M.V.	DOUGLAS, B.I. - GDN.	73
MARLOW, ZACHERY - DECD.	DUBOSE, SAMUEL - ADMR.	32
MARR, or Mann, LEWIS - DECD.	MARR, or Mann, J.M. - ETAL ADMR.	32
MARSH, MILDRED & M.L. JR.	PRITCHETT, CARRIE	98
MARSHALL, ANNIE - ETAL	MARSHALL, W.S. - GDN.	71
Marshall, Bobbie L. - Etal Minors	Marshall, W.S.; Wm. E. Dixon, decd.	82
MARTIN, BENJ. - DECD.	MARTIN, J.C. - ADMR.	34
MARTIN, CARLOS	MARTIN, JAMES - ADMR.	137
MARTIN, Charlie, Finnie & Sam L.	FARNELL, J.D. - Apprenticeship	83
MARTIN, JOHN - DECD.	MARTIN, JOHN Y. - ADMR.	34
MARTIN, JOHN - MINOR	MCLEOD, A.G. - APPRENT.	11
MARTIN, LEO	PENNINGTON, A.L. - GDN.	62
MARTIN, MARTHA - DECD.	WHITE, WYLEY - ADMR.	33
MARTIN, MARY A. - MINOR	HILL, BENJ. A.	11
MARTIN, Mattie & Willie - Minors	MARTIN, W.D. - GDN.	50
MARTIN, Y. - DECD.	MARTIN, J.H. - ADMR.	32
MARTIN, YERBY - DECD.	MARTIN, JAS. H. - ADMR.	9
MASSEY, J.A. - DECD.	MASSEY, ETHEL - EXEC. WILL	159
MATHEWS, ARTHUR - DECD.	MATHEWS, EDWARD - ADMR.	32/3
MATHEWS, ARTHUT - DECD.	MATHEWS, SARAH - ADMR.	34

MATHEWS, DAVE - DECD.	Homestead Exempt.; Florence Mathev	144
MATHEWS, LEROY - MINOR	STEPHENSON, WM. H. - GDN.	24
MATHEWS, LOUISE - MINOR	RODGERS, ANNIE - GDN.	119
MATHEWS, MOLLIE - ETAL	TENANTS IN COMMON	71
MATHEWS, NANCY E.	BASHINSKY, L.M. - GDN.	86
Mathews, Nancy E.; Non Comp. Ment	MINUTE BOOK O or Q, PAGE 101	86
MATHEWS, PRUDENCE - DECD.	SHIRLEY, J.S. - ADMR.	52
MATHEWS, RUBY LEE - DECD.	MATHEWS, IDA F. - ADMR.	89
MATHEWS, SMITH - ETAL MINOR	CAIN, HIX - GDN.	24
MATTHEWS, JOHN H. - DECD.	MATHEWS, JOEL - ADMR.	11
MATTHEWS, NANCY E. - DECD.	WHITE, D.J. - ADMR.	88
MAUGHON, MITCHELL D. - DECD.	LIGHTFOOT, M. - WILL	85
Maughon, Robert, Jesse, Cora; Minor	MAUGHON, M.T. - GDN.	82
MAXWELL, ARTHUR	CLARK, W.J. - ADMR.	113
MAXWELL, J.F. - DECD.	MCDOWELL, ALEX - ADMR.	34
MAXWELL, JOHN F. - DECD.	MCGUIRE, JAMES - ADMR.	32
MAY, BARBARA S. - DECD.	NEFF, MAUDE E. - WILL	90
MAY, CHASTENE - DECD.	Buchanan, Lillie A. - Etal Exec. Will	143
MAY, JAMES - DECD.	ARRINGTON, J.N. - ADMR.	10
MAY, W.H. - DECD.	MAY, MARY M. - EXEC. WILL	161
MCADAMS, THOMAS - DECD.	FOLMAR, I.S. - ADMR.	35
MCAFEE, FLORENCE A. - MINOR	EDWARDS, J.J. - GDN.	9
MCAFEE, JOSEPH - DECD.	MCAFEE, W.S. - ADMR.	9
MCAFEE, W.S. - ETAL	TENANTS IN COMMON	62
MCBETH, Neil & Sarah A. - Minor	MCLEAN, JOHN B. - GDN.	9
MCBETH, WALTER - DECD.	LOVE, A.P. - ADMR.	32
MCBRYDE, A.J. - DECD.	MCBRYDE, KANNIE - WILL	90
MCBRYDE, JAS. - DECD.	MCBRYDE, J.C.	92
MCBRYDE, MARTHA - MINOR	BUTLER, PEARL MCBRYDE - GDN.	81
MCBRYDE, MATTIE E. - DECD.	MCBRYDE, B.R. - EXEC.	162
MCBURNEY, DeHUGH - DECD.	MCBURNEY, JOS. C. - ADMR.	33
MCCALL, CHARLES R. - DECD.	MCCALL, EMILY FOSTER - WILL	67
MCCALL, G.A. - DECD.	CROSSLEY, E.A. - EXEC.	53
MCCALL, KATHERINE R. - DECD.	WILKERSON, J.H. - EXEC. WILL	152
MCCALL, MARTHALEEN - MINOR	WILLIFORD, LUTHER F.	134
MCCALL, SARAH - DECD.	JOHNSON, WM. - ADMR.	34
MCCARA, FREDERIC A.	KEY, Hortense M. - Gdn. (Equity Ct.)	103
MCCARRA, W.T. - DECD.	LAW, JOHN A. - ADMR.	33
MCCARTHA, C.L. SR. - WILL	MCCARTHA, C.L. JR.	94
MCCARTHA, CLARENCE L. - Decd.	MCCARTHA, MABEL T. - Exec. Will	158
MCCARTHA, LOULA L. - DECD.	MCCARTHA, CLARENCE L. - Admr.	119
MCCARTY, JACK	EXPARTE	58
MCCASKELL, D.C. - DECD.	MCLEOD, N. - ADMR.	31

MCCASKELL, GILBERT A. - DECD.	TERRY, CLIFF - ADMR.	9
MCCASKILL, CHRISTIAN - DECD.	MCCASKILL, DAN'L. - ADMR.	34
MCCASKILL, KENNETH - DECD.	JOINER, J.A. - ADMR.	49
MCCASKILL, LEWIS	MCCASKILL, MRS. C.A. - ADMR.	92
MCCOMB, VEOLA	ANDERSON, W.M. - GDN.	96
MCCOMMACK, MARVIN - MINOR	HORN, F.C. - GDN.	95
MCCORMICK, JOHN C. - DECD.	SMITH, WILBORN - ADMR.	34
MCCRARY, ELMIRA - MINOR	MCCRARY, AMANDA - GDN.	9
MCCRARY, J.W. - DECD.	MCCRARY, L.J. - ADMR.	10
MCCRARY, T.K. - DECD.	COLLINS, C.B. - ETAL	32
MCCRARY, THOMAS - MINOR	COLLINS, C.B. - GDN.	9
MCCRUMMIN, ALEX - DECD.	MOORE, DAN'L. - ADMR.	33
MCCRUMMIN, HENRY - MINOR	DOWNING, H.J. - GDN.	9
MCCRUMMING, R. - DECD.	WILLBANKS, E. - ADMR.	32
MCCULLOUGH, E.A. & A.A. - Minor	MCCULLOUGH, ELIZA - GDN.	24
MCCULLOUGH, FANNIE - DECD.	MCNEIL, A.O. - ADMR.	167
MCCULLOUGH, JAMES - DECD.	MCCULLOUGH, WILLIAM - ADMR.	24
MCCULLOUGH, JOS. - DECD.	MCCULLOUGH, WM. M. - ADMR.	24/3.
MCCULLOUGH, SALLIE C. - ETAL	TENANTS IN COMMON	10
MCDANIEL, MARTHA - MINOR	MCDANIEL, A.M. - GDN.	9
MCDANIEL, MATTIE G. - MINORS	MCDANIEL, W.F. - GDN.	72
MCDANIEL, WEBSTER - Etal Minor	MURPHY, W.O. - GDN.	77
MCDONALD, ELIZA - DECD.	MCDONALD, JOHN - ADMR.	109
McDonald, J.H. & Margaret - Decd.	WINDHAM, W.T. - ADMR. WILL	130
MCDONALD, J.W. & T.W. - ETAL	TENANTS IN COMMON	9
MCDONALD, NELL - ETAL MINOR	MCDONALD, EMMA - GDNSHIP.	84
McDonald, Thomas - Heirs of; Minors	MCDONALD, AGNES - GDN.	24
MCDORRELL, SMITH		35
MCDOWELL, ALEX - DECD.	MCDOWELL, JOHN S. - ADMR.	8
MCDOWELL, ALEX - DECD.	MCDOWELL, J.S. - ADMR.	34
MCDOWELL, JAMES - DECD.		35
MCDOWELL, MABLE R. - DECD.	MCDOWELL, M.L. - ADMR.	151
MCDOWELL, MARY T. - DECD.	JACKSON, J.H. - ADMR.	118
MCDOWELL, Oscar Kyle - Minor	McDowell, M.L.; Gdn. (Trans. Cir. Ct.)	151
MCDOWELL, W.D. - DECD.	MCDOWELL, JANE - ADMR.	34
MCDOWELL, WM. D. - DECD.	MCDOWELL, JAMES - ADMR.	32
MCDUFFEE, JOHN - DECD.	JOHNSON, WM. M. - ADMR.	33
MCDUFFEE, JOHN - MINORS	NALL, JAMES P. - GDN.	24
MCEACHERN, HADLEY A. - DECD.	WALLACE, WILL B. - EXEC. WILL	150
MCEACHERN, J.D. - ETAL MINOR	MCEACHERN, J.D. - GDN.	9
MCEACHERN, JOHN A. - DECD.		89
MCEACHERN, WM. C. - DECD.	MCEACHERN, C.P. - ADMR.	118
MCELVEY & NEAL	TENANTS IN COMMON	81

MCGHEE, MATTIE L. - DECD.	MCGHEE, J.A. - ADMR.	73
MCGILVRAY, J.W.	McGilvray, W.A. - Admr. (Equity Ct.)	95
MCGILVRAY, J.W.	McGilvray, H.T., De Bonis Non (Eq. C	133
MCGILVRAY, JOHN A. - DECD.	MCGILVRAY, SALLIE E. - ADMR.	113
MCGOURTS, JAS. & WM. - MINOR	HAYS, JOS. - GDN.	24
MCGOWEN, JOHN - DECD.	WORTHY, A.C. - ADMR.	58
McGowen, Thadeus A. - Etal Minor	YOUNGBLOOD, JNO. B. - GDN.	9
MCGOWEN, THOMAS D.S. - Decd.	TAYLOR, EZEKIEL - ADMR.	32
MCGOWIN, Everett & Jack - Minors	MCGOWIN, JOSEPHINE - GDN.	140
MCGRADY, ROBERT - DECD.	RHODES, JOHN F. - ADMR.	33
MCGUIR, Nancy Jane - Etal Minors	RAMAGE, JAS. T. - GDN.	94
MCGUIRE, DANIEL SR. - DECD.	MCGUIRE, GABE & STEVE - EXEC.	85
MCGUIRE, HOWARD D. - DECD.	MCGUIRE, JAMES - Gdn. (Equity Ct.	128
MCGUIRE, STEPHEN - DECD.	MCGUIRE, GABRIEL - ADMR.	92
MCILHENNY, SARAH G. - DECD.	GOLDTHWAITE, Charles B. - Will	76
MCINTYRE, ED L. - DECD.	GARDNER, JNO. D. - ADMR.	9
MCKAY, JOHN - DECD.	MCKAY, ALEXANDER - ADMR.	9
MCKEE, A.J. - MINORS	SCARBROUGH, J.N. - GDNSHIP.	61
MCKINNEY, BEAUFORD L. - DECD.	MCKINNEY, IDA L. - ADMR.	147
MCKINNIS, FRANK - DECD.	MCKINNIS, MATTIE LEE - ADMR.	145
MCKINNON, DANIEL - DECD.	MCKINNON, LAUCHLAN - ADMR.	9
MCKINNON, JNO. B. - ETAL MINOR	MCKINNON, LAUCHLIN - GDN.	9
MCKINNON, JOHN - MINOR	MCKINNON, LAUCHLON - ADMR.	32
MCKNIGHT, DR. T.D. - DECD.	GRIFFIN, H.P. - ADMR.	143
MCKOWN, JOHN - DECD.	WORTHY, A.C. - ADMR.	56
MCLANE, FRANCIS - ETAL MINOR	MCLANE, CATHARINE - GDN.	9
MCLANE, JNO. BILL - DECD.	MCKINNON, LAUCHLAN - ADMR.	9
MCLANEY, ELIZA J. - MINOR	DAVIS, EDWARD - GDN.	9
MCLANEY, F.F. - MINOR	BOSWELL, F.A. - GDN.	9
MCLANEY, JAMES - DECD.	MCLANEY, MARGARET - EXEC.	9
MCLANEY, JAMES - DECD.	MCLANEY, JAMES - ADMR.	63
MCLANEY, JAMES D.	MCLANEY, MRS. ANNIE - GDN.	97
MCLANEY, JAS. M. - ETAL MINOR	BEAN, JOHN - GDN.	9
MCLANEY, JOS. J. or Jr. - J.P.		68
MCLANEY, ROBERT - MINOR	MCLANEY, LILLIE P. - GDN.	94
MCLEAN, CHARLES - DECD.	MCLEAN, EFFY - ADMR.	35
MCLEAN, DUNCAN - DECD.	BLUE, ARCHIBALD - ADMR.	31
MCLEAN, EMMETT J. SR. - DECD.	MCLEAN, EMMETT J. JR. - ADMR.	165
MCLEAN, HENRY A.	BASS, F.C. - WILL	85
MCLEMORE, CORINE - MINOR	BAUGH, T.M.	9
MCLENDON, A.G.	MCLENDON, MITTIE - ADMR.	100
MCLENDON, BRYANT - DECD.	YOUNGBLOOD, J.B. - ADMR.	33
MCLENDON, CHARITY - DECD.	HUEY, W.P. - ADMR.	87

MCLENDON, E. - DECD.	BROOKS, JOSEPH - ADMR.	34
MCLENDON, EVERETT - DECD.	STANLEY, J.W. - ADMR.	32
MCLENDON, G.G. - DECD.	HOMESTEAD EXEMPT	64
MCLENDON, JAMES - DECD.	MCLURE, JOHN - ADMR.	32
MCLENDON, John M. - Etal Minor	LAWRENCE, W.T. - GDN.	9
MCLENDON, JOHN S. - DECD.	KEENER, JAMES M. - ADMR.	10
MCLENDON, Jos. A. - Etal Minors	MCLENDON, MATILDA W. - GDN.	24
MCLENDON, JOSEPHINE - MINOR	CLAYTON & PRUITT - GSN.	9
MCLENDON, Josiah G. - Etal Minor	MCLURE, JOHN - GDN.	24
MCLENDON, NANCY - DECD.	VEASEY, P.J. - EXEC.	57
MCLENDON, SARAH - DECD.	MCLENDON, BRYANT	10
MCLENDON, WM. H. & M. - MINOR	BERRY, M.E. - GDN.	24
MCLEOD, ALEX - DECD.	NEWMAN, WM. - ADMR.	9
MCLEOD, ANGUS - DECD.	MENEFEE, WM. C. - ADMR.	32
MCLEOD, BEN R. - DECD.	MCLEOD, KATE - ADMR.	114
MCLEOD, BRYANT - DECD.	MCLEOD, WM. - ETAL	33
MCLEOD, BRYANT - DECD.	YOUNGBLOOD, JOHN B.	29
MCLEOD, CHARLES F. - DECD.	McLeod, Jack & J.B., Trans. Cir. Ct.	157
MCLEOD, ELIJAH	Ross, Freeman & Darby, Oscar; Appt.	82
MCLEOD, H.C. - DECD.	MCLEOD, HERBERT - EXEC. WILL	114
MCLEOD, HERBERT - DECD.	MCLEOD, Evelyn Knox - Exec. Will	149
MCLEOD, IDA - MINOR	MCLEOD, M.F. - GDN.	74
MCLEOD, NEIL - DECD.	BARTON, J.F. - ADMR.	73
MCLEOD, NORMAN - DECD.	Menefee, W.C. & McLeod, S. - Exec.	9
MCLURE, E.E. & W.F. - MINOR	MCLURE, D.A. - GDN.	9
MCLURE, GUSTAVOS Y.	WILL	68
MCLURE, J.J. - DECD.	MCLURE, R.U. - ADMR.	64
MCLURE, M.K.	WILL	68
MCLURE, MARTHA A.	WILL	68
MCLURE, R.R. - DECD.	MCLURE, J.W. & THOMAS - ADMR.	32
MCLURE, R.U. - ETAL	TENANTS IN COMMON	53
MCLURE, RAY or ROY	MCLURE, FLORA - GDNSHIP.	82
MCLURE, SARAH E.	MCLURE, R.U. - ADMR.	106
MCLURE, WILBERT - DECD.	NICHOLS, PLEAS A. - ADMR.	118
MCMICHAEL, JOHN - DECD.	HILL, J. - ADMR.	35
MCMILLAN, A.R. - MINOR	MCMILLAN, M. - GDN.	9
MCMILLAN, EDWARD - DECD.	McMillan, Dan'l & Margaret - Admr.	32
MCMILLAN, MARGARTT - DECD.	MCMILLAN, DAN'L. - ADMR.	10
MCMILLAN, MARTHA J.	TENANTS IN COMMON	93
McMillan, Pink, Polly & Will - Minors	THOMPSON, J.D. - GDN.	89
MCMILLAN, WILLETTE	BASHINSKY, L.M. - ADMR.	108
MCMORRIS, DAN'L. - DECD.	HOBBIE, M.E. - ADMR.	9
MCNABB, BOISEY	PARK, R.F. - Admr. (Circuit Ct.)	118

MCNEAL, EASTER EPSIE	MCNEAL, E.L. - GDNSHIP.	77
MCNEAL, LINCOLN - DECD.	CATRETT, MARY AGNES - ADMR.	132
MCNEAL, MARY AGNES - MINOR	MCNEAL, EFFIE JANE - GDNSHIP	112
MCNEAL, MRS. M.E. - DECD.	MCNEAL, E.L. - ADMR.	156
MCNEIL, ANN - MINOR	HOBDY, HARRELL - GDN.	24
MCNEIL, CATHERINE - MINORS	WILLIAMS, JUDGE S. - GDN.	24
MCNEIL, I.H. - WILL	MCNEILL, W.M. - EXEC.	101
MCNEIL, JOHN - DECD.	MCNEIL, NANCY - ADMR.	35
MCNEIL, JOHN - MINORS	COX, EMANUEL - GDN.	24
MCNEIL, JOHN A. - DECD.	MCNEIL, SARAH C. - ADMR.	31
MCNEIL, MARY - MINOR	MCNEIL, NANCY - GDN.	24
MCNEIL, S.C. - ETAL	TENANTS IN COMMON	9
MCNEIL, W.M. - ETAL MINOR	MCNEIL, SARAH C. - GDN.	9
MCNEILL, LIZZIE - WILL	GIBSON, V.A. - EXEC.	96
MCNEILL, W.M. - DECD.	MCNEILL, EADIE - EXEC.	135
MCPHAUL, M.C. - DECD.	MCPHAUL, MATTIE C. - ADMR.	155
MCPHERSON, E.A. - WILL	MCPHERSON, Mrs. Huron - Exec.	137
MCRAE, JOE - VS.	STATE AL. - JUDGEMENT	53
MCREE, IDA - MINOR	MCREE, CHAS. - GDN.	75
MCREE, IDA J. - MINORS	MCREE, D.J. - GDN.	65
MCSWAIN, COLLEY - DECD.	McSwain, Leana; Homestead to widov	165
MCSWAIN, MRS. ELIZABETH		145
MCSWEAN, DR. COLIN - DECD.	MCSWEAN, MARGARETT A. - WILL	82
MCVEY, MATTIE - ETAL	Tenants in Com. (Henry Briggs, decd.	81
MCWATERS, MARILDA & MEDA	MCWATERS, W.P. - DIS. NON-AGE	77
MCWATERS, MRS. S.L. - DECD.	1ST F & M NAT'L. BK. - EXEC. WILL	136
MCWATERS, WILLIE G. - LEASE	THOMPSON, W.L. - GDN.	148
MCWATERS, WILLIE G. - VS.	THOMPSON, W.L. - GDN.	137
MCWHORTER, JOHN C. - DECD.	MATHESON, N.A. - ADMR.	35
MEADOWS, JOSHUA - DECD.	MULLINS, T.K. - ADMR.	35
MEADOWS, TEBITHA - Etal Minor	MEADOWS, SUSAN - GDN.	9
MEDLOCK, ANDERSON - DECD.	PICKETT, FREDERICK - ADMR.	33
MEDLOCK, BENJ. - DECD.	PICKETT, FRED - ADMR.	31
MEDLOCK, WM. - DECD.	MEDLOCK, SAM'L. - ADMR.	34
MEDLOCK, WM. JAMES - MINOR	PICKETT, FRED - GDN.	24
MEIRS, DAN'L. T. - DECD.	MEIRS, E.P. - ADMR.	34
MENEFEE, C.E. - DECD.	MENEFEE, W.C. - ADMR.	136
MENEFEE, EMILY E. DECD.	BOWER, W.H. - ADMR.	90
MENEFEE, ERVIN E.	MENEFEE, C.E. - ADMR.	95
MENEFEE, ERVIN L. - DECD.	MENEFEE, W.C. - ADMR.	130
MENEFEE, GUSSIE L. - DECD.	MENEFEE, W.C. -.ADMR.	122
MENEFEE, NORMAN M. - ETAL	TENANTS IN COMMON	82
MENEFEE, RACHEL M. - DECD.	MENEFEE, JAS. H. - ADMR.	34

MENEFEE, W.C. - DECD.	MENEFEE, MARGARET - ADMR.	63
MEREDITH, EZEKIEL - DECD.	SANDERS, JERE - ADMR.	32
MESSICK, ELI - ETAL	TENANTS IN COMMON	114
MESSICK, W.F.		155
METCALF, DAISY C. - DECD.	RYALS, MACKIE M. - ADMR.	144
METCALF, WM. F.	METCALF, JEWEL - ADMR.	105
MIDDLEBROOKS, H.S. - DECD.	FOLMAR, W.D. - ADMR.	76
MIDDLEBROOKS, JOS. B.	MIDDLEBROOKS, MACIE - ADMR.	105
MILES, D.D. - DECD.	MAHONEY, CHAS. T. - ADMR.	35
MILES, D.W.	MAHONEY, CHAS. T. - ADMR.	35
MILES, MARION GRAVES - MINOR	MILES, W.W. - GDN.	95
MILLER, EURALIE S. - DECD.	BOWDEN, ALICE - ADMR.	148
MILLER, FRANK HAMPTON - Minor	MILLER, EURALE - GDN.	145
MILLER, THOMAS - DECD.	MILLER, MARTHA A. - EXEC.	31
MILLER, U.L.	MILLER, MARIE - EXEC. WILL	161
MILLS, ABIJAH H. - MINOR	MILLS, M.A. - GDN.	9
MILLS, ALICE - DECD.	MILLS, G.W. - ADMR.	138
MILLS, ANDREW - DECD.	MILLS, NANCY - ADMR.	34
MILLS, BARBARA - DECD.	JORDAN, ERIN - EXEC. WILL	137
MILLS, EMMA - DECD.	F & M NAT'L. BK. - ADMR.	111
MILLS, HENRY L. - ETAL	TENANTS IN COMMON	9
MILLS, J.H. - DECD.	MILLS, ALICE - ADMR. (CIR. CT.)	120
MILLS, JAMES B. - DECD.	MILLS, M.A. - ADMR.	34
MILLS, M.E. - ETAL	TENANTS IN COMMON	63
MILLS, MARGIE ANN - ETAL	TENANTS IN COMMON	90
MILLS, MINNIE - ETAL VS.	JORDAN, CLINT - SALE OF LAND	138
MILLS, NANCY - DECD.	YOUNGBLOOD, E.J.	33
MILLS, WM. P. - DECD.	MILLS, WM. - ETAL	9
MILNER, SAMANTHA - MINOR	MILNER, WM. - GDN.	9
MIMS, LARKIN N. - DECD.		33
MIMS, THOMAS - DECD.	MIMS, SHADRACK - ADMR.	34
MINCHENER, F.	MINCHENER, W.H. - WILL	92
MINCHENER, GRACE	TENANTS IN COMMON	98
MINCHENER, MARY E. - DECD.	MINCHENER, F. - WILL	79
MINCHENER, MRS. W.H. - DECD.	Minchener, Grace Lee - Exec. Will	150
MINCHENER, W.H. - DECD.	MINCHENER, ALICE - ADMR. WILL	116
MING, HENRY M. - NON COMPOS	MING, A.J. - GDN.	33
MING, NELSON - DECD.	MING, CALLIE - EXEC. WILL	112
MING, T.E.	CHANCE, S. LUTHER - ADMR.	104
MING, WILLIAM - DECD.	ALLEN, WALLACE - ADMR.	33
MING, WILLIAM - NON COMPOS	MING, HENRY M. - GDN.	24
MITCHAM, E.L. - DECD.	MITCHAM, ETHEL L. - ADMR.	155
MITCHELL, ELEANOR	SHIRLEY, H.D. - ADMR.	130

MITCHELL, H.T. & JESSE - MINOR	BAGENTS, JAMES - GDN.	24
MITCHELL, J.F. - DECD.	MITCHELL, ELLEN S. - WILL	96
MITCHELL, J.R. - ETAL MINORS	MITCHELL, WILLIAM	9
MITCHELL, James Arthur - Minor	LAWSON, WM. - GDN.	88
MITCHELL, L.M. - INSANE	MITCHELL, M.L. - GDN.	51
MITCHELL, L.M. - INSANE	MITCHELL, J.F. - GDN.	63
MITCHELL, LUCY - MINOR	BUSH, M.C. - APPRENTICESHIP	62
MITCHELL, MATHEW - DECD.	TAYLOR, E. - ADMR.	33
MITCHELL, R.L.	EXPARTE	9
MITCHELL, REBECCA (LLOYD)	HOMESTEAD EX.	66
MITTENTHAL, DAVID - DECD.	MITTENTHAL, SAM - ADMR.	85
MITTENTHAL, TILLIE W. - DECD.	MITTENTHAL, SAM - ADMR.	117
MIZE, WM. A. - DECD.	MIZE, A.J. - ADMR.	35
MOBILE & GIRARD R.R. CO. - VS.	Henderson, Maggie C. - Etal Condem	58
MOBILE GIRARD R.R.		70
MOBLEY, BELLE - DECD.	MOBLEY, DOC - ADMR.	157
MOBLEY, BRADY - DECD.	MOBLEY, RUBY E. - ADMR.	149
MOBLEY, CLYDE - DECD.	MOBLEY, C.M. - ADMR. (CIR. CT.)	139
MOBLEY, MRS. LUVERNE - DECD.	MOBLEY, BURNICE - ADMR.	136
MONK, MINNIE - ETAL	COLLEY, J.O. - GDN.	118
MOODY, WILBURN CECIL - MINOR	MOODY, MRS. B.M. - GDN.	82
MOONEY, SAM'L. N. - MINORS	CARLISLE, DAN'L. - GDN.	9
MOORE, ADELINE - ETAL MINOR	O'DEY, ANDREW - GDN.	25
MOORE, ANN - DECD.	STINSON, M.B. - ADMR.	31
MOORE, BENJ. F. - DECD.	MOORE, J.C. - ETAL ADMR.	32
MOORE, EZEKIEL - DECD.	ROSS, R.A. - ADMR.	52
MOORE, JAMES C. - DECD.	MOORE, JOHN E. - ADMR.	61
MOORE, JAS. E. - ETAL	TENANTS IN COMMON	67
MOORE, JOHN C. - DECD.	BROWN, J.B. - ADMR.	63
MOORE, JOHN E.	MOORE, JAS. E. - ADMR.	92
MOORE, JOHN R. - DECD.	FRAZER, ALLEN - ADMR.	34
MOORE, John T. & Mary A. - Minors	WINGARD, B.T.A. - GDN.	49
MOORE, JOHN T. - DECD.	ROWELL, R.M. - ADMR.	31
MOORE, JOHN W. - DECD.	MOORE, ELVA J. - ADMR.	10
MOORE, L.D. - DECD.	MOORE, S.B. - ADMR.	9
MOORE, MARGARETT - DECD.	MCLURE, J.A. - ADMR.	67
MOORE, S.H. - MINOR	BRANNEN, W.M. - GDN.	9
MOORE, W.C. - ETAL VS.	MOORE, Clarence, Etal. - sale of land	138
MORELAND, E.L. - DECD.	TAYLOR, M.S. - ADMR.	32
MORELAND, E.N. - DECD.	TAYLOR, M.S. - ADMR.	34
MORELAND, JOHN F. - MINOR	MORELAND, NANCY - GDN.	9
MORELAND, JOSEPH - DECD.	KING, G.W. - ADMR.	34
MORGAN, BENTON	MORGAN, MONROE - GDN.	131

MORGAN, EVA - ETAL	MORGAN, S.M. - GDN.	101
MORGAN, JOE KIRBY - MINOR	HARRELL, J.E. - GDN.	160
MORGAN, JOHN W.	EXPARTE AD QUOD DAMNUN	53
MORGAN, R.R. - DECD.	SELLERS, J.D. - ADMR.	50
MORGAN, S. MONROE - DECD.	MORGAN, MAGGIE - EXEC. WILL	139
MORRIS, CLAUD - MINOR	MORRIS, L.B. - GDN.	9
MORRIS, J.P. - DECD.	COLLIER, J.M. - ADMR.	70
MORRIS, J.P. - DECD.	COLLIER, J.M. - ADMR.	70
MORRIS, RUTH - MINOR	Tenants in Common - V.A. Wise, Gdn	73
MORRIS, RUTH - MINOR	Wise, V.A. - Gdn. sale for reinvestmer	73
MORRISON, A.D. - DECD.	MYERS, IRA - ADMR.	34
MORRISON, ALEX D. - DECD.	MCNAIR, GILBERT - ADMR.	32
MORRISON, JEFF D. - ETAL	TENANTS IN COMMON	68
MORRISON, JOHN (ANNIE J.)	HOMESTEAD EX.	67
MORROW, MARY - DECD.	YOUNGBLOOD, JOHN B. - ADMR.	31
MORROW, PETER G. - DECD.	BEAN, JOHN - ADMR.	31
MOSELEY, WILLIAM - DECD.	TRICE, THOMAS C. - ADMR.	32
MOSELEY, WM. - DECD.	TRICE, THOS. C. - ADMR.	32
MOSER, BOLINDA - DECD.	COOK, RICHARD - EXEC.	33
MOSSER, MARY - ETAL	TENANTS IN COMMON	10
MOSSER, SAMUEL - DECD.	TAYLOR, EZEKIEL - ADMR.	31
MOSSER, SAMUEL B. - MINOR	MOSSER, SAMUEL - GDN.	24
MOTES, ALICE A. - ETAL	TENANTS IN COMMON	98
MOTES, D.H. - DECD.	MOTES, ONA - EXEC. WILL	154
MOTES, DAVID E. - DECD.	MOTES, RAY C. - ADMR.	162
MOTES, DENDY - DECD.	MOTES, WM. N. - ADMR.	31
MOTES, ISAAC	TENANTS IN COMMON	107
MOTES, J.A. - DECD.	MOTES, D.H. - ETAL EXEC. WILL	121
MOTES, JAMES C. - DECD.	MOTES, D.H. - ADMR.	121
MOTES, M.A. - DECD.	MOTES, IRA JEPTHA - EXEC. WILL	156
MOTES, MACKLIN - DECD.	Motes, P.A.; Etal Tenants in Common	9
MOTES, MARTHA A. - DECD.	GRIFFIN, J. LEONARD - WILL	83
MOTES, MORRIS - DECD.	BARNES, L.F. - EXEC.	53
MOTES, P.A. - ETAL MINORS	MOTES, MARTHA - GDN.	53
Motes, Pressley A. - Etal Minor	MOTES, MARTHA - GDN.	24
MOTLEY, NED M.	SELMAN, JOHN L. - EXEC.	166
MT. HILLIARD BAPTIST CHURCH	INCORP.	85
MULKEY, F.G. & SNEED, LETTIE	TENANTS IN COMMON	49
MULKEY, FELIX G. - ETAL	TENANTS IN COMMON	9
MULKEY, HULDY	Mulkey, W.G. - Gdn. Non Comp Ment	78
MULKEY, HULDY - ETAL	TENANTS IN COMMON	74
MULLICAN, W.H. - DECD.	MULLICAN, LILLIE - EXEC.	144
MUNN TRADING CO.	CORP.	84

NICHOLSON, DUNCAN - DECD.	Nicholson, Mary A. & Carter, Jas. M.	34
NILSON, JOHN - DECD.	HAYES, WM. C. - ADMR.	10
NIX, GEO. WASHINGTON - DECD.	WILLIFORD, Sallie Lou Nix - Admr.	164
NIXON, J.L. - DECD.	Jordan, Robert; etal tenants in com.	10
NIXON, JNO. H. - MINORS	JORDAN, J.L. - GDN.	8
NIXON, TINA - MINORS	FITZPATRICK, M.A. - GDN.	8
NOBLES, JOHN - DECD.	NOBLES, J.M. - ADMR.	35
NOBLES, MARK - DECD.	NOBLES, S. & STILL, BENJ. - Admr.	35
NOLAN, ANNIE M. - ETAL	TENANTS IN COMMON	74
NOLAN, BENNIE - ETAL	PARTITION	93
NORDON, A.B. - ETAL	TENANTS IN COMMON	10
NORDON, CLEMENTINE - MINORS	SANDERS, JERE - GDN.	8
NORRIS, F.L.		157
NORTON, GEO. W. - MINORS	LINTON, G.W. - GDN.	8
Norwood, Cornelius C. - Etal minors	DEWBERRY, J.H. - GDN.	8
NORWOOD, M.M. - DECD.	NORWOOD, ELIZA - ADMR. WILL	53
NUNNELEE, J.A. - DECD.	NUNNELEE, JENNIE - ADMR.	94
O'DEY, A.L. & M.A. - MINOR	O'DEY, ANDREW - GDN.	25
O'DEY, CINTHIA - MINOR	O'DEY, ANDREW - GDN.	25
OFFICER, THOMAS - DECD.	THOMPSON, J.M. - ADMR.	10
OGLESBY, Charles Ross - Decd.	SHEFFIELD, James Talbot - Admr.	155
OGLETREE, W.A. - DECD.	OGLETREE, O.C. - ADMR.	144
OLIVER, JAMES C. - DECD.	WINGARD, MARY L. - ADMR.	35
OLIVER, JAMES C. - DECD.	OLIVER, MARY C. - ADMR.	36
OLIVER, MARY - DECD.	OLIVER, WM. J. - ADMR.	35
OLIVER, RICHARD - DECD.	ROSS, R.A. - ADMR.	54
OLIVER, SARAH - ETAL MINOR	OLIVER, WM. J. - GDN.	24
OSTEEN, H.A.	Osteen, Emma B. & Rutherford, Lela	158
OSTEEN, J.I. - DECD.	OSTEEN, MARY - ADMR.	85
OSTEEN, J.I. - ETAL MINORS	OSTEEN, W.M. - GDN.	73
OSTEEN, W.R. - DIS. NON AGE	MINUTE BOOK O, PAGE 127	89
OUSLEY, DAVE & WILL - MINORS	OUSLEY, IRVIN - GDNSHIP.	66
OUSLEY, J.C. - DECD.	JOHNS, LEROY J. - ADMR.	35
OWENS, A.H. - DECD.	EXEMPTIONS	90
OWENS, ARABELLA - ETAL	TENANTS IN COMMON	74
OWENS, ARABELLA - ETAL	TENANTS IN COMMON	74
OWENS, ARTHUR H. - DECD.	OWENS, Arthur Joseph - Exec. Will	167
OWENS, B.M.	OWENS, GEORGE E. - EXEC. WILL	158
OWENS, CORNELIA W. - DECD.	OWENS, B.M. - ADMR.	90
OWENS, IDA - ETAL MINORS	OWENS, R.R. - GDN.	8
OWENS, Jule & Margaret; minors		94
OWENS, M.A.K. - DECD.	OWENS, CHAS. A. - ADMR.	35
OWENS, MRS. C.A.	SALE OF LANDS	132

PAUL, MOSES SR. - DECD.	PAUL, MOSES JR. - ADMR.	37
PAUL, RAY - MINOR	PAUL, OTIS - GDN.	96
PAUL, ROBERT - DECD.	PAUL, MOSES - ADMR.	36
PAULK, FORBES - DECD.	PAULK, JOSHUA - ADMR.	36
PAULK, WM. A. - DECD.	PAULK, JOSHUA - EXEC.	11
PAYNE, THE J.M. MEDICINE CO.	CORPORATION	89
PEA RIVER POWER CO. - VS.	CARROLL, ALMIRA - Etal Condem.	104
Pea River Valley & Gulf R.R. Co.	BAKER, HUFF - Etal Articles of Inc.	75
PEACH, W.F. & G.W. - MINORS	KIRKLAND, N.C. - GDN.	14
PEACOCK, DANIEL W.	PEACOCK, W.R. - ADMR.	97
PEACOCK, JOHN L. - DECD.	PEACOCK, PEARL S. - Exec. Will	167
PEAK, TULA - DECD.	PEAK, S.T. - ADMR.	114
PEARCE, ELIZABETH - MINOR	WHITE, J.M. - GDN.	24
PEARSON, THOS. J. - MINOR	PEARSON, W.R. - GDN.	35
PEARSON, THOS. T. - DECD.	CARLISLE, G.W. - ADMR.	37
PEEK, ZACK - DECD.	COSBY, A.Y. - ADMR.	11
PELHAM, CHAS. W. - ETAL	PELHAM, A.L. - GDN.	67
PELHAM, G.A. - DECD.	PELHAM, A.L. - ADMR.	67
PENICK, MARY A. - DECD.	CARTER, JOSEPH - ADMR.	110
PENN, WILLIAM F. - DECD.	PENN, J.E. - ADMR.	143
PENN, WILLIE - DECD.	PENN, RUBY - ADMR.	158
PENNINGTON, ANNIE K.	WILLIAMSON, HELEN - EXEC. WILL	99
PENNINGTON, C.	Grider, W.E. & Sorrell, J.F. - Exec.	95
PENNINGTON, C.C. - DECD.	PENNINGTON, HENRY - ADMR.	10
PENNINGTON, F.M.	PENNINGTON, A.K. - ADMR.	89
PENNINGTON, F.M.	FAIR FIELD - PLAT OF LAND	76
PENNINGTON, JOHN R. - DECD.	PENNINGTON, HENRY - ADMR.	37
Pennington, Lula (Townsend) - Decd.	PENNINGTON, JULY - ADMR.	110
PENNINGTON, M. & O. - MINORS	PENNINGTON, E.L. - GDN.	11
PENNINGTON, M.W. - DECD.	PENNINGTON, J.H. - EXEC. WILL	111
PENNINGTON, MARY - ETAL	TENANTS IN COMMON	51
PENNINGTON, T.J. - DECD.	PENNINGTON, VERA - ADMR.	131
PENNY SAVINGS BANK	INCORP.	66
PEOPLES BLDG. & LOAN ASSN.	CORP.	61
PERDUE, EASTER - DECD.	BARRON, M.N. - ADMR.	36
PERDUE, ELVIRA - DECD.	PERDUE, J.S. - ADMR.	37
PERDUE, LEROY - DECD.	PERDUE, M.A. - ADMR.	37
PERDUE, M.E. - DECD.	COWART, STEPHEN - ADMR.	36
PERKINS, H.W. - MINOR	TALBOT, HAIL - GDN.	11
PERKINS, JARDINE C. - DECD.	PERKINS, W.L. - EXEC. WILL	143
PERKINS, P.H. - DECD.	PERKINS, L.H. - ADMR.	54
PERKINS, WM. - DECD.	LEE, S.P. - ADMR.	37
PERSONS, AMOS - DECD.	PERSON, JANE B. - ADMR.	36

RHODES, BEATRICE - ETAL	TENANTS IN COMMON	101
RHODES, H.L. - DECD.	RHODES, MRS. HELEN L. - ADMR.	135
RHODES, JOHN - DECD.	RHODES, LILLIE - ADMR.	166
RHODES, JOHN D. - DECD.	RHODES, J.P. & M.A. - ADMR.	62
RHODES, JOHN F. - DECD.	RHODES, S.E. - ADMR.	110
RHODES, JOSIE	EVANS, JOHN C. - ADMR.	72
RHODES, JOSIE MADGE - MINOR	JONES, W.W.D. - GDN.	86
RHODES, M.A. - DECD.	RHODES, MRS. C.B. - ADMR.	119
Rhodes, Madge (alias Josie) - Minor	JONES, V.O. - GDNSHIP.	72
RHODES, S.F. - ETAL	Tenants in Common - Part. of Land	76
RHODES, T.J.	EXEMPTION	91
RHODES, W.J.	EXPARTE	53
RHODES, WM. - DECD.	RHODES, JOHN D. - ADMR.	37
RICHARD, LOUIE - DECD.	Homestead to Vella Richards	159
RICHARDSON, H.B. - DECD.	RICHARDSON, E.S. - ADMR.	72
Richardson, Mary, heirs of - Minors	JONES, LITTLETON - GDN.	24
RICHARDSON, R.	LOCKE, JESSE	24
Richardson, Rebecca - Etal Minor	MAIN, ALLEN M. - GDN.	11
Richardson, S. & A. & E.W. - Minors	RICHARDSON, E.S. - GDN.	72
RICHARDSON, S.J. - DECD.	MCCALL, D.A. - ADMR.	38
RICHBOURG, DAVID S. - DECD.	RICHBOURG, SARAH - ADMR.	38
RICKS, JESSE	Boswell, Williams, Stripling	38
RITCH, EDWARD R. - DECD.	MCKINNON, LAUCHLIN - ADMR.	37
RIVER FALLS POWER CO. - VS.	LINTON, J.A. - ETAL COND.	113
RIVER FALLS POWER CO. - VS.	JONES, GUSSIE H. - ETAL COND.	113
ROADS	PETITIONS, ETC.	148
ROBERSON, S.C. - MINOR	BELSER, C.C. - GDN.	118
ROBERTS, JESSE H. - DECD.	WHALEY, M.F. - ADMR.	51
ROBINSON, CLAVINIA - Etal Minor	ROBINSON, C. - GDN.	74
ROBINSON, CLUSTER - MINOR	ROBINSON, JAMES - GDN.	88
ROBINSON, HENRY D. - DECD.	WHITE, GEORGE - ADMR.	38
ROBINSON, LOTTIE - DECD.	PENNINGTON, PIERCE - EXEC.	111
ROBINSON, VIOLA	NON AGE REMOVAL	77
RODGERS, EARNEST - DECD.	RODGERS, ERIC - EXEC. WILL	159
RODGERS, ELI - ETAL	RODGERS, ELIZABETH	24
RODGERS, HUGH R. - DECD.	RODGERS, TABITHA A. - ADMR.	39
RODGERS, LIZZIE - ETAL	TENANTS IN COMMON	74
RODGERS, PHILLIP - DECD.	SPIVEY, J.W. - GDN.	37
RODGERS, ROBERT - DECD.	RODGERS, Sarah & Dennis - Admr.	37
RODGERS, T.M.H. - DECD.	RODGERS, EARNEST - ADMR.	133
ROGERS, GEO. W. - DECD.	COWART, ALBERT W. - ADMR.	114
ROGERS, NOAH - DECD.	ROGERS, SHEPHERD - ADMR.	38
ROGERS, THOMAS P. - DECD.	ROGERS, SHEPPHERD - ADMR.	38

ROLIN, JOHN - DECD.	FLOYD, T.S. - EXEC.	38
ROLING, A.V. - WIDOW	HUSSEY, J.F., DECD. - EXEMP.	72
ROLLINS MUTUAL AID SOCIETY	HOOTEN, JAMES - ETAL INCORP.	66
ROLLO, SOPHRONIA - MINOR	ROLLO, MILTON A. - GDN.	58
ROSE, JOHN B.	ROSE, EULA I. - ETAL ADMR.	101
ROSEBERRY, GEO. W. - DECD.	CARLISLE, C.M. - ADMR.	39
ROSEBERRY, J.T.	WILL	86
ROSEBERRY, ROBT. L. - DECD.	REDDOCH, J.D. - ADMR.	73
ROSENBERG, ABRAHAM - DECD.	Rosenberg, Sigmund & Marvin - Exec	143
Ross, Freeman & Darby, Oscar	MCLEOD, ELIJAH - APPRENT.	82
ROSS, M.J.	ROSS, S.T. - ADMR.	103
ROSS, MARCUS J. - MINOR	ROSS, R.A. - GDN.	52
ROSS, TARVER - MINORS	ROSS, M.J. - GDN.	85
ROSS, WM. T. - DECD.	ROSS, ANN C. - ADMR.	38
ROUNTREE, CASEY - MINOR	BENTON, G.C. - GDNSHIP.	81
ROUNTREE, THOMAS CASEY	NON AGE - Min. Book 0, Page 119	88
ROUR, MALISSA - DECD.	WILL	93
ROUSE, WM. H. - DECD.	CALLOWAY, ROBT. - EXEC.	39
ROWE, J.P. - DECD.	ROWE, MELISSA A. - ADMR.	51
ROWE, J.P. - ETAL	TENANTS IN COMMON	52
ROYAL THEATRE CO.	CORP.	85
ROYAL THEATRE CO.	DISSOLUTION	88
RUFFIN, SHEPHERD - DECD.	RUFFIN, ELI - ADMR.	38
RUGG, ALEX & HENRY - MINORS	LONG, JOHN J. - GDN.	24
RUGG, ELI S. - DECD.	RUGG, JAS. & ELI S. - ADMR.	39
RUGG, J.C. - DECD.	RUGG, ELI & J.C. - ADMR.	38
RUGG, JAMES C. - DECD.	FRAZIER, ALLEN - ADMR.	39
RUSHING, L. & M. - MINORS	HINSON, M.A. - GDN.	54
RUSHING, M.R. & R.H. STEVENS	Rushing, M.R. - Tenants in Common	80
RUSHING, S.M. - DECD.	HOMESTEAD	92
RUSHING, WILLIAM C. - DECD.	RUSHING, J.E.H. - ADMR.	49
RUSHTON, FRANCIS M. - DECD.	RUSHTON, OLIVER C.	48
RUSS, ANN - DECD.	DUBOSE, JOHN - ADMR.	38
RUSSELL, HOMER D. - MINOR	REEVES, D. - GDN.	51
RUSSELL, HOMER DAVID	RUSSELL, MATTIE P. - GDN.	98
RUSSELL, RITA DENISE - MINOR	RUSSELL, JESSIE J. - GDN.	167
RUSSELL, SAREPTA A. - DECD.	SANDERS, W.S. & J.M. - Exec. Will	118
RUSSELL, W.F. - DECD.	RUSSELL, MRS. VESA - ADMR.	77
RUTLAND, EMANUEL - MINOR	HIGHTOWER, THOS. A. - Etal Gdn.	36
RUTLAND, Valera Henrietta - Minor	RUTLAND, MRS. HENRIETTA J.	83
RUTLAND, W.J. - DECD.	BOATNER, E.L. - ADMR.	97
SACKS, A. - DECD.	SACKS, H. - ADMR.	72
SALTER, ANGUS E. - DECD.	SALTER, WM. B. - ADMR.	42

SEALS, Helen & Regina - Minors	SEALS, J.W. - GDN.	107
SEALS, J.D. - DECD.	SEALS, N.C., Widow - Homestead	67
SEALS, JOHN M.	SEALS, MRS. L.J. - WILL	75
SEALS, MRS. L.J. - DECD.	WRIGHT, T.R. - WILL	83
SEALS, MRS. L.J. - ETAL	TENANTS IN COMMON	82
SEALS, PETER - MINOR	SEALS, J.W. - GDNSHIP.	65
SEALS, S.J. - DECD.	MORGAN, JOHN H. - ADMR.	54
SEALS, S.J. - DECD.	MORGAN, JOHN H. - ADMR.	80
SEALS, S.P. - DECD.	WILLIAMS, SAM A. - ADMR.	88
SEAMOUR, WILLIAM	BAKER, D.A. - ADMR.	94
SEAY, A.G. - DECD.	SEAY, MARY A. - EXEC. WILL	144
SEAY, CATHERINE, ETAL	TENANTS IN COMMON	67
SEAY, EMMA B.	EXPARTE - HOMESTEAD	71
SEAY, EMMA B. - DECD.	GRAVES, LULA - WILL	82
SEAY, WILLIAM A.	EXPARTE	12
SEBASTIAN, L.J. - DECD.	HALL, I.N. - ADMR.	11
SEGARS, HUGH J. - DECD.	SEGARS, THELMA L. - ADMR.	164
SEGARS, MARY LEE, ETAL	TENANTS IN COMMON	61
SEGARS, SARAH A. - DECD.	SEGARS, MARY LEE - EXEC.	50
SEGARS, WILLIE BELLE, ETAL	SEGARS, W.J. - GDNSHIP.	62
SELLERS, GERTRUDE - DECD.	SELLERS, LULA - WILL	76
SELLERS, HEPSEBETH	GRIFFIN, H.H. - WILL	79
SELLERS, JACOB M. - DECD.	Sellers, Hepsybeth, Pet. to set apart a	74
SELLERS, R.W. - DECD.	PARTIN, T.F. - ADMR.	153
SELLERS, SAMUEL - DECD.	SELLERS, E.M. - ADMR.	42
SELLERS, VIRGINIA	WILL	96
SELLERS, W.R. - DECD.	SELLERS, HUBERT & R.L. - EXEC.	104
Selligsberg, William - Naturalization	EXPARTE	24
SELMAN, MARY M. - DECD.	Selman, John L. & Elizabeth - Exec.	156
SENN, C.T. - DECD.	SENN, HUME & EMORY - Exec. Will	138
SENN, ROSA BELL	BERRY, MALINDA	84
SENN, T.S. - VS.	SHIVER, M.A. - Crop Settlement	143
SENN, W.H. - VS.	GRIFFIN, TALTON	146
SENN, WILLIAM - DECD.	YOUNGBLOOD, J.B. - ADMR.	11
SESSIONA, W.H. - DECD.	SESSIONS, S.J. - ADMR.	77
SESSIONS, A. - MINORS	NORSWORTHY, PRESSLEY - GDN.	24
SESSIONS, ABSALOM - DECD.	SESSIONS, JOHN - ADMR.	44
SESSIONS, GERTRUDE - MINOR	SESSIONS, JOHN H. - GDNSHIP.	77
SESSIONS, J.A. - DECD.	MILLER, U.L. - ADMR.	119
SESSIONS, J.M. & J.R. - MINOR	SESSIONS, JASPER - GDN.	12
SESSIONS, JOHNIE HUBBARD	DIS NON AGE	76
SESSIONS, S.A. & M.J. - MINOR	JOHNSTON, SOLOMON - GDN.	12
SESSIONS, WILLIAM - DECD.	SESSIONS, JOHN - ADMR.	44

SIKES, MRS. ALLICE	LAWSON, WM. - GDN.	80
SIKES, MRS. C.A. - DECD.	LAWSON, WILLIAM - ADMR.	87
SIKES, MRS. JOHNIE - ETAL	TENANTS IN COMMON	97
SIKES, THOS. A. - DECD.	FAULK, TIMOTHY - ADMR.	40
SIKES, W.J. - DECD.	HOMESTEAD EXEMPT	147
SILER, ALLEN T. - DECD.	SILER, JOHN - ADMR.	39
SILER, JANE O.G. - DECD.	PICKETT, JAS. F. - ADMR.	11
SILER, JOE FRANK, ETAL	TENANTS IN COMMON	63
SILER, MAGGIE G., ETAL - MINOR	SILER, M.A. - GDN.	58
SILER, MARY A. - MINOR	SILER, Q.P. - DECD.	66
SILER, MINNIE A. - DECD.	SILER, J.F. - EXEC.	101
SILER, Q.P. - DECD.	SILER, M.A. - ADMR.	55
SILER, Q.P. - DECD.	SILER, MRS. M.A. - DOWER	62
SILER, SALLIE A. - DECD.	MURPHREE, JOEL D. - ADMR.	11
SILER, SOLOMON - DECD.	SILER, J.O.G., ETAL - ADMR.	42/4:
SIMMONS, ALTO - DECD.	CARROLL, W.C. - ADMR.	97
SIMMONS, DANIEL JR. - DECD.	LIVINGSTON, S.B. - ADMR.	40
SIMMONS, DORCAS - Etal Minor	LOE, S.P. - GDN.	15
SIMMONS, FANNIE - DECD.	Simmons, J. & Stroud, Emma - Exec.	88
SIMMONS, GEO. B., ETAL	TENANTS IN COMMON	59
SIMMONS, JOHN - DECD.	SIMMONS, ISAAC - ADMR.	41
SIMMONS, MARGARET - DECD.	SIMMONS, MATTIE - EXEC. WILL	117
SIMMONS, MRS. T.A. - ETAL	TENANTS IN COMMON	81
SIMMONS, SIMPSON - DECD.	JEFFCOAT, WM. E. - ADMR.	44
SIMMORS, L.R. - DECD.	MILLS, WILLIAM - ADMR.	41
SIMPSON, CHARLIE A. - DECD.	SIMPSON, MINNIE B. - ADMR.	143
SIMPSON, I.B. - DECD.	SIMPSON, MAMIE MARIE - ADMR.	167
SIMS, B.F. - DECD.	SIMS, J.R. - EXEC.	101
SIMS, B.F. - DECD.	SIMS, J.R. - EXEC.	111
SIMS, B.F. - ETAL	Pet. for part. of land - Tenants in Com	77
SIMS, JACOB - DECD.	SIMS, ELIZABETH - ADMR.	39
SIMS, JACOB A. - DECD.	SIMS, J.L. - ADMR.	77
SIMS, JAMES - DECD.	SIMS, JACOB & S. - ADMR.	42
SIMS, MARY A. - ETAL	TENANTS IN COMMON	12
SIMS, MRS. A.E. - DECD.	MCLEOD, DARBY - EXEC.	99
SIMS, R.J.	SIMS, R.L. - ADMR. (CIR. CT.)	114
SIMS, SALLIE L. - MINOR	SIMS, R.L. - ADMR.	114
SIMS, W.A. - DECD.	SIMS, A.E. - EXEC. WILL	88
SINGERFIELD, MOSES - DECD.	SINGERFIELD, FRANCIS A. - EXEC.	12
SITERAS, GEORGE E. - DECD.	BALAKO, MARY - EXEC.	155
SKEINS, PETER & THOS. - DECD.	SKEINS, ADAM - ADMR.	40
SKINNER, LEMUEL - DECD.	SKINNER, W.R. - ADMR.	42
SKINNER, S.J. - DECD.	SKINNER, CHARLOTTE R. - ADMR.	48

SKINNER, SARAH W. - DECD.	SKINNER, S.J. - ADMR.	133
SKINNER, SEABORN J. - DECD.	BASSETT, EWELL C. - EXEC. WILL	146
SKINNER, WILLIE B., Etal - Minors	SKINNER, MAUD A. - GDNSHIP.	78
SKINNER, WM. J. - DECD.	SKINNER, MARTHA J.	63
SLATON, HENRY - DECD.	SLATON, ANNIE J. - ADMR.	100
SLATON, JOHN WALTER - DECD.	SLATON, HENRY - ADMR.	79
SLAUGHTER, A.R. - DECD.	KINNON, R.W.H. - ADMR.	40
SMALL, WILLIAM - DECD.	SMALL, NANCY - ADMR.	40
SMART, ADDIE BELLE	NON AGE DECREE	75
SMART, ED F. - DECD.	SMART, Shirley Vernetta - Exec.	165
SMART, EMILY C. - DECD.	SMART, S.F. - ADMR.	112
SMART, JOHN W. - DECD.	SMART, S.F. - ADMR.	112
SMART, SHELBY F. - DECD.	BRUCE, J.L. - ADMR.	153
SMART, VICTOR - DECD.	MCGHEE, R.A. - ADMR.	162
SMART, VICTOR L. (INC.)	Powell, L.C. & McGhee, R.A. - Admr.	152
SMEDLEY, ALIN - NON COMPOS	SMEDLEY, DAVID B. - GDN.	40
SMILEY, JACOB & WM. J. - MINOR	TALBOT, JAMES B. - GDN.	15
SMILEY, STEPHEN D. - DECD.	HENDERSON, J.A. - ADMR.	11
SMILIE, ELLA - DECD.	HURLEY, D.P. - ADMR.	11
SMILIE, HENRY - DECD.	TALBOT, J.B. - ETAL	39
SMILIE, HIRAM A. - DECD.	SMILIE, S.D. - ADMR.	40
SMILIE, ROBERT - DECD.	SMILIE, OLIVER P. - ADMR.	41
SMILIE, WYLY - MINOR	JONES, W.M. - GDN.	12
SMITH, A.M. - DECD.	POWELL, R.F. - Admr. Sale of land	82
SMITH, ALEX - DECD.	SMITH, G.W. - ADMR.	11
SMITH, ALFA	APPRENTICESHIP	68
SMITH, ALONZA - DECD.	LIGHTFOOT, TUPPER - ADMR.	139
SMITH, ANN - DECD.	KNOX, O.F. - ADMR.	44
Smith, Anna, Arthur & Daniel; Minors	TICER, SAMUEL - GDN.	59
SMITH, ARTHUR - DECD.	Smith, Ann & Henderson, W.D.; Admr	54
SMITH, AUBREY - MINOR	APPRENTICESHIP	67
SMITH, C.C.	Pet. to sell land - Tenants in Common	80/81
SMITH, C.P. - DECD.	BENSON, O.L. - ADMR.	89
SMITH, D.J. - DECD.	WHATLEY, LABAN - ADMR.	41
SMITH, DAVIS		34
SMITH, ISAAC B. - DECD.	SMITH, JOHN O. - ADMR.	63
SMITH, J.D. - DECD.	COLQUITT, W.B. - ADMR.	41
SMITH, J.H.	EXPARTE	50
SMITH, J.M. - ETAL	TENANTS IN COMMON	93
SMITH, JAS, ISAAC - DECD.	Smith, Pennie C. - Pet. for exemption	90
SMITH, JOHN C. - DECD.	TAYLOR, W.G. - ADMR.	40
SMITH, JORDAN - DECD.	SMITH, A.J. - ADMR. WILL	41
SMITH, LOLA - DECD.	MACK, JOHN - EXEC. WILL	157

SPEIR, G.W. - HEIRS OF - MINOR	SPEIR, H.K. - GDN.	15
SPEIR, JOHN - DECD.	SPEIR, JOHN M., ETAL - ADMR.	40
SPENCE, FITZ J. - ETAL MINOR	HILLIARD, C.W. - GDN.	12
SPENCER, C.E. & HENRY; Minors	SPENCER, GEO. E. - GDN.	48
SPENCER, CHARLES V. - DECD.	SPENCER, MAY - ADMR.	87
SPENCER, E.H. - DECD.	FOSTER, M.A. - ADMR.	66
SPENCER, FRANCIS - ETAL	TENANTS IN COMMON	12
SPENCER, H & C - MINORS	SPENCER, G.E. - GDN.	12
SPENCER, HENRY - DECD.	SPENCER, G.L. - ADMR.	119
SPENCER, J.G. - MINOR	LAW, JNO. A. - GDN.	49
SPENCER, JOSEPH G. - MINOR	LAW, JOHN A. - GDN.	54
SPENCER, MARTHA A. - ETAL	TENANTS IN COMMON	12
SPENCER, PETER - DECD.	DARBY, S.P. - ADMR.	12
SPENCER, W.F. - DECD.	SPENCER, EFFIE B. - ADMR.	156
SPHEERIS, ANDREW - DECD.	SPHEERIS, JUANITA GARY - Admr.	162
SPIVEY, CEPHUS (Non Age) Minor	SPIVEY, MARY EMMA - EXPARTE	82
SPIVEY, EDMOND - DECD.	HODGES, B.W. - ADMR.	40
SPIVEY, ELISHA - DECD.	SUMMERSETT, Alexander - Admr.	41
SPIVEY, J.G. - DECD.	SPIVEY, M.S. - ADMR.	99
SPIVEY, J.L. - DECD.	SPIVEY, MINNIE L. - ADMR.	136
SPIVEY, J.M.		158
SPIVEY, M.S. - DECD.	SPIVEY, S.E. - EXEC. WILL	131
SPIVEY, MRS. S.E.		163
SPIVEY, Priscilla D. & Theodore M.		158
SPIVEY, WILEY - DECD.	SPIVEY, DR. M.S. - ADMR.	82
SPLAWN, RICHARD - DECD.		22
SPRINGHILL GIN CO.	INCORPORATION	59
SPURLIN, ELIJAH - DECD.	DUNN, URIAH - ADMR.	11
STAGNER, JOHN - DECD.	CARTER, W.O. - ADMR.	52
STALLINGS, DR. H.S.	Stallings, Rubye Lee - Gdn. (Cir. Ct.)	132
STALLINGS, DR. H.S. - DECD.	1st F & M Nat'l. Bk. (Cir. Ct.)	150
STALLINGS, J.J. - DECD.	STALLINGS, J.A., Etal - Exec. Will	73
STALLINGS, JAS. L. - DECD.	STALLINGS, LIZZIE - ADMR.	88
STALLINGS, MRS. S.A.F. - DECD.	STALLINGS, HOMER S. - EXEC.	113
STALLWORTH, JAMES - DECD.	STALLWORTH, E.M. - ADMR.	41
STALLWORTH, THOMAS T. - Decd.	STALLWORTH, AMON A. - ADMR.	41
STANALAND, Billy Joyce - Minor	STANALAND, O.L. - GDN.	146
STANDARD CHEMICAL & OIL CO.	EXPARTE - CORP.	72
STANFIELD, E.E. & J. - MINORS	WALKER, FELIX - GDN.	12
STANLEY, JAMES M. - DECD.	STANLEY, MARTHA A. - ADMR.	42
STANLEY, JAS., Heirs of - Minors	STANLEY, THOMAS - GDN.	24
STANLEY, JOHN, Heirs of - Minors	SWANNER, CARRIE - GDN.	24
STARK, FANNIE A. - DECD.	GARDNER, L.D. - ADMR.	86

STARK, FANNIE C. - DECD.	STARK, S.J. - EXEC.	94
STARKE, A.W. - DECD.	GARDNER, BENJ. - ADMR.	11
STARKE, MAMIE M. - DECD.	STARKE, S.J. - EXEC. WILL	145
STARKE, MARY A. - DECD.	ADAMS, HUGH - EXEC. WILL	151
STARKE, SAMUEL J. - DECD.	MURPHREE, SAM - EXEC.	164
STARKE, WILEY - DECD.	EXEMPT. TO MATTIE STARKE	99
STARKE, WM. C. - DECD.	STARKE, MARY - EXEC.	113
STARKES, LEROY - DECD.	SANKEY, JOHN M. - ADMR.	133
STARLING, GEORGIA IDA	REEVES, BEN, SHERIFF - ADMR.	158
STARLING, J.M. - ETAL	TENANTS IN COMMON	94
STARLING, SARAH E. - DECD.	STARLING, J.M. - GDNSHIP.	63
STEPHENS, A.T. - DECD.	STEPHENS, ODELL - ADMR.	146
STEPHENS, F.L. - DECD.	STEPHENS, R.H. - ADMR.	80
STEPHENS, JOHN - DECD.	STEPHENS, JOSIAH - ADMR.	40
STEPHENS, JOHN; Heirs of - Minor	STEPHENS, JANE - GDN.	24
STEPHENS, NEEDHAM - MINORS	STEPHENS, JANE - GDN.	24
STEPHENSON, J.T.	EXPARTE	59
STEPHENSON, MARY P. - DECD.	HOLLINGSWORTH, M.E. - ADMR.	64
STEVENS, BERNICE	REESE, C.L. - GDN.	96
STEVENS, H.V. - DECD.	WOULFOLK, J.M. - EXEC. WILL	143
STEVENS, JAMES - ETAL. MINOR	STEVENS, ELANDER - GDN.	12
STEVENS, JAMES E. - DECD.	STEVENS, MATILDA - ADMR.	11
STEVENS, NEEDHAM - DECD.	STEVENS, JAS. E. - ADMR.	11
STEVENS, NEWTON J. - DECD.	STEVENS, JOHN W. - ADMR.	44
STEVENS, R.H. SR. - DECD.	BOROM, S.B. - ADMR.	96
STEVENS, W.H. - DECD.	STEVENS, R.H. - ADMR.	51
STEWART, A.G. - MINOR	HAYGOOD, J.W. - GDN.	6
Stewart, Buddie, Girther L., A.D., Cec.	STEWART, ANNIE	84
STEWART, C.P. - DECD.	TENANTS IN COMMON	33
STEWART, CHARITY - DECD.	STEWART, JAMES S. - ADMR.	40
STEWART, G.W. - DECD.	MURPHREE, D.B. - ADMR.	48
STEWART, G.W. - DECD.	STEWART, M.O. - GDN.	50
STEWART, JOSHUA W. - DECD.	GIBSON, JAMES M. - ADMR.	41
STEWART, MARTHA J. - MINOR	BRYANT, T.H. - GDN.	48
STEWART, MATILDA - DECD.	STEWART, J.W. - EXEC. WILL	108
STEWART, WILEY - DECD.	HENDERSON, GEO. W. - ADMR.	119
STINSON, ALONZA	TENANTS IN COMMON	85
STINSON, Carroll & Calvin - Minors	FLOWERS, J.F. - GDN.	93
STINSON, GREEN B. - DECD.	STINSON, R.W. - ADMR.	55
STINSON, J.B. - DECD.	STINSON, M.C. - ADMR.	44
STINSON, J.T. - DECD.	STINSON, M.B. - ADMR.	41
STINSON, J.T., ETAL	TENANTS IN COMMON	61
STINSON, JASON - DECD.	STINSON, JOHN, ETAL - ADMR.	42

STINSON, JOHN L. - DECD.	STINSON, JOHN	39
STINSON, MICAJAH - DECD.	STINSON, JORDAN B. - ADMR.	42
STINSON, ROBT. M. - DECD.	STINSON, JOHN - ADMR.	42
STOUDENMIRE, Dallas - Etal Minor	MAY, SIMEON R. - GDN.	15
STOUGH, Bruness & Robert - Minors	STOUGH, MRS. SUSIE - GDN.	89
STOUGH, D.J. - DECD.	ROLLO, SARAH - ADMR.	41
STOUGH, LENA B.	CHESSER, WILLIAM B. - EXEC.	160
STOUGH, MARTIN - DECD.	RUSH, JOHN S. - ADMR.	40
STOUGH, MARTIN - DECD.	Stough, S.J., Etal Tenants in Commor	48
STOUT, E.J. - DECD.	STOUT, T.H. JR. & SR.	52
STOWE, HENRY - MINOR	GOLDSMITH, J.M. - GDN.	15
STOWE, THOMAS J. - MINOR	GARRETT, HENRY A. - GDN.	15
STRICKLAN, J.W. - DECD.	ROSS, C.J. - ADMR.	56
STRICKLAN, JOHN - DECD.	ROSS, C.J. - ADMR.	59
STRICKLAN, KATE - MINOR	PENNINGTON, W.H. - GDN.	59
STRICKLAN, SALLIE - MINOR	HIGGINS, R.J. - GDN.	48
STRICKLAN, W.H. - DECD.	HIGGINS, R.J. - ADMR.	65
STRICKLAN, W.H. - HEIRS	TENANTS IN COMMON	59
Strickland, Joseph L. - Etal Minor	STRICKLAND, LUCINDA J. - GDN.	15
STRINGER, BILL - MINOR	FOLMAR, THOS. J. - Apprenticeship	51
STRINGER, ELLEN - ETAL	TENANTS IN COMMON	94
STRINGER, JAMES	ENZOR, J. LANE - ADMR.	108
STRINGER, JAMES - DECD.	1ST F & M BK. - ADMR.	120
STROM, JOHN - DECD.	STROM, WM. - ADMR.	39
STROM, JOSEPH - DECD.	STROM, WILLIAM - ADMR.	40
STROTHER, HENRY T. - DECD.	STROTHER, J.B. - ADMR.	138
STROUD, DAVID - DECD.	STROUD, MARTHA L. - ADMR.	88
STROZIER, ELIZABETH - DECD.	WILLIAMS, J.W. - ADMR.	41
STRUM, H.S. - DECD.	STRUM, WM. - ADMR.	40
STRUM, LUCY - DECD.	STRUM, WM. & J.H. - ADMR.	42
STUART, JAS. D. - ETAL MINOR	STUART, C.P. - GDN.	15
STUBBS, LEWIS - DECD.	STUBBS, THOMAS J. - ADMR.	39
STUBBS, WM. - ETAL MINOR	TAYLOR, H.H. - GDN.	15
STUBBS, WM. E. - DECD.	STUBBS, THOMAS J.	39
STUDDARD, S.W.	STUDDARD, Jack Bogart - Exec.	158
STURGEON, LOWRY - Admr. - vs.	SILER, Mrs. Wm., Etal - Sale of land	89
SUGGS, ALPHA - ETAL. MINOR	SUMMERSETT, WM. - GDN.	24
SULLINS, S.B. - DECD.	SULLINS, MARTHA - ETAL EXEC.	11
SUMMERSETT, A.P. - DECD.	SUMMERSETT, A. - ADMR.	11
SUMMERSETT, ELIZABETH - Decd.	SUMMERSETT, A. - ADMR.	11
SUMMERSETT, J.W. & J.M. - Minors	SUMMERSETT, ELIZABETH - GDN.	15
SUMMERSETT, JOHN W. - DECD.	SUMMERSETT, ALEXANDER; Admr	41
SUMMERSETT, SUSAN - MINOR	FAULK, J.T. - GDN.	11

153

THORNTON, JOB - DECD.		45
THORNTON, JOHN L. - MINOR	CHILDS, ELISHA - GDN.	14
THORNTON, THOMAS - DECD.	CHILDS, ELISHA - ADMR.	45
THREADGILL, LUTHER E. - MINOR	THREADGILL, MINNIE LEE - GDN.	130
THURMAN, DINK - HOMESTEAD	THURMAN, MITTIE B. - WIDOW	149
THWEATT, Lilian & Sonora - Minors	THWEATT, G.R. - GDN.	65
TICER, ANIS - DECD.	PHILLIPS, DELLA - EXEC. WILL	142
TICER, ROXIE - ETAL	TICER, S.S. - GDN.	67
TICER, SAM S. - DECD.	Hightower, Harold F.; Admr. (Equity C	131
TICER, SAM S. -DECD.	Hightower, J.F.; Admr. (Equity Ct.)	117
TILLERY, ELIZABETH - IDIOT	BYRD, JOHN R. - GDN.	23
TILLEY, Virginia & Sarah T. - Minor	EDWARDS, BENJAMIN - GDN.	23
TINER, EMMA - DECD.	HENDERSON, FOX - ADMR.	82
TINER, JAMES W., ETAL	TENANTS IN COMMON	45
TOMLINSON, HARRISON - DECD.	BRUNSON, I.J.	44
TOMLINSON, PRISCILLA - MINORS	WILLIAMSON, B.F. - GDN.	12
TOMPKINS, H.H., ETAL - MINOR	LOVE, A.P. - GDN.	14
TOMPLIN, MARTHA & JOS. - Minor	NOBLES, SYNTHA - GDN.	23
TOWER, GOODE - DECD.	BOSWELL, M.V.	45
TOWN OF BRUNDIDGE - VS.	Haisten, Mrs. S.E., Etal Cond. (Cir. Ct	122
TOWNSEND, ELI	BOSWELL, F.A.; Admr. - Min. Bk J	
TOWNSEND, ELIZABETH	WILL	98
Townsend, Lula Pennington - Decd.	PENNINGTON, JULY - ADMR.	110
TOWNSEND, MARTHA J.A. - Minor	TOWNSEND, S.J. - GDN.	12
TOWNSEND, MATTIE E.	TOWNSEND, IDA L. - NON AGE	76
TOWNSEND, ORRIE - ETAL	TENANTS IN COMMON	93
TRAVATHAN, ELI - DECD.	GRAVES, ARCHIBALD - ADMR.	45
TREVATHAN, ELI, Heirs of - Minor	LYNCH, JACOB - GDN.	23
TRICE, THOMAS - DECD.	CANTERBERRY, C.R.	44
TROTMAN, JOHN L.	TROTMAN, ERIN - WILL	83
TROTMAN, JOHN P.	WILL	159
TROTTER, A.B. - EXPARTE	TENANTS IN COMMON	78
TROTTER, E.C. - ETAL	Tenants in Common - Sale of land	81
TROTTER, E.H. & WIFE - VS.	PIKE COUNTY	159
TROTTER, F.M.	HOMESTEAD	66
TROTTER, GEORGE	YOUNG, J.C. - ADMR.	96
TROTTER, JOHN W. - DECD.	TROTTER, C.T. - ADMR.	73
TROTTER, MILES & NEAL	SKINNER, S.J. - GDN.	73
TROTTER, MILES, ETAL - MINORS	SKINNER, S.J. & C.T. - GDN.	73
TROTTER, NEAL	SKINNER, S.J. - Gdn. Dis Non Age	81
TROTTER, S.J. - NON COMPOS	TROTTER, J.W. - GDN.	71
Trotter, Samantha; Non Comp. Mentis	FANNIN, J.B. - GDN.	73
TROTTER, SAMUEL - DECD.	WILL	63

TURNER, L.O. - ETAL	Tenants in Common - Part. of land	75
TURNER, Laura A. & Ida L. - Minors	FARMER, GEO. W. - GDN.	54
TURNER, LOLA - MINOR	TURNER, J.R. - GDN.	130
TURNER, MARTHA E.	TURNER, J.R. - ADMR.	95
TURNER, MARTHA E. - DECD.	BOROM, T.L.	95
TURNER, MARY EMMA - DECD.	TURNER, W.T. - ADMR.	136
TURNER, MRS. LEMIE L. - DECD.	WEIDENBACK, W.H.	118
TURNER, NATHANIEL - MINOR	TURNER, SOPHIA E. - GDN.	12
TURNIPSEED, J.T. - DECD.	TURNIPSEED, Susan Caroline - Exec	71
TURNIPSEED, SAMUEL - DECD.	ELLIS, ISAAC N.	44
TUTTLE, AMOS G. - DECD.	MOORE, NUBIL A.	44
TYLER, J.F. - DECD.	ROSS, R.A. - ADMR.	53
TYNER, ARMILLE - DECD.	Culpepper, Carlos; Admr. (Equity Ct.	123
UNDERWOOD, BENJAMIN - DECD.	Underwood, James & Wiley - Admr.	45
UNDERWOOD, JOSIAH - DECD.		45
Union Christian Graveyard Protection INC.		64
VANCE, W.R.	GILMORE, W.G. - ADMR.	104
VAUGHN, EMMA J.	GDN.	84
VEAZEY, MARSELLA, ETAL	TENANTS IN COMMON	54
VENDRICK, J.C.	TENANTS IN COMMON	84
VINCENT, G.W. SR. - DECD.	VINCENT, F.F. - ADMR.	128
Vincent, Geo. Washington Jr. - Decd.	VINCENT, JOE C. - ADMR.	129
VINCENT, PENNINGTON - DECD.	VINCENT, CAROLINE - ADMR.	45
WADE, W.S. - DECD.	WADE, GENIE - PROBATE OF WILL	76
WAGES, JOE - DECD.	PARISH, J.H. - ADMR.	131
WAGES, MARY	SEAY, A.G. - ADMR.	94
WALDEN, C.M. - DECD.		59
WALDEN, W.M. - EXPARTE		74
WALKER, ALER	SIMMONS, ALTO - EXEC.	160
WALKER, ANNIE - DECD.	WILL	96
WALKER, DICK - DECD.	EXEMPTION for AMANDA WALKER	87
WALKER, FELIX - DECD.	WALKER, W.R. - DECD.	50
WALKER, GARTHA - MINOR	WALKER, LILLA - GDN.	98
WALKER, INEZ - ETAL	GAMBLE, JOHN - CUSTODIAN	114
WALKER, JOHN BUFFORD - Decd.	WALKER, JESSIE K. - ADMR.	139
WALKER, NOVIE - DECD.	WALKER, LILLA - ADMR.	98
WALKER, RICHARD - DECD.	Exempt. to widow Amanda Walker	87
WALKER, ROBERT H. - DECD.	COLLEY, J.O., ETAL - EXEC. WILL	120
WALL, E.J. - DECD.	COSBY, A.Y. - ADMR.	12
WALTERS, ETTA H. - DECD.	WALTERS, JOE F. - EXEC. WILL	155
WALTERS, J.W. - DECD.	WALTERS, ETHEL - ADMR.	88
WALTERS, JAMES	Bently, S.M. & W.C. Walters - Exec.	96
WALTERS, JAMES - DECD.	WALTERS, B.L. - ADMR.	46

WATSON, W.E.	ANDERSON, L.K. - Apprenticeship	77
WEBB, C.W.	WEBB, Nettie; Homestead Exempt.	134
WEBB, WILLIAM W. - DECD.	WARNOCK, JAMES T. - ADMR.	45
WEED, Charles & Louie - Minors	HELMS, FRANCES E. WEED; Gdn.	138
WEED, CHAS. H. - ETAL MINORS	WEED, FRANCES ESTHER - GDN.	99
WEED, WINNIE DAVIS - MINOR	WEED, J.A. - GDN.	91
WEEDON, H.M. - DECD.	WEEDON, JULIA H., ETAL - EXEC.	98
WEEKS, ALICE JONES - DECD.	TRANSFERED TO CIRCUIT COURT	147
WELCH, DRICILLA - DECD.	DICKINSON, R.C. - ADMR.	89
WELDON, FANNIE	BOSWELL, SAM - ADMR.	135
WELDON, REBECCA - DECD.	WELDON, D.R. - ADMR.	65
WELDON, W.A. - DECD.	WELDON, J.J. & D.R. - ADMR.	51
WELDON, W.W. - ETAL	DOCKET 2	100
WELLS, M.D. - DECD.	YOUNGBLOOD, M. - ADMR.	46
WELSH, JOHN - DECD.	MOTES, NOAH - ADMR.	46
WESLEY, H.B.	WESLEY, H.C. - ADMR.	120
WESLEY, R.H. - DECD.	JORDAN, JNO. J. - ADMR.	11
WESLEY, Z.E. - DECD.	ANDERSON, J.A. - ADMR.	51
WESLEY, Z.E. - DECD.	ANDERSON, J.A - ADMR.	56
WEST VIRGINIA LAND CO.	PLAT OF LAND	75
WEST, B.J. - DECD.	MORGAN, D. & E.M. WEST - ADMR.	12
WEST, J.B. - DECD.	TATE, J.C. - ADMR.	83
WEST, JOHN F.	TENANTS IN COMMON	12
WEST, JOSEPH W. - DECD.	Harrell, Louis & Mary A. West - Admr	47
WHALEY, ARCHIBALD - DECD.	ROBERTS, MARY W. - ADMR. WILL	45
WHALEY, ELIJAH S. - DECD.	MCPHERSON, ELI ALONZO - WILL	79
WHALEY, J.M. - DECD.	WHALEY, MARY E. - EXEC.	59
WHALEY, J.R. - ETAL	TENANTS IN COMMON	50
WHALEY, JAMES C. - DECD.	WHALEY, MARY W. - ADMR.	45
WHALEY, JAS. - ETAL	TENANTS IN COMMON	115
WHALEY, JOE - DECD.	Whaley, Ola & J.L. Giddens - Admr.	134
WHALEY, JOHN S. - MINOR	WHALEY, JAMES A. - GDN.	54
WHALEY, L.E.	TRANS. TO CIR. CT.	164
WHALEY, MALON - DECD.	CARROLL, W.C. - SPEC. ADMR.	101
WHALEY, RUTH - DECD.	WHALEY, J.M. - ADMR.	12
WHALEY, SAM - DECD.	WHALEY, A.P. & W.D. - EXEC. WILL	153
WHATLEY, LABAN - DECD.	HILL, J.P. - EXEC.	48
WHATLEY, WILLIS - DECD.	WHATLEY, R.N. - EXEC.	12
WHEELER, ISABELLA	PET. FOR EXEMPTION	64
WHEELER, R.E. - DECD.	WHEELER, DOCK W. - ADMR.	119
WHEELER, REBECCA - ETAL	TENANTS IN COMMON	63
WHIDBY, NEBO	NON AGE MIN. BOOK O, PAGE 123	89
WHIDBY, ROBERT	NON AGE MIN. BOOK O, PAGE 120	88

WILSON, S.D. - DECD.	WILSON, JULIA A. - ADMR.	50
WILSON, SAM P. - ETAL	WILSON, A.J. - GDN.	110
WILSON, W.A. - DECD.	SMITH, S.F. - GDN.	50
WILSON, W.E.	BARNES, W.G. - ADMR.	75
WILSON, W.H. - DECD.	WHITE, W.R. - EXEC	88
WINDHAM, D.O. - MINOR	YELVERTON, J.R. - GDN.	53
WINDHAM, E.I. - DECD.	ROLLO, MOLLIE - WILL	139
WINDHAM, E.P. - MINOR	RICHARDSON, BROOKS - GDN.	53
WINDHAM, J.E. - DECD.	WINDHAM, FANNIE - ADMR.	59
WINDHAM, JOHN E. - DECD.	WINDHAM, MARTHA E. - Exec. Will	142
WINDHAM, L.M. - ETAL	TENANTS IN COMMON	76
WINFIELD, RAYMOND, Etal - minors	WINFIELD, W.H. - GDN.	119
WINFIELD, ROAN - DECD.	NICHOLS, PLEASANT - GDN.	134
WINGARD, DAVID, ETAL - VS.	WINGARD, T.B., ETAL	128
WINGARD, G.F.	WINGARD, Samuel Andrew - Exec.	158
WINGARD, GEORGE - MINOR	WINGARD, JACK - GDN.	12
WINGARD, JAMES C. - DECD.	WINGARD, MARY E. - ADMR.	35
WINGARD, JOHN - MINOR	CARROLL, W.C., SHERIFF - GDN.	98
WINGARD, RICHARD W. - DECD.	STEVENS, JAMES E. - ADMR.	46
WINGARD, ROCHELLE	CARROLL, W.C., SHERIFF - GDN.	98
WINGARD, SALLIE B. - DECD.	CARROLL, W.C. - ADMR.	97
WINSLETT, JNO. G. - DECD.	JONES, V.D. - ADMR.	77
WINSLETT, JOEL - DECD.	COLEMAN, W.S. - ADMR.	12
WINSLETT, JOEL - DECD.	WINSLETT, JOHN G.	53
WINSLETT, JOEL A. - DECD.	WINSLETT, MARGARET A. - WILL	81
WINSLETT, M.W. - DECD.	WINSLETT, PEARL - ADMR.	143
WINSLETT, MARGARET - ETAL	TENANTS IN COMMON	79
WINSLETT, MARY C. - DECD.	WINSLETT, MARGARET A. - WILL	81
WINSLETT, MARY NELL - MINOR	WINSLETT, PEARL - GDN.	143
WINSLETT, SARAH J.	WILL	98
WINSLOW, CHAS. - Exparte - vs.	FOLMAR, G.A.	67
WISE, V.A. - ETAL	TENANTS IN COMMON	73
WITHERINGTON, NATHAN - DECD.	PUGH, JAMES - ADMR.	46
WITHERSPOON, Sam'l. - Freedman	EXPARTE	47
WOOD, A.E. - DECD.	WOOD, J.P. - ADMR.	73
WOOD, ALICE GRACE - MINOR	WOOD, F.S. - GDN.	66
WOOD, ANNIE, ETAL - MINORS	WOOD, CLARA B. - GDN.	62
WOOD, E.H. - DECD.	WOOD, J.H. - ADMR.	56
WOOD, F.S. - DECD.	Wood, J.P. Sr. & J.P. Trotman - Admr	98
WOOD, F.S. - DECD.	MCSWAIN, BETTIE T. - ADMR.	98
WOOD, GEO. A. - MINOR	WOOD, CATTIE B. - GDN.	82
WOOD, ISAAC M. - DECD.	BRYAN, JOHN - ADMR.	12
WOOD, J.C. - ETAL	TENANTS IN COMMON	59

ABERCROMBIE, M.E.	11	522 - 532
ADAM, HARMON	1	114 - 141
ALFORD, ALLEN	12	589 - 603
ALFORD, TABITHA	12	557 - 581
ALLEN, CHARLES, JAMES A.	5	806
ALLEN, J.F.	10	115
ALLEN, JAMES	1	468 - 471
ALLEN, M.G.	12	4 - 50
ALLEN, MARY J.	12	432 - 457
ALLEN, ROBERT, DAVID, WM. J.	5	806
AMOS, BEVERLY	1	197
ANDERSON, JAMES	1	178 - 195
ANDERSON, SARAH	1	158
ANDERSON, W.C.	1	1 - 12
ANDRESS, JAMES	11	540 - 541
ANDRESS, SARAH J.	1	142 - 157, 196
ANDREWS, ISAAC	11	823 - 832
ANDREWS, WILLIAM	12	674 - 694
ANGLIN, JOHN M.	12	604 - 622
ARMSTRONG, A.J.	11	769 - 774
ARMSTRONG, CLEMENTINE	5	243 - 259
ARMSTRONG, H.P.	10	60 113
ARMSTRONG, M.F. & H.P.	12	85 - 163
ARMSTRONG, SALLY	12	164 - 196
ARNOLD, MARY E.	1	477 - 489
ARNOLD, MARY E.	10	344 - 345
ARNOLD, SIMPSON	10	116
ASBELL, SOLOMON	12	622 - 648
ATHEY, HENRY	11	603 - 660
ATKINSON, P.W.	1	13 - 20
BAILEY, JAMES	2	88 - 99
BAILEY, LUCINDA	18	771 - 787
BAKER, J.M.B.	10	203 - 220
BALDWIN, GEORGE E.	1	562 - 623
BALDWIN, WILLIAM	10	114
BALLARD, NANCY	1	408 - 434
BANKS CANNING CO.	16	389 - 390
BARNES, JAMES etal	18	260 - 262
BARNES, JOHN	13	322 - 377
BARNETT, ASA	1	21 - 98, 731
BARNETT, ASA	16	323 - 325
BARNETT, JOHN J.	2	114 - 177
BARNETT, KATHARINE	10	231 - 234

BARNETT, M.J.	12	649 - 671
BARNETT, M.M.	13	222 - 226
BARNETT, M.M.A. etal	16	740 - 768
BARRON, CHARLES	10	387 - 438
BARRON, JAS.	13	136 - 139
BARRON, THOS.	13	583 - 621
BARTLETT, ANNA (now Stewart)	3	798
BARTLETT, ELIZABETH	18	819
BATTLE, ELIZABETH A.	17	443 - 460
BATTLE, JOHN M.	12	695 - 741
BAXTER, WILLIAM R.	1	246 - 249
BAYGENTS, JOHN D.	13	110 - 128
BAYLEY, SARAH	10	237 - 252
BEAMAN, ABRAHAM	3	41 - 198
BEAMAN, OLIVER	9	291 - 343
BEAN, ALEXANDER	13	32 - 39
BEAN, JAMES F.	1	283 - 284
BEAN, JAMES F.	10	342 - 343
BEASELEY, H.T.E.V.	4	561 - 563
BEASLEY, ELIZABETH	18	29 - 32
BEASLEY, H.T.E.V.B.	3	561 - 563
BEASLEY, JAMES	10	173 - 202
BEASLEY, WILLIAM	13	100 - 101
BECK, JOURDAN	3	2 - 40
BECKWITH, H.C.	2	224 - 225
BEECHER, MARIAH	13	142 - 149
BELL, EMANUEL	13	378 - 398
BELL, SAMUEL	13	1 - 16
BELSER, WILLIAM	13	78 - 99
BENBOW, ANN E.	10	235 - 236
BENBOW, J.H.	10	489 - 514
BENBOW, JAMES H.	1	435 - 439
BENBOW, JOS. R.	18	117 - 126
BENBOW, MARGARET N. etal	17	378 - 379
BENBOW, RICHARD	13	622 - 686
BETHANEY, JOHN	10	221 - 229
BETHUNE, JOHN	12	197 - 354
BETSILL, HARRIET	10	289 - 303
BLACK, H.L.	9	447 - 496
BLACK, HENRY L.	1	701
BLACKBURN, THOS.	13	534 - 582
BLACKMON, JAMES S.	13	105 - 109
BLAIR, JOHN L.	18	794 - 798

BLAIR, L.M.	10	158 - 165
BLEDSOE, WILLIAM	1	516 - 561
BLUE, DANIEL	10	253 - 288
BLUE, FLORA E.	18	816 - 817
BLUE, JOHN	10	439 - 488
BLUE, M.M.	10	166 - 172
BLUE, PETER	10	515 - 570
BOND, ALFRED C.	1	472 - 476
BOND, WILLIAM B.	1	287 - 330, 490 - 515
BOND, WILLIAM M.	1	631 - 659
BOSWELL, F.A.	12	794 - 921
BOSWELL, JOHN	14	1 - 69
BOSWELL, JOHN W.	12	742 - 793
BOSWELL, M.A. etal	18	367 - 382
BOSWELL, M.V.	8	746 - 750
BOSWELL, MARCELLOUS etal	9	497 - 574
BOSWELL, STEPHEN	10	346 - 386
BOSWELL, THOMAS C.	12	937 - 942
BOUTWELL, JANE	10	304 - 339
BOUTWELL, NOEL	8	765 - 774
BOUTWELL, THOS.	13	130 - 135
BOUTWELL, WILLIAM	2	1 - 23
BOWERS, BENJAMIN	1	198 - 245
BOYD, ALICE	1	341 - 361
BOYD, CASPER	13	399 - 401
BOYETT, M.A. & CHARLES	8	758 - 764
BRABHAM, MARTIN	8	753 - 757
BRABHAM, REBECCA	2	24 - 39
BRADLEY, MARY C.	10	117 - 157
BRADLEY, RHODA C.	1	250 - 282
BRADLEY, RICHARD	18	33 - 34
BRADSHAW, ELIZA & H.J.	16	689 - 710
BRADSHAW, JOHN	10	1 - 59
BRADSHAW, JOHN J.	9	344 - 386
BRADSHAW, LIZZIE	18	788 - 790
BRADSHAW, SARAH	18	110 - 116
BRADY, JAS. T.	2	100 - 108
BRASWELL, JAMES W.	12	582 - 588
BRAZIL, WILLIAM	12	370 - 415
BRISTOW, MARY	13	50 - 64
BRISTOW, WM. F.	16	711 - 739
BROOKS, CALEB S.	12	458 - 488
BROOKS, E.S.	12	416 - 431

BROOKS, JAMES A.	13	28 - 31
BROOKS, JOSEPH C.	12	672 - 673
BROOKS, JOSIAH	12	922 - 936
BROOKS, ROBERT	13	150 - 155
BROOKS, WILLIAM C.	1	660 - 700
BROWDER, HARDY	13	263 - 316
BROWN, BENJAMIN G.	1	331 - 340
BROWN, CAROLINE	18	320
BROWN, JOHN	13	174 - 190
BROWN, JONATHAN	2	109 - 113
BROWN, WM.	13	191 - 206
BROWNING, EDWARD	13	140 - 141
BRUCE, A.	13	65 - 70
BRUNDIDGE, E.M.	18	383 - 399
BRUNDIDGE, ELECTION	2	875
BRUNSON, BENJAMIN	13	437 - 484
BRUNSON, EPSEY A.	1	362 - 407
BRUNSON, WILLIAM W.	1	624 - 630
BRYAN, LUCY A.F.	18	490 - 516
BRYANT, S.L.	10	571 - 598
BUCHAN, D.T. & W.A.S.	1	702 - 715
BULLARD, JAS. R.	13	129
BULLARD, NANCY	1	408 - 434
BUNDY, JOHN L.	1	440 - 467
BURGESS, ESQUIRE etal	17	1 - 85
BURGESS, JAMES	2	40 - 87
BURGESS, WILLIAM	14	70 - 151
BUTLER, ROBERT A.	13	317 - 321
CADE, IGNATIUS	2	294 - 304
CAISON, FRANCES J.	2	826
CALLOWAY, WILLIS M.	17	885 - 953
CAMERON, ARCHIBALD M.	2	564 - 568
CAMPBELL, ALEXANDER	2	844 - 846
CAMPBELL, BENJ. W.	14	335 - 341
CANADY, ELIZABETH	11	276 - 288
CANADY, ELIZABETH	17	374 - 376
CANNON, JOHN F.	19	1030 - 1033
CAPPS, G.F.	2	226 - 253
CARGILE, CHARLES M.	2	482 - 548
CARGILE, JASON	2	808 - 825, 827 - 828
CARGILE, JASON	14	725 - 886
CARGILE, M.M. etal.	2	591 - 596
CARGILE, MARGARET etal	17	738 - 744

CARGILE, WILLIAM A.	2	849 - 856
CARLISLE, EDMUND L.	2	332
CARLISLE, JOHN	13	102 - 104
CARLISLE, JOHN	19	295 - 316
CARNLEY, GEORGE	20	398 - 424
CARNLEY, SARAH ANN etal	17	966
CARNLY, LEWIS	13	156 - 173
CARNLY, LEWIS	13	207 - 221
CARNLY, LEWIS	13	485 - 533
CARPENTER, IDA L.	2	268 - 275
CARPENTER, JESSE	14	228 - 269
CARR, ANSLEY	1	862 - 885
CARR, DANIEL	2	869 - 874
CARR, DANIEL	14	412 - 414
CARR, ROSANNA P.	2	410 - 424
CARROLL, AMANDA etal.	1	836 - 846
CARROLL, CLAUDINE	14	388
CARROLL, D.L.	1	962 - 967
CARROLL, JOHN	1	738 - 777
CARROLL, JOHN	1	778 - 801
CARROLL, JOHN	2	616 - 636
CARROLL, JOHN SR.	1	802 - 808
CARROLL, M.E. & G.W.	2	637 - 657
CARROLL, M.J.	1	809 - 835
CARROLL, MARTHA B.	2	472 - 476
CARROLL, S.B.	14	571 - 651
CARROLL, S.M. etal.	2	191
CARROLL, SAMUEL	14	411
CARTER, CHARLES A.	2	409
CARTER, CYNTHIA	2	195 - 223
CARTER, DARLING	14	277 - 300
CARTER, FRANCIS	2	399 - 408
CARTER, HENRY S.	2	597 - 615
CARTER, HENRY S.	21	893
CARTER, HENRY S.	17	517 - 576
CARTER, JOHN	13	227 - 262
CARTER, JOHN	13	432 - 436
CARTER, LEE	17	629 - 641
CARTER, S.F.	18	1046 - 1076
CASON, FRANCIS	17	788 - 795
CASON, FRANCIS JANE	2	563
CASON, HENRY	14	652 - 724
CASON, HENRY	17	677 - 683, 843 - 847

CASTLEBERRY, DRUCILLA & DANIEL	1	959 - 961
CASTLEBERRY, ISAAC	14	524 - 570
CATRETT, JOHN	3	200 - 201
CATRETT, JOHN JR.	14	369 - 387
CATRETT, THOMAS	1	936 - 958
CATTRETT, MELISSA etal.	2	192
CHANCELLER, W.W.	14	342
CHANCEY, JOHN A.	2	848
CHESSER, JOHN	14	343 - 365
CHILDS, G.L.	14	205 - 227
CHILDS, RAIBON etal	17	388 - 391
CHILDS, RUBIN	2	847
CHILDS, WILLIAM	2	569 - 582
CHRISTIAN, W.T.	18	941 - 976
CHRISTIAN, WM. F.	19	33 - 36
CHRISTIAN, WM. F.	17	582 - 591
CLARK, BETHANY etal	17	498 - 515
CLARK, HOSEA	14	416 - 438
CLARK, JOHN	14	415
CLARK, JOHN J.	14	389 - 410
CLARK, SARAH MARTHA	20	45 - 52
CLARY, W.S.	19	23
CLARY, W.S.	20	95 - 97
CLAYTON, I.B.	2	350 - 370
COBLER, SAM	17	777
COCHRAN, T.G. & L.L.	17	569 - 579
COCKRAN, T.G. & L.L.	1	971 - 972
COCKROFT, HENRY	14	366 - 368
COGBURN, CYNTHIA	14	270 - 276
COGBURN, MARTHA etal.	2	583 - 590
COKER, JOHN	17	827
COLE, ALIA etal	17	377
COLE, MASON	14	152 - 171
COLEMAN, P.J.	19	12 - 22
COLEMAN, W.S.	17	819 - 820
COLLIER, BENJAMIN	19	110 - 160
COLLINS, GEO. W.	17	826
COLLINS, GEORGE W.	13	40 - 49
COLLINS, W.B.	2	428 - 469
COLLINS, WILLIAM B.	2	371 - 398
COLLINSWORTH, ZACH	14	193 - 204
CONNELL, SARAH E. HARTER	5	198 - 213
COOK, ARCHIBALD	2	193

COOK, JAMES G.	2	305 - 307
COOK, JOHN E.	2	425 - 427
COOK, JOHN E.	11	735 - 736
COOK, M.O.G.	13	17 - 27
COOKSEY, AMANDA etal	17	821 - 822
COOPER, ENOCH	14	476 - 477
COPE, H. & T.	17	837 - 838
COPE, SAMUEL	20	356 - 388
COPELAND, ISAAC	1	886 - 935
COPELAND, NANCY B.	2	308 - 331
CORBETT, LOT	13	854 - 869
CORLEY, ABRAHAM etal.	2	658 - 677
CORLEY, ALABAMA	1	968 - 970
CORLEY, JOHN C.	2	733 - 773
COSBY, SAMUEL	2	861 - 865
COWART, JAMES	2	194
COWART, JOHN W.	2	254 - 267
COWART, NATHANIAL	2	477 - 481
COX, WM. R.	13	797 - 828
CRAIG, DAVID	14	478 - 523
CRAIG, MARTHA	2	779 - 807
CRANSWELL, ADA	2	866 - 867
CRASWELL, REBECCA	14	301 - 334
CRAUSWELL, JAMES S.	14	172 - 192
CRAWFORD, EDWARD A.	2	868
CRAWFORD, MARY	2	842 - 843
CRIBB, THOMAS	14	439 - 475
CROSWELL, ELI	13	402 - 431
CROW, JOHN etal.	2	276 - 293
CROWDER, JOHN M.	13	71 - 77
CUMMING, JOHN	1	847 - 861
CURETON, JOHN	3	199
CURRY, CLARINDA	2	829 - 841
CURTIS, JOHN D.	2	678 - 733
DANIEL, ISAAC B.	15	479 - 491
DARBY, B.F. etal	16	1 - 9
DARBY, JAMES	13	745 - 796
DARBY, SUSAN	15	678 - 704
DARBY, WILLIS	9	823 - 824
DASSINGER, JOSEPH	14	887 - 910
DAVENPORT, ELIZABETH	13	829 - 853
DAVIS, ELLANDER	3	1
DAVIS, ENOCH	15	829 - 836

DAVIS, GEORGE F. etal	15	867 - 885
DAVIS, JAS. D.	15	795 - 816
DAVIS, JOHN P.	9	718 - 720
DAVIS, JOHN P.	15	244 - 261
DAVIS, JOSIAH	3	228 - 296 & 559
DAVIS, PRESSLEY	15	121 - 193
DAVIS, WILLIAM	13	737 - 744
DAVIS, WM.	15	817 - 828
DAWKINS, A.T.	15	841 - 866
DAWKINS, M.A.C.	3	202 - 209
DAY, MARTIN H.	16	10 - 175
DEAN, JOSEPH L.	2	880 - 887
DEAN, STEPHEN B.	15	705 - 774
DEFFEE, JOHN	15	886 - 924
DENNIS, CHAS. A.	15	262 - 432
DENNIS, DANIEL	8	317 - 329
DENNIS, JOEL	8	330 - 384
DICKEY, THOMAS S.	1	99 - 113
DILLARD, L.R. etal.	9	830
DINKINS, A.J. & D.D.	9	387 - 446
DINKINS, EDWARD	3	297 - 322
DORMAN, JOHN A.	9	831 - 838
DORMAN, LEVERETT	15	535 - 592
DORNE, ABNER	15	194 - 243
DORRIS, WM.	16	533 - 556
DOWNING, A.J.	15	492 - 498
DOWNING, REBBECA F.	8	775 - 783
DOWNING, THOMAS	15	1 - 120
DRIGGERS, ANZA etal.	9	798 - 807
DUBOSE, JEREMIAH	15	645 - 677
DUBOSE, W.H. heirs	9	703 - 713
DUKE, M.C. & M.F.	11	77 - 114
DUNCAN, JULIUS M.	3	210 - 227
DUNN, DAVID A.	16	176 - 315
DYER, JOHN F.	15	593 - 618
EASTERLING, HENRY	15	775 - 794
EASTERS, CLARINDA	3	392 - 394
EASTERS, ERNSLEY	16	522 - 532
EAVES, JANE B.	3	323 - 344
EDDINS, JOHN S.	3	396 - 399
EDDINS, JOSEPH	11	177 - 192
EDWARDS, BENJAMIN	16	557 - 688
EDWARDS, J.J.	3	391, 560

EDWARDS, JOHN	3	345 - 390
EDWARDS, JOSEPH	15	619 - 644
ELLIS, WM. S.	17	236 - 273
ELLIT, DAVIS	15	837 - 840
EMERSON, JOHN	3	199
EMMERSON, F.M.	3	400 - 413
EMMERSON, JOHN	15	433 - 478
ETHRIDGE, GEORGE W. etal.	9	808 - 810
ETHRIDGE, PHILIP Z.	16	416 - 432
EUBANKS, GEORGE & M.F.	9	673 - 693
EUBANKS, JOHN	17	47 - 112 or 67 - 112
EUBANKS, M.F. & GEO.	15	673 - 693
EVANS, WILLIS J.	17	113 - 152
EVANS, WM. P.	15	516 - 534
EVERETT, D.J.	15	499 - 575
EVERHART, SUSAN	3	395
FANNIN, JOSEPH B.	4	1 - 4
FARIOR, T. & ANN	18	83 - 95
FARRIOR, WM.	18	318 - 366
FARRIOR, WM.	18	94 - 95
FAULK, JOSEPH T.	3	550
FAULK, MARY A. etal	18	35 - 40
FAULK, SARAH	16	874 - 881
FAULKNER, MARTHA J. (was Stewart)	3	536 - 548
FAULKNER, W.F.	4	86 - 103
FAY, PATRICK	4	14 - 16
FERRELL, THOS.	17	274 - 305
FERRILL, THOMAS	3	551 - 553
FIELDER, L.B.	17	306 - 332
FIELDER, MARY L.	16	870
FIELDER, THOS. L.	16	394 - 413
FILDER, THOMAS L.	3	456 - 461
FINLAYSON, M.A.	18	143 - 169
FINLAYSON, WM. N.	3	549
FITZGERALD, P.D.	17	234 - 235
FITZPATRICK, BIRD	2	982 - 1004
FITZPATRICK, JAMES & BIRD	3	468 - 496
FITZPATRICK, JAMES F.	3	497 - 519
FITZPATRICK, SARAH	18	8 - 28
FLEMING, ADAM	4	17 - 18
FLOURNOY, JONATHAN C.	2	934 - 981
FLOWERS, A.F.	4	19 - 24
FLOWERS, A.F. etal.	8	255 - 316

FLOWERS, J.I.W.	8	254
FLOWERS, JAMES L. & LILLA P.	2	470 - 471
FLOWERS, JOHN	8	255 - 316
FLOWERS, JOHN I.W.	3	554 - 558
FLOWERS, SILAS R.	4	25 - 66
FLOWERS, SILAS W. etal	18	127 - 142
FLOWERS, W.W.	2	178 - 190
FLOWERS, WINGATE	2	894
FLOYD, JETHRO	18	227 - 237
FLOYD, LEWIS J.	20	93 - 94
FLOYD, SAM	17	333 - 342
FLOYD, SAMUEL	3	454 - 455
FLOYD, WM.	16	515 - 521
FOLMAR, ISAAC S.	18	517 - 568
FOLMAR, JACOB	18	569 - 576
FOLMAR, JOEL	18	44 - 73
FOREMAN, DAVID	3	520 - 534
FOREMAN, JACOB O.	2	888 - 893
FORTUNE, JOSHUA	18	412 - 449
FOWLER, BURRELL	16	368 - 376
FOWLER, BURRELL	17	191 - 230
FOWLER, N.S.	3	200 - 201
FRANKLIN, BARNETT	16	872 - 873
FRANKLIN, H.D.	16	391 - 393
FRANKLIN, JOHN	18	603 - 622
FRAZER, ALLEN	3	414 - 452
FRAZER, WM.	18	732 - 770
FRAZER, WM. H.	3	414 - 452
FRAZIER, MODINA	18	103 - 109
FRIZEL, JASON	16	440 - 514
FRIZEL, JASON	18	74 - 92
FRIZLE, ELIZABETH J.	18	623 - 639
FRIZLE, EPHRAIM	18	648 - 683
FRIZZLE, EPHRAIM	3	453
FRIZZLE, TEMPERANCE	2	895 - 933
FRIZZLE, THOMAS	18	779 - 815
FRYER, A. & J.	16	868
FRYER, ALEXANDER	18	577 - 602
FRYER, LEWIS A.	4	67 - 85
FRYER, THOMAS L.	3	462 - 467
FRYER, THOMAS L.	7	491 - 514
FRYER, WM. Y.	18	264 - 319
FUQUA, JAMES M.	4	5 - 13

FURLOW, JAMES M.	3	535
GAINES, W.J.	4	785 - 786
GALLOWAY, F.S.	3	564 - 569
GALLOWAY, MARY A.	4	431 - 435
GAMBLE, S.A. etal.	4	372 - 387
GANEY, R.E.	19	24 - 32
GANEY, STEPHEN	20	394 - 397
GANEY, STEPHEN	18	1012 - 1045
GARDNER, F. & S.H.	18	255 - 256
GARDNER, JAMES C.	3	535
GARNER, J.L.	3	583 - 657
GARNER, JEFFERSON L.	3	570 - 581
GARRETT, S.L.	4	215 - 217
GARRETT, SARAH E.	3	582
GERALD, ALEX	4	359 - 363
GERALD, FRANKLIN	16	882 - 929
GERALD, POLINA	4	352 - 358
GERALD, SARAH M.	20	81 - 92
GIBSON, ROBERT J.	4	218 - 228
GIBSON, SAMUEL	18	1105 - 1119
GIBSON, SAMUEL R.	4	110 - 214
GIBSON, SYLVANUS	3	658 - 693
GILES, SAMANTHA	4	427 - 430
GILLIS, M.I. or M.J.	20	1 - 12
GILMORE, ARCHIBALD	18	238 - 246
GILMORE, HUGH G.	4	399 - 424
GILMORE, JAMES W.	3	694 - 698
GLAWSON, JAMES	4	289 - 351
GODDIN, NATHAN	18	400 - 411
GODWIN, EPHRAIM	18	684 - 731
GODWIN, S.P.	17	59
GODWIN, WILEY	16	866
GODWIN, WILEY	20	13 - 24
GOFF, D.A.	4	388 - 393
GOLDEN, ELIZABETH	4	394 - 398
GOMMILLION, HENRY	16	425 - 427, 769 - 783
GOODE, BETTIE	4	364 - 371
GOODMAN, JOHN	4	425 - 426
GOOLSBY, MICAJAH	18	450 - 489
GOOLSBY, WOOTEN	19	1 - 11
GRADY, H.M.	3	699 - 709
GRAHAM, EMMA JANE	3	710 - 711
GRAHAM, M.J. etal.	3	711

GRANGER, JOHN	18	170 - 226
GRANT, SARAH	3	717 - 729
GRAVES, ARCHIBALD	3	730 - 745
GRAVES, DAVID	4	229 - 288
GRAVES, ELIJAH D.	20	25 - 44
GRAVES, GEORGE W.	3	754 - 758
GRAVES, HARDY	18	884 - 940
GRAVES, JOHN J.	3	748 - 753
GRAVES, JOHN J.	3	746
GRAVES, M.E. & J.W.	3	747
GRAVES, MARY E. & JAMES W.	3	747
GRAVES, THOS.	16	319 - 322
GRAY, ELI B.	3	712 - 716
GRAY, MARY	7	397 - 403
GREEN, JOHN O.	3	759 - 760
GREEN, NANCY B.	4	104 - 109
GRIDER, BENJAMIN	18	821 - 882
GRIFFIN, A.A.	16	865
GRIFFIN, BURELL W.	18	1077 - 1104
GRIFFIN, LUNSFORD	20	69 - 80
GRIFFIN, WM. H. & JASPER	3	761 - 762
GRIMES, DOSON	18	977 - 1011
GRIMES, W.F.	16	863
GRIMES, W.F.	18	41 - 43
GRIMMER, MARY J.	3	763
GRIMMER, MARY J.	12	355 - 357
GUNTER, MAE	17	56 - 58
HAIL, DAVID	19	338 - 345
HAIR, PETER	16	867
HALL, ISAAC	5	305 - 346
HAMILTON, DANIEL	17	1082
HAMILTON, J.A.	19	1024 - 1025
HAMM, THOMAS	20	415 - 436
HAMMONDS, JOHN	20	624 - 625
HANCHEY, JOHN W.	16	808 - 861
HARDAMAN, CHARLES etal.	9	257 - 390
HARDAMAN, LEE	8	738 - 745
HARDEMAN, U.	20	513 - 529
HARDIE, JOS. E.	19	905
HARP, W.	20	606 - 616
HARRELL, HENRY	3	776 - 777
HARRIS, AMOS	19	231 - 241
HARRIS, FRANCIS	7	483 - 484

HARRIS, J.D.	3	776 - 777
HARRIS, J.W. etal.	8	784 - 787
HARRIS, WILLIAM D.	8	109 - 156
HARRIS, WILLIAM T.	5	347 - 401
HARRISON, MARY	3	767 - 775
HARRISON, WM. etal	18	818
HARTER, SARAH (CONNELL)	5	198 - 213
HARTER, WM. H.	19	717 - 731
HARTSFIELD, GEORGIA E.	3	764 - 766
HARTSFIELD, J.W. etal.	5	290 - 304
HARTSFIELD, W.W.	20	274 - 318
HARVEY, D.	11	115 - 164
HARWELL, J.W.	5	402 - 424
HARWELL, T.C.	19	346 - 355
HATAWAY, DANIEL	20	437 - 469
HAWKINS, WM. C.	20	559 - 578
HAYGOOD, J.W.	3	798 - 807
HENDERSON Admr's. Vs. HENDERSC	3	949 - 955
HENDERSON, ELI	5	1 - 197
HENDERSON, J.A.	3	956 - 1009
HENDERSON, MATTHEW	19	317 - 326
HENDERSON, SHADRACK	17	857 - 884
HENDERSON, SUSAN E. etal.	9	627 - 672
HENDRICK, T.H. etal.	5	232 - 239
HERNDON, JAMES	5	426 - 452
HERNDON, JOHN P.	20	485 - 512
HERNDON, SYLVIA	20	547 - 558
HERRIN, HENRY	19	37 - 109
HERRIN, MICHAEL	19	909 - 923
HICKS, MARY A.	4	431 - 435
HICKS, W.H.	20	243 - 273
HIGDON, TERRILL	19	327 - 337
HIGHTOWER, LUCINDA REBECCA	3	810 - 812
HILL, HILSMON	11	602
HILL, JAMES	3	813
HILL, R.H.	3	814
HILLIARD, ANNIE V. & LENORA L.	3	808 - 809
HILLIARD, WILLIAM	5	260 - 282
HIXON, DANIEL A. etal.	5	214 - 231
HIXON, JEREMIAH A.	3	956 - 1009
HIXON, SAMUEL	3	815 - 894
HIXON, W.L.	19	1026 - 1028
HIXON, WM. L.	3	895 - 903

HOBDY, EDMUND	19	629 - 651
HOBDY, IVEY	20	105 - 166
HOBDY, JAMES M.	3	904 - 905
HOBDY, JOHN & C.	16	785 - 807
HOBDY, JOHN etal	19	1034 - 1036
HOBDY, JOHN etal.	5	243 - 259
HOBDY, JOHN R. etal	16	866
HOBDY, THOMAS (minor of JOHN E. H	3	906 - 909
HODGES, B.W.	19	161 - 190
HOLENHEAD, A.P.	3	915
HOLLAND, THOMAS J.	3	910 - 914
HOLLEY, BEASANT	19	516 - 540
HOLLOWAY, M.E. etal	16	864
HOLLOWAY, M.E. etal	20	389 - 393
HOOK, HILLERY SR.	17	954 - 1051
HOOKS, CHARLES A.	3	916
HOOKS, DANIEL	19	213 - 230
HOOKS, DANIEL	20	167 - 208
HOOKS, FRANCIS M.	3	916
HOOKS, GEORGE	19	985 - 1023
HOOKS, JAMES	11	63 - 68
HOOKS, R.M.	5	240 - 242
HOOKS, RACHEL	11	1 - 61
HOOKS, THOMAS J.	19	191 - 212
HORN, ISAAC	17	1082
HORN, MICHAEL	20	617 - 623
HOUGH, JOSEPH D.	11	172 - 176
HOUGH, NANCY	20	530 - 546
HOUGHTON, F.R.	20	626 - 630
HOWARD, JNO. A.	5	282 - 289
HUDSON, A.R.	17	365 - 373
HUDSON, ELIZABETH A.	11	431 - 521
HUGHES, WM. S.	17	1052 - 1081
HUNT, HOLLIS, JACKSON, & EMELINI	5	624 - 625
HURLEY, FREEMAN B.	19	242 - 273
HURLEY, JOEL	20	388 - 414
HURLEY, L.J.G.	3	917 - 931
HURLEY, W.F.	8	751 - 759
HURST, HOLLIS etal	17	360 - 361
HURST, PRISCILLA	19	593 - 622
HURT, JAMES	19	1029
HURT, JOHN	20	593 - 605
HURY, RICHARD or Henry, Richard	16	871

HUTCHINSON, J.B. etal.	3	933 - 948
HUTCHISON, J.B.	20	319 - 351
HUTCHISON, JAMES	20	209 - 242
HUTCHISON, JOHN	20	579 - 592
HUTCHISON, W.W.	20	352 - 375
HUTCHISON, WM. B.	19	274 - 294
HUTTO, CHARLES	20	470 - 484
HUTTO, NANCY ANN	3	932
HYATT, MARY M.	3	904 - 905
JACKSON, A.A.	5	739
JACKSON, A.L., F.M., & N.E.	5	757 - 759
JACKSON, ALEXANDER	19	569 - 587
JACKSON, DANIEL	19	588 - 592
JACKSON, J.T.	5	542 - 602
JACKSON, J.T.	5	621 - 622
JACKSON, JNO. T.	20	1070 - 1081
JACKSON, RANDALL	12	2 - 3
JACKSON, ROBERT	19	441 - 457, 875 - 904
JACOBS, JOHN	5	626 - 632
JAMES, MARY	5	912 - 952
JARRELL, MARGARET L.	5	882
JEFCOAT, AVIS	5	734 - 738
JEFCOAT, JACOB	5	639 - 661
JEFFCOAT, H. & S.	11	675 - 677
JEFFCOAT, JOHN	19	428 - 440
JEFFCOAT, RHEUBIN	5	502 - 509
JEFFCOAT, SAMUEL	5	453 - 496
JENERETT, ELIAS	5	662 - 733
JENKINS, WILEY	19	707 - 765
JOHNS, L.J.	19	732 - 786
JOHNS, THOMAS W.	5	750 - 755
JOHNS, WM. M., LEROY B., MARY	5	510 - 521
JOHNSON, A.D.	5	835 - 838
JOHNSON, BOB	20	1090 - 1096
JOHNSON, ELIAS	5	756
JOHNSON, J.A.	19	652 - 688
JOHNSON, JARRED	5	760 - 805
JOHNSON, O.S.	5	884 - 911
JOHNSON, S.D.	19	623 - 628
JOHNSON, SOLOMON	19	669 - 716
JOINER, JONES A. heir of Nathan R. Jc	5	741
JOINER, LEWIS	5	740
JOINER, NATHAN	19	458 - 515

JONES, AMANDA M. etal.	5	623
JONES, B.M.	5	746 - 747
JONES, DAVID	5	748 - 749
JONES, E.H.	19	939 - 963
JONES, ELIZABETH	21	158 - 159
JONES, JAMES etal.	5	522 - 541
JONES, JAMES H.	21	145 - 156
JONES, JAMES M. etal. Heirs of W.A. J	5	810 - 834
JONES, JAS. D.	21	1 - 111
JONES, M.J.	11	701 - 706
JONES, MARY E., WM. W., LOUISA J.	5	633
JONES, MINTON J., WM. A., & MARY	5	883
JONES, S.F., B.M., & MARY A.	12	489 - 556
JONES, SETETON	17	850
JONES, SUSAN A.	5	634 - 638
JONES, URBAN L.	11	681 - 683
JONES, WILLIAM A.	5	839 - 881
JORDAN, CHARLIE	5	425
JORDAN, JAMES H.	5	603 - 620
JORDAN, JOEL	5	497 - 501
JORDAN, JOSIAH	19	964 - 984
JORDAN, ROSS	5	742 - 745
JORDAN, SAMUEL B.	19	924 - 938
KEATON, N.B.	6	1
KEENER, JAMES M.	10	340 - 341
KEILS, ISAAC	21	157
KELLY, ELIAS	20	675 - 1002
KELLY, G.J. etal.	9	811 - 822
KELLY, J.M.	9	736
KELLY, J.P.D.	4	528 - 530
KELLY, JAMES MICHAEL	4	525 - 530
KERSEY, JOHN	11	69 - 72
KEY, JOHN	20	1041 - 1069
KINDRED, F.L. & J.H.	20	631 - 674
KING, GEORGE W. Gdn. of Susan King	4	554 - 563
KING, J.F.	4	550 - 553
KING, WILLIAM	4	564 - 599
KING, WILLIAM R. & N.D.	9	694
KNOWLES, JOSEPH B.	4	436 - 524
KNOWLES, RICHARD	6	1
KNOWLES, ROBERT	20	1003 - 1040
KNOWLES, THOMAS	21	112 - 144
KNOX, O.F.	4	531 - 547

KOKER, THOMAS	13	687 - 736
KYLE, W.B.	20	1081 - 1090
LAMM, SARAH A.	21	866 - 874
LATIMER, JOSEPH A.	4	669 - 700
LAWHORN, JOHN	9	714 - 715
LAWRENCE, SARAH	4	711 - 716
LAWSON, ELIZA	11	74 - 76
LEACH, JAMES M.	4	701 - 704
LEAKE, WM. B.	21	247 - 276
LEDDON, JACOB J.	4	801 - 807
LEE, BENJAMIN	4	625 - 629
LEE, BETSY A. etal.	4	600 - 620
LEE, JAMES	21	851 - 860
LEE, MATILDA E.	16	328 - 346
LEE, W.P.	21	413 - 424
LEE, WILLIAM	4	630 - 637
LEVERETT, HIRAM J.	21	491 - 541
LEWIS, ELISHA	4	732 - 763
LEWIS, JAMES L.	4	621 - 624
LEWIS, LODERICK L.	5	809
LIGON, D.W. etal.	4	793 - 800
LINDSAY, NATHAN H.	4	771 - 784
LINDSEY, JORDAN	4	710
LINDSEY, WM.	21	437 - 440
LINTON, C.P.	4	810
LINTON, JOHN & WINNIE	4	808 - 809
LINTON, WM. etal	17	840
LIPTROTT, KIZIAH & MARTHA W.L.	4	787 - 792
LIPTROTT, WM. A.	21	805 - 850
LITTLE, JOHN N.	21	343 - 345
LLOYD, LEROY	21	297 - 342
LOCK, RICHARD	21	876 - 886
LOCKARD, PHOEBE J.	17	684 - 692
LOCKE, ELIAS H. & RICHARD D.	4	765
LOCKHART, RICHARD M.	21	887 - 892
LONG, DAVID A.	21	425 - 436
LONG, JAMES B.	21	346 - 363
LONG, MARY A.	4	766 - 770
LORD, JUDSON etal.	8	227 - 228
LOVELESS, DAVID J.	4	764
LOW, WM. & JOHN A.	21	578 - 615
LOWE, WILLIAM	5	807 - 808
LOWRY, JOHNNIE	4	785 - 786

LOYD, LEROY etal.	9	721 - 735
LUCKIE, JAMES B.	4	717 - 731
LUDLAM, JEREMIAH	21	542 - 577
LUDLAM, JOHN	21	667 - 690
LUDLOW, ELIZABETH	4	705 - 709
LUDLUM, MARTHA	9	716 - 717
LYNN, L.W.	4	638 - 659
LYNN, W.K. & JOSEPHINE	4	660 - 668
MADISON, JAMES	17	828
MAHONEY, C.T.	22	230 - 274
MAHONEY, MARTHA etal.	6	552
MANCELL, CHRISTOPHER etal.	6	559 - 575
MANN, LEWIS	23	457, 854 - 884
MANN, ROBT.	17	764 - 765
MANNING, W.H.	24	477 - 493
MANNING, W.H.	17	392 - 438
MANSELL, JOHN	22	486 - 519
MANSELL, SAM'L. J. etal	17	745 - 750
MARLOW, ZACHERY	23	447 - 453
MARTIN, JOHN	7	472 - 476
MARTIN, MARY A.	7	469 - 471
MARTIN, Y.	23	461
MARTIN, YERBY etal.	6	576 - 592
MATHEWS, ARTHUR	23	456, 717 - 730
MATHEWS, JOHN H.	8	89 - 96
MATHEWS, LEROY	17	693
MATHEWS, SMITH	17	831
MAY, JAMES etal.	6	616 - 701
MCADAMS, THOS.	24	146 - 159
MCAFEE, FLORENCE A.	6	16 - 18
MCAFEE, JOSEPH	6	337 - 377
MCBETH, WALTER	23	368 - 446
MCBURNEY, DE HUGH	22	212 - 229
MCCALL, SARAH	23	685 - 698
MCCASKELL, D.C.	21	755 - 804
MCCASKILL, GILBERT A.	6	34 - 75
MCCOLLOUGH, SALLIE C. etal.	6	748 - 759
MCCRARY, AMANDA E.	6	430 - 437
MCCRARY, J.W.	6	731 - 741
MCCRARY, T.K.	23	38 - 164
MCCRARY, THOMAS K.	6	416 - 424
MCCRIMMINE, HENRY	6	450 - 453
MCCRUMMING, R.	23	165 - 200

MCCULLOUGH, JAMES	17	516 - 549
MCCUMMIN, ALEX	22	199 - 211
MCDANIEL, A.D.	23	731 - 762
MCDANIEL, AGNES	6	202 - 229
MCDONALD, J.W. etal.	6	378 - 398
MCDOWELL, ALEX	21	1037 - 1049
MCDOWELL, ALEXANDER	4	811 - 905
MCDOWELL, JAMES	24	507 - 511
MCDOWELL, W.D.	23	589 - 600
MCDOWELL, WM. D.	21	894
MCDUFFEE, JOHN	17	800 - 804
MCEACHERN, J.D.	6	86 - 87
MCGOURTS, JAS. & WM.	17	849
MCGOWEN, THOMAS L.	6	81 - 85
MCGOWEN, THOS. D.S.	23	317 - 335
MCGRADY, ROBERT	22	520 - 584
MCINTYRE, ED L.	24	518
MCINTYRE, EDWARD L.	6	399 - 415
MCKAY, JOHN	6	90 - 96
MCKINNON, DANIEL	6	76 - 80
MCKINNON, DANIEL	6	97 - 201
MCKINNON, REBECCA etal	18	791 - 793
MCKOWN, JOHN	23	201 - 316
MCLANE, FRANCIS etal.	6	494
MCLANEY, F.F.	6	495 - 498
MCLANEY, HENRY C.	6	490 - 491
MCLANEY, JAMES	6	454 - 460
MCLANEY, JAMES M. W.	6	501 - 507
MCLEAN, CHARLES	24	500 - 502
MCLEAN, DUNCAN	21	636 = 666
MCLEAN, JOHN BILL	6	230 - 306
MCLEMORE, CORINE	6	19 - 33
MCLENDON, E.	23	674
MCLENDON, EVERETT	21	895 - 907
MCLENDON, JAMES	23	1 - 37
MCLENDON, JOHN M. etal.	6	438 - 449
MCLENDON, SARAH etal.	7	137 - 278
MCLENDON, WM. H. & M.	17	694 - 709
MCLEOD, ALEX	6	9 - 15
MCLEOD, ANGUS	23	336 - 367
MCLEOD, BRYANT	19	1037 - 1062
MCLEOD, NORMAN	6	325 - 335
MCLURE, E.E. & W.F.	6	336

MCLURE, R.R.	21	980 - 1010
MCMICHAEL, JOHN	24	359 - 384
MCMILLAN, ANGUS R. etal.	6	88 - 89
MCMILLAN, EDWARD	21	908 - 928
MCMILLAN, MARGARET	6	702 - 706
MCMILLAN, MARGARET	7	279 - 304
MCMORRIS, DANIEL	6	425 - 429
MCNEIL, ANN	17	839
MCNEIL, CATHERINE	17	758
MCNEIL, JOHN	24	503 - 506
MCNEIL, JOHN	17	757
MCNEIL, JOHN A.	21	441 - 491
MCNEIL, M.M. etal.	6	2 - 8
MCNEIL, MARY	17	767
MCNEIL, S.C. etal.	6	307 - 324
MCWHORTER, JOHN C.	24	185 - 256, 410 - 422
MEADOWS, JOSHUA	24	257 - 283
MEADOWS, TELITHA etal.	6	593 - 594
MEDLOCK, ANDERSON	22	1 - 126
MEDLOCK, ANDERSON	23	462 - 485
MEDLOCK, BENJAMIN	21	616 - 635
MEDLOCK, WM. JAMES	17	832 - 836
MEIRS, DAN'L. T.	23	763 - 831
MENEFEE, RACHAEL M.	23	673 - 684
MEREDITH, EZEKIEL	21	1050 - 1060
MILES, D.D.	24	99 - 145
MILLER, THOMAS	21	472 - 490
MILLS, ABIJAH H.	6	553
MILLS, HENRY L. etal.	6	512 - 551
MILLS, NANCY	22	347 - 399
MILLS, WILLIAM P.	6	486 - 489
MILNER, SAMANTHA	6	595 - 599
MING, HENRY M.	22	127 - 198
MING, THOMAS	22	580
MING, WM.	17	768 - 776
MITCHELL, MATHEW	22	400 - 417
MITCHELL, RICHARD L.	6	492 - 493
MITCHELL, RICK etal.	6	554 - 558
MIZE, WM. A.	24	519
MONEY, SAMUEL N.	6	507
MOORE, BENJAMIN F.	21	1011 - 1036
MOORE, HOLLAND	6	510 - 511
MOORE, JOHN T.	21	160 - 246

MOORE, JOHN W.	6	829 - 935
MOORE, L.D.	6	600 - 615
MOORE, S.H.	6	508 - 509
MORELAND, E.L.	23	458 - 460
MORELAND, JOHN FRANKLIN	6	505 - 506
MORRIS, CLAUD	6	461 - 468
MORRISON, ALEX D.	23	454 - 455
MORROW, MARY	21	861 - 865
MORROW, PETER G.	21	719 - 754
MOSELEY, WM.	21	929 - 936
MOSER, BALINDA	22	418 - 485
MOSSER, MARY etal.	7	99 - 136
MOSSER, SAMUEL	18	7
MOSSER, SAMUEL	21	364 - 412
MOTES, DENDY	21	691 - 718
MOTES, PRESSLEY A.	18	263
MULKEY, FELIX G. etal.	6	475 - 485
MURCHIN, JAS. S.	23	832 - 853
MURPHREE, B.F.	23	699 - 717
MURPHREE, T.F.	6	499
MURPHREE, THOMAS M.	17	362 - 363
MURPHREE, W.M.	6	500
MURPHY, ROBERT	21	957 - 979
MYHAND, JAMES	6	469 - 474
NASH, W.A.	24	160 - 184
NELSON, JOHN	6	707 - 730
NEUGENT, G.W.	7	1 - 2
NEWBERRY, J.C.	24	385 - 409
NEWTON, JASPER	17	824
NICHOLSON, DUNCAN	23	486 - 588
NIXON, J.L.	6	776 - 802
NIXON, JOHN H.	4	911
NIXON, TINA	4	912 - 920
NOBLES, JOHN	24	284 - 304
NOBLES, MARK	24	63 - 98
NORDAN, A.B. etal.	6	760 - 775
NORDAN, A.B. etal.	8	253
NORDAN, CLEMINTINE	4	906 - 909
NORTON, GEORGE W.	4	910
NORWOOD, CORNELIUS C. & ANNA.	4	914 - 920
O'DAY, CINTHIA	18	638 - 648
OFFICER, THOMAS	16	316 - 318
OLIVER, JAMES C.	22	585 - 603, 423 - 476

OLIVER, MARY	24	494 - 499
OUSLEY, J.C.	24	1 - 62
OWENS, IDA etal.	4	921
OWENS, NETTIE & WALTER	4	922
OWENS, SMITH J.	5	806
OWENS, W.J.K.	17	439 - 442
PADGETT, C.J.	7	404 - 406
PADGETT, NANCY	11	289 - 358
PADGETT, NELSON	8	1 - 5
PARISH, WILLIAM J.	8	52 - 55
PARK, FRANK	25	234 - 259
PARK, JAS. D.	22	682 - 688
PARKS, E.F. & I.H.	11	73
PAUL, ROBERT	22	806 - 838
PAULK, FORBES	22	788 - 805
PAULK, WILLIAM A.	7	388 - 396
PEACH, W.F. & G.W.	11	165 - 171
PEARCE, ELIZABETH	17	815 - 841
PEARSON, THOS. J.	25	1 - 123
PEEK, ZACKARIAH	8	216
PENNINGTON, C.C.	6	803 - 828
PENNINGTON, M. & P.	7	703 - 704
PERDUE, EASTER	22	639 - 647
PERDUE, LEROY	25	260 - 298
PERDUE, M.E.	22	750 - 787
PERSONS, AMOS	22	648 - 676
PETERS, HARRIETT	25	179 - 191
PHILLIPS, JAMES	22	839 - 854
PHILLIPS, JOHN	22	709 - 749
PHILLIPS, MARY	7	3 - 34
PHILLIPS, MATILDA etal	18	560
PHILLIPS, MATILDA M. etal.	8	200 - 215
PICKETT, H.F.	25	124 - 146
PICKETT, JAMES	8	186 - 188
PICKETT, MARY A.	8	244 - 245
PICKETT, RICHARD M.	11	359 - 430
PIERCE, ELISHA R.	22	689 - 708
PIERSON, THOMAS N.	9	737
PITMAN, HIRAM	11	258 - 275
PITTS, HENRY W.	25	166 - 169
PITTS, LEE etal.	9	825 - 829
PITTS, LOU etal.	7	485 - 490
PITTS, MARTHA E.	11	193 - 205

SESSIONS, S.A. & M.J.	8	627 - 643
SESSIONS, S.A. & M.J.	12	368 - 369
SHANKS, JOSEPH E.	11	674
SHAW, A.S.	7	366 - 387
SHAW, MARY & JOHN R.	11	725 - 728
SHELL, J.W.	8	189 - 193
SHIRLEY, H.D. or. W.D.	8	247 - 251
SHIRLEY, MONTEREY etal.	7	477 - 482
SHULTZ, FREDRICK	7	695 - 702
SILER, J.O.G.	8	60 - 77
SILER, SALLIE A.	7	407 - 409
SIMMONS, DORCAS	11	542 - 563
SIMMONS, WILLIAM J.	11	724
SIMS, MARY A. etal.	8	337 - 361
SIMS, WILLIAM	11	714 - 716
SINGNIFIELD, MOSES	8	659 - 664
SMILEY, JACOB & WM. J.	12	51 - 84
SMILEY, STEPHEN D.	7	521 - 694
SMILIE, ELLA	7	461 - 468
SMILIE, WYLY	8	376 - 378
SMITH, ALEX	7	705 - 813
SMITH, ALEX	12	367
SMITH, D.M.	11	718 - 719
SMITH, SARAH B.	11	722
SMITH, W.J. heirs	8	393
SMITH, WM. N. & J.J.	11	775 - 780
SMYTH, S.M.	7	305 - 330
SNELL, D.W.	8	220 - 226
SNIDER, ELIZABETH	11	723
SNIDER, EZEKIEL	4	923 - 925
SNIDER, EZEKIEL	7	331 - 352
SOLES, TIMOTHY L.	8	435 - 445
SPAULDING, A.P.	8	584 - 619
SPEAR, G.W.	11	684 - 685
SPENCE, FITZ J. etal.	8	538 - 563
SPENCER, H. & C.	8	362 - 373
SPENCER, MARTHA A. etal.	8	717 - 734
SPENCER, PETER	9	1 - 116
SPLAWN, RICHARD	16	381 - 388
SPURLIN, ELIJAH	8	229 - 243
STANFIELD, E.E. & J.	8	715 - 716
STANLEY, JAS.	17	561 - 568
STANLEY, JOHN	17	784 - 787

STARKE, A.W.	8	104 - 108
STARKE, RITA	4	364 - 371
STEPHENS, JOHN	17	805 - 811
STEVENS, JAMES E.	8	97 - 103
STEVENS, JAMES etal.	8	428 - 434
STEVENS, JOSHUA	11	707 - 710
STEVENS, NEEDHAM	8	162 - 185
STEVENS, NEEDHAM	12	365 - 366
STEWART, ANNA BARTLETT	3	798
STEWART, MARTHA J. (now Faulkner)	3	536 - 543
STINSON, EMMA L.	11	711 - 713
STONE, WALTER	11	661 - 673
STOUDENMIRE, DALLAS	11	781 - 822
STOWE, HENRY	11	678 - 680
STRICKLAND, JOSEPH L.	12	1
STUART, JAMES D.	11	533 - 534
STUBBS, WILLIAM	11	564 - 601
SUGGS, ALPHA etal	17	759 - 763
SULLINS, S.B.	7	353 - 358
SUMMERSETT, A.P.	8	217 - 219
SUMMERSETT, ELIZABETH	8	6 - 51
SUMMERSETT, J.W. & J.M.	11	535 - 539
SUMMERSETT, S.	8	78 - 83
SUMMERSETTE, S.	12	358 - 364
TAYLOR, E.H.	18	257 - 259
TAYLOR, LOUISA M. heirs	8	571 - 582
TEAT, M.J. & WM. O.	8	453 - 455
TEAT, O.W.	8	157 - 161
THADDEUS, MARY J.	8	714
THOMAS, CORA	4	17 - 18
THOMAS, CORA	4	17 - 18
THOMAS, HENRY B. heirs	8	710 - 713
THOMAS, JAMES	9	575 - 625
THORINGTON, MARTHA	18	247 - 250
THORNTON, AURORA M. etal.	8	520
THORNTON, ELIAS	18	1 - 6
THORNTON, JOHN L.	9	695 - 702
TILLERY, ELIZABETH	18	253 - 254
TILLERY, ELIZABETH	17	343 - 347
TOMLINSON, PRISCILLA	8	421 - 426
TOMPKINS, H.H. etal.	9	738 - 797
TOWNSEND, MARTHA J.A.	8	521 - 526
TREVATHAN, ELI	18	251 - 252

TUCKER, CATHERINE T.	16	869
TUCKER, PERRY	8	706 - 709
TUCKER, T.C.	8	246
TURNER, NATHANIEL	8	335 - 336
WALL, E.J.	8	518 - 519
WARD, JOHN B.	8	374 - 375
WESLEY, R.H.	8	194
WEST, JOHN F. etal.	8	644 - 658
WHALEY, RUTH	8	427
WHATLEY, WILLIS	8	620 - 626
WHITE, GEORGE J.	8	665 - 672
WILKERSON, W.S.	8	394 - 412
WILKES, MOSES P.	8	379 - 392
WILLIAMS, BURGESS heirs	8	413 - 420
WILLIAMS, SIMEON	8	465 - 471
WILLIAMS, V.A.	8	564 - 568
WILLIAMS, W.J.	16	377 - 380
WILSON, ADDIE E.	4	364 - 371
WILSON, ADDIE E.	4	364 - 371
WILSON, JAMES M.	8	673 - 693
WILSON, M.T.	8	527 - 537
WILSON, ROBERT E. etal.	8	694 - 705
WILSON, S.D.	8	569 - 570
WILSON, SAMUEL H.	9	246 - 256
WINGARD, GEORGE	8	735 - 737
WINSLETTE, JOEL	9	117 - 245
WOOD, ISAAC M.	8	472 - 517
WOOD, JAMES	8	456 - 464
WRIGHT, JANE	8	446 - 452

9781639140633